BOTH BARRELS FROM BRAZIL

BOTH BARRELS FROM BRAZIL

MY WAR ON THE NUMPTIES

ALAN BRAZIL WITH **MIKE PARRY**

A *RACING POST* COMPANY

DEDICATION

To my parents Mary and Ben, who gave up a lot to help my
brother Michael and me on our way in life.

Published in 2008 by Highdown,
an imprint of Raceform Ltd
Compton, Newbury, Berkshire RG20 6NL

A catalogue record for this book is available from the British Library.

ISBN 978-1-905156-44-3

Cover designed by Adrian Morrish
Interiors designed by Fiona Pike

Printed by Creative Print and Design, Wales

CONTENTS

1   We're Only Here for a Visit   7

2   Putting the Boot In   53

3   The Road to Nowhere   79

4   Where Have All the Policemen Gone?   107

5   Vodka on the Menu   141

6   The Fairway to Heaven   173

7   The Health of Nations   203

8   The Men Who Would Be King   239

9   Flower of Scotland   267

Index   297

CHAPTER ONE

WE'RE ONLY HERE FOR A VISIT

'The person I have always most admired in football is George Best ... one thing you learnt from him was that life is for living.'

THE YOUNG LAD burst into the studio in a clear state of agitation. It was just before 6.30 a.m. and we were only half an hour into our four-hour breakfast show at talkSPORT. He was an assistant producer out on the floor, and he had about twenty seconds during our first break to tell me something which seemed, to him at least, to be important.

'Do you know a James Steel?' he asked me quickly.

'No,' I said. 'Should I?'

'He's just called for you. He wants me to pass a message to you but I don't know if he's a nutter.'

'What's the message?'

Just then the red 'On Air' light flashed twice, indicating that there were five seconds before we were back live.

The lad spat something out very quickly which I didn't quite catch. But as I returned to my microphone and opened up again with 'Welcome back, you're listening to the Alan Brazil Breakfast Show on talkSPORT' there was a very strange collection of words whirling around in the back of my head.

I could have sworn that the assistant had said to me, 'Alan Ball is dead.'

I shivered at such a wicked thought. Legendary World Cup

hero Bally was one of my best mates on the racing and celebrity golf circuit. But I could see the lads through the glass screen in the control room were getting agitated about something. I had to find out what was going on. Mild panic was starting to engulf me. I waved frantically to the producer and indicated to him to go to a break.

When I got into the production room, Dave, the lad who had given me the message, was white and breathless.

'What did you say to me?' I asked, pursing my lips and shaking my head.

'I'm sorry, Al, but this guy James Steel rang up. He was in a right state. He said he had to get hold of you because Alan Ball is dead.'

'James Steel ...' I muttered.

And suddenly my brain clicked into gear. A distinctly unpleasant shiver went down my spine. James Steel was in fact Jim Steel, my old footballing pal who was one of the architects of my doom when I got sacked after the infamous Cheltenham incident. He had played for Southampton when Alan Ball was ending his career and he had become one of his playing partners in golf tournaments. He was very close to Bally, and if anybody was going to be in charge of the devastating information I now realised I had just received, it was Jim.

My lips parted. I was about to say 'I can't believe this' when another of our young producers came in and said, 'A bloke called Jimmy Ball is trying to get hold of you.' Jimmy is Alan's son. I knew in that instant that Alan Ball was indeed dead.

The phones in our office then started ringing in unison. Mutual friends were calling to alert me to the tragedy. Alan had been found dead in the garden of the family's luxury home in Warsash, Hampshire, in the early hours of the morning. He had apparently been trying to quell a small fire in the garden, the remnants of an earlier compost bonfire that had re-ignited. He had collapsed and died, and was found by firemen who had been called to the house by neighbours. I also learnt that Jimmy had been speaking to his dad after midnight about a spectacular game that had been on the telly between Manchester United and AC Milan. Alan had been raving about the performance of Paul Scholes and his inch-perfect passes.

Even more tragically, my 61-year-old pal had been making plans to move house – which may have been the reason for clearing up the garden – following the death of his wife. Lesley, to whom he had been married for nearly 37 years. She had died of ovarian cancer three years earlier. Alan was devastated because his family – Jimmy, his two daughters, his wife and grandchildren – were the centre of his universe. He used to talk about playing football with the little ones in the garden. But, as with everything else that confronted him in his life, Bally met his despair with stoicism, knowing that he had to lead from the front for the rest of the family.

My eyes filled with tears. I was incapable of speech for a few moments, and I didn't know what to do. I didn't know how widespread this terrible information was. I worked at the hub of a news operation, and Alan Ball was one of the most famous footballers in Britain, if not the world. Surely I wasn't going to have to go through the ordeal of telling the world of his death? I was in shock. I didn't know if I could manage it. But I realised I had a responsibility. Jimmy had put his trust in me by ringing me.

I composed myself and went back into the studio. As I sat

down I suddenly saw a strapline come up on the bottom of the Sky News monitor. I think it said 'World Cup hero Alan Ball dies at home'. My producer told me in my earphones that we were going straight over to breaking news. Suddenly I was listening to more or less the same information that I had just been given.

I don't know how I got through the rest of the show but I thought I had a duty to stay. As the show came to an end I asked the boys to play 'Back Home', the theme tune for the England team – including, of course, Alan Ball – at the 1970 World Cup in Mexico.

This song now holds a special significance for me. My life seems to exist in concentric circles. The very day before Bally died I went to a pal's 50th birthday party at Langan's, my regular London restaurant. On the table was a Scotsman I had met a few times before. His name was Bill Martin, and he's a songwriter. He wrote the Sandy Shaw hit that won the 1967 Eurovision Song Contest, 'Puppet on a String'. He has had six number one hits, and one of them was 'Back Home'. We sang it at the table, little knowing that one of the men to whom it was dedicated was in the last twelve hours of his glorious life.

Immediately after the show I jumped in the car and headed home to Suffolk. I wanted to be with my family.

One of the mantras by which I have lived my life is 'We're only here for a visit'. That might sound trite, but the fickle hand of fate can strike at any time. I've thought that since my days as a youth footballer. Maybe it was a reaction to the glorious life I had as a young pro and the fear that it could all end at any time. Take life as it comes, and enjoy every day. Don't waste a minute.

I thought about it all deeply as I drove home that day. I was having great difficulty taking in what had happened. Why Bally? There was nobody on this earth who least deserved to die suddenly of natural causes.

Alan Ball was a much worthier man than me. I played for my country in a World Cup. He won a World Cup. He was only 21 in 1966, the youngest member of the England team. On the day of the final, he was roundly acknowledged as the best player on the pitch. He went on to win top honours with Everton. Despite our fourteen-year age gap I was lucky enough to play against him – though he didn't think so at the time. It was the night I scored five goals against his Southampton team at the end of his career. Three of them came in a seventeen-minute hat-trick. A newspaper took my picture the following day at the stables of the legendary racehorse Shergar. Alan and I met up regularly in later years at racecourses, and when playing golf. He would often recall that Shergar picture and tell people with a huge smile on his face, 'I wish Brazil had been kidnapped instead of the horse.'

It wasn't just that he was a great footballer, he was a wonderful human being too. He was so full of humility that I don't think he ever realised just what a huge star he was. Wherever we went people would stop and gape open-mouthed at him. I never saw that sort of reaction for anybody else except George Best. But Bally was unaware of it. If we were in a restaurant and people were gazing over at him, he wouldn't have dreamt of calling a waiter or asking to be moved. He was far more likely to get up, go over to the people concerned and ask them if they were enjoying their meal. He was more worried that his presence might make other customers feel uneasy, and he wanted them to feel comfortable. If somebody summoned up the courage to approach him and ask for an autograph or a picture, they never got turned away. He must have been asked thousands of times about the day in 1966 when England won the World Cup, but he never once failed to talk about it. He liked talking about it. As he told me, he felt tremendously privileged to have been on the pitch that day and he felt he had a duty to share it with all Englishmen – and anybody else who enquired.

One of the best indicators of Alan Ball's personality was the reverence in which he held other great footballers. Every year I go to Vila Sol on Portugal's Algarve to take part in the Bobby Robson Classic, and Bally was always there. But as far as he was concerned he was just another footballer helping out at a charity event. He regarded Bobby Robson, the most successful England manager since Alan's boss, Alf Ramsey, as the star of the show. Bobby, of course, was my gaffer during the glory years at Ipswich, and he used to confide in me. He was constantly amazed at the utter respect Bally showed him. Everybody in the game respects Bobby, but as far as Alan was concerned Robson was on a pedestal. He was to be revered for having led the England team to the semi-finals of the World Cup in 1990. It never occurred to him for a moment that he was due more respect because he'd actually gone a lot further and won the competition.

Grown men adored Alan Ball. My broadcasting pal Mike 'Porky' Parry was one of them. The day after Bally's death we met at the Four Seasons Hotel in Canary Wharf. Poor old Porky was in a sort of daze, clutching a colour picture of Alan Ball that was about 35 years old. He had cut it out of one of his schoolboy scrapbooks that morning. Bally's signature was quite clearly embossed across his white Everton shorts. It was the same signature I had seen on score-cards after a round of golf on many occasions.

After a bottle of wine, Porky started crying. He had once fallen at Alan's feet as a gesture of worship in the Owners and Trainers' bar at Newmarket. Through his blubs, he said, 'I'm so glad I had the chance to grovel to him.'

I will miss Alan terribly.

A week later I was still musing on Bally's sudden demise when my 'we're only here for a visit' life theory was put to the test again, in an equally shocking manner.

It was almost seven days exactly to the hour since I had spoken to Jimmy Ball about his father's death, and again I was in the studio. One of the many monitors we have in front of us suddenly threw up a strapline which read 'Helicopter carrying Chelsea FC executives reported missing'.

What a shock. The previous night Chelsea had played at Liverpool's ground, Anfield. The information we were now getting was that a chopper taking some of the bigwigs back south had gone down somewhere en route. The London club is owned by Russian billionaire Roman Abramovich, so it was no surprise that helicopters were involved. But surely, I thought, it couldn't be the oligarch himself.

A sudden bolt of fear such as I had experienced a week earlier hit me again when I saw a graphic displayed on one of our screens showing the route of the helicopter. It had certainly taken off from John Lennon airport in Liverpool, but instead of heading due south to London it had gone across country to Peterborough. I had a great friend called Phil Carter who lived on a country estate just outside Peterborough. He was a very wealthy self-made man who commuted regularly in a helicopter. He was not an official of Chelsea Football Club, but he was a lifelong Chelsea fan. He had in fact very nearly launched a bid for the club just before Abramovich swooped with his unbeatable billions. For his devotion to the club he had been made an executive vice-president. I'd been with him at games at Stamford Bridge on many occasions.

My head started spinning. The circumstances were too coincidental for Phil not to be involved in some way, but I started wondering whether perhaps another helicopter had planned to use his landing pad.

I couldn't concentrate. Just like a week earlier, I had to get out of the studio. I have another very good friend who is a wealthy Chelsea fan, and a big friend of Phil Carter's. I figured he must be aware of the issue because the helicopter had now been missing for nine hours. The minute my pal answered the phone I knew that my worst fears were about to be realised. There was no confirmation yet of identities but the police had been to Phil's house and he was missing. He had travelled back from the game the previous night with three other people. Everybody was praying that Phil's seventeen-year-old son Andrew was not one of them. I could only think of the terror that Phil's lovely wife Judith was going through.

I couldn't go back into the studio. I was too shocked. Just a few nights earlier I had enjoyed a drink with Phil in the five-star Lanesborough Hotel in London. I had just come out of a meeting involving my racing club, and as I moved through the lobby I spotted Phil. He was a very distinctive man. Invariably dressed in a pinstripe suit, he always had a broad smile on his well-tanned face that displayed a set of ivory-white teeth.

His company was infectious too. Even though I was due somewhere else we hugged each other and, without even needing to raise the issue, retired to the bar and sank a couple of bottles of champagne.

Phil and Judith ran a vocational training business that had grown to employ more than 2,000 people. For a man who is listed as the 770th wealthiest person in the *Sunday Times* Rich List and who must have been very tough to have got to that position, he was just such a pleasant bloke. He was always considerate to everybody, whether they were selling him a newspaper or signing off another multi-million-pound deal.

I remembered when Porky and I were in Monaco in April 2004, lunching together with millionaires in Casino Square on the day of Chelsea's European Cup semi-final. It was the time I tricked Porky into paying the bill; I wrote about it in *There's an Awful Lot of Bubbly in Brazil*. One of the diners was a well-known singer from the group Tenors Unlimited – not as famous as Placido Domingo, but still a class act, and widely appreciated in operatic circles. People were trying to goad him into singing, but as he quite fairly pointed out, a table full of well-lubricated albeit wealthy football fans was not really the sort of audience he worked with. Presumably thinking that he had some sort of equivalent talent, Porky then jumped on the table and sang the Beatles song 'When I'm Sixty-Four'. He was met with a barrage of bread rolls and abuse – all except for one person, Phil. He stood up and warmly clapped my mate, whom he hardly knew, and praised him for being a sport. That's the sort of guy Phil Carter was.

Tragically, his son was on board that helicopter, along

with one of Phil's good pals, Jonathan Waller, who I had met several times.

After Phil's death I was wandering around in a daze. To see two such close friends lose their lives in the space of a week had rocked me on to my heels. It had also reinforced my belief in my mantra. A few years ago a pal and I were on the golf course when one of the players in front of us dropped dead in a bunker. I had to steer in the air ambulance on my mobile phone. And just a few weeks before the deaths of Alan and Phil I attended the memorial service of my good pal and fellow broadcaster Mike Dickin, who died in a road accident. Many years ago I used the mantra as a quip to justify my boisterous lifestyle, but the chord it strikes within me is sounding deeper the longer life goes on. It first struck me that you can be alive one moment and dead the next at a very early stage of my life.

***

I always loved playing in evening games. The atmosphere always seemed extra special under the lights. Night games for me are synonymous with a European campaign, and as I have two UEFA Cup medals with Ipswich Town and Spurs I associate them with the best of times. But even as a youth-team player I liked evening kick-offs – and part of the reason was that we would all go out afterwards because we didn't have to go into training the following day. One fateful night will remain in my memory for ever because I'm certain the events of that evening had a major bearing on my 'we're only here for a visit' attitude to life.

Young players are always full of 'buzz' after a match. The adrenalin is coursing through your veins for hours afterwards, and even if you want to go home to bed you would find it impossible to sleep. I wasn't even a regular drinker in those days, and neither were most of the other lads. Our careers were just starting, many of us had already made our first-team debuts and we were all desperate to make the grade as established professionals. We'd drink a few pints of lager and shandies. We weren't interested in getting drunk. Another factor in our thinking was that you soon became known as a Town player in rural Suffolk and both the youth bosses and Bobby Robson were sticklers for behaviour.

We had notched up a convincing victory on the pitch next to the stadium, and four of us jumped into two cars and headed out to a night-club called the Windmill in Copford, a couple of miles west of Colchester on the A12. We didn't get there until about eleven o'clock. I arrived with Eric Gates, a Geordie whom I always found great company, and we met up with Peter Canavan and David Geddis. Geddis was one of the more competitive apprentices at the club, and Canavan was a kid with a very bright future. He had been the England under-19 captain.

Eric and I drank halves of lager, but the other two were on the Cokes. Believe it or not, that was perfectly normal in those days. The other two left earlier than us on their twenty-minute drive back to Ipswich. I know that neither of them had a single drop of alcohol that night. A bit later, Eric and I left. He dropped me at my digs in Capel St Mary, a village off the A12 on the way to Ipswich, where Eric lived. It had been an unremarkable night, and I went to bed.

The next morning I was woken by my landlady. She was weeping uncontrollably.

'Wake up, Alan. Please, wake up.'

I stirred myself, puzzled as to why she was crying. She held her pinny in her hands and was wiping her eyes.

'What's wrong?' I asked.

She could hardly get her words out, but between the sobs she spluttered, 'Peter's dead.'

'Don't be silly,' I replied. 'I was with him last night. He was at the game and we went for a drink afterwards.'

I turned over and pulled the covers up. I couldn't figure out what she was talking about.

But she started shaking my shoulder. 'No, you don't understand. He was killed in a car crash on the A12. David Geddis is injured and he's in hospital.'

A terrible wave of fear swept through me. Peter had been in a car last night. Dave Geddis had been with him. And they would have gone home down the A12.

I sat bolt upright in bed. 'Who told you?'

'I heard the news about a crash on the radio and I didn't pay much attention,' the landlady explained, 'but I've just had a call from the club and they've told me the dreadful news. It happened on the main road.'

The road was just a couple of miles from the house. I didn't know what to think. I thought back to the previous evening. It was very difficult to take in the way events had unfolded. Just a few minutes after I had bid my pals farewell at the Windmill, one of them had been killed and the other had gone through a near-death experience. Tears welled up in my eyes, and now, instead of crying herself, the landlady was comforting me.

Details of what happened that night remain sketchy. The car had run off the road into a fence and was smashed to pieces. There was some talk that it might have clipped a kerb. Nobody was ever found to be responsible. It was simply a road accident, like the dozens of others we read about in the papers. It is a routine happening, until it involves somebody you know.

Not long after the crash David was back in training. He had, by all accounts, had a very lucky escape. But something like that is bound to have a long-term effect on a young man and within months he had moved on to pursue his football career elsewhere. Still, he can truly be called a hero in the annals of Ipswich Town because at the age of only twenty he played a major role in the FA Cup-winning side of 1978. In a masterstroke the manager, Bobby Robson, played him down the right-hand side in a bid to unsettle Arsenal's Irish full-back Sammy Nelson. It worked, because Geddis supplied the cross that was blocked by Arsenal's Willie Young only for Roger Osborne to seize on the ball faster than the other Arsenal defenders and lash it home with his left foot.

I still see Dave occasionally. I've never asked him about that night, and I never will. If he ever wants to talk to me about it I am sure he knows he can. But I suspect that he has probably put what must have been an horrendous experience to the back of his mind. I admire him for coping with it all these years.

I thought about visiting the crash site to pay homage to my mate, but I couldn't bring myself to go. When you're young, it's something you do not want to face up to. I pass the exact location of the crash three or four times a week on my journeys to London and back, and every time I do a shudder goes through me. One of the strangest aspects of the business is that Eric and I must have driven right past the scene of the crash that night. We never saw a thing. As we were only about half an hour behind Peter and David, I have had to assume ever since that the crashed car was lying on its side in the undergrowth, or in a dip, and that hundreds of motorists must have passed by unknowingly in the darkness. I don't torment myself by wondering if Peter could have been saved had the crash been discovered earlier. I just don't know.

Looking back, I realise what a profound effect Peter's death had on me. Young men of that age believe they are immortal. I know I did. Not only was I fit and healthy, I was a budding footballer, and I felt like one of God's chosen people. I had never even thought about dying. But I had had previous experience of death. You will read later about my pal at the ice-skating rink. I had always believed that that was a horror that would never visit me again, but just a few years on, here I was again, mourning another pal.

What is happening? I asked myself. I certainly believed in God, and I wondered why two of my mates had been taken. Would it be me next? From that moment my attitude to life started to change. I began to question the perceived wisdom that had been drummed into me by my parents (as is the case with most young people) about planning for the future. That didn't seem quite as important to me in the wake of Peter's death. I wasn't feeling morbid, I certainly had a great love of life, but psychologically I decided that every day had to count. Even if a few risks had to be taken along the way.

Yes, there's absolutely no doubt that during the weeks following Peter's death my attitude to life changed. I remember thinking when we had a short memorial service for Peter at the ground, 'What's it all about?' It's a common expression these days because of the success of the Monty Python film, but I really did start wondering about the meaning of life. Peter had obeyed all the rules. He was a model professional. He didn't drink and I never saw him place a bet in an era when most footballers spent more time in the bookie's than they did on the training ground. His reward was an early death. And it was so terribly sudden. One minute he was chatting up a girl and dancing to soul music in a night-club, the next he was dead. I figured that nobody could ever predict how many more days they had on earth, and gradually I began to live my life accordingly.

The person I have always most admired in football is George Best. I'm sure I'm not alone, but I was lucky enough to know George, as a player and a pal. And one thing you learnt from him was that life is for living.

I assumed I would never grace the same football field as the Irish genius because by the time I became a professional he had virtually retired. He had won the European Cup with Manchester United in 1968, the year after Celtic had lifted the trophy. As far as I was concerned he was the greatest player in the world. But by 1972 he had started to miss training at the club, and he played his last game for them in January 1974. He was playing in a poor United side that had simply not replaced the players from the legendary team of the sixties. As Law, Charlton and Crerand bowed to age, the team fell apart. It was no surprise that they were relegated from the First Division in the season George left, just six years after being crowned European champions. By that time George's life seemed to be careering all over the place. On one occasion after doing a runner from United he turned up in Marbella and confessed that he was drinking a bottle of vodka a day.

The stories about George's life are legendary. Booze, girls, newspaper headlines, sackings, career changes, financial problems, missed appointments, and even more missed opportunities. (Take out the girls – I enjoy one of the longest marriages I know of in football – and a lot of those factors have cropped up in my life.) George came to a shocking end when he succumbed to total organ failure following his lifelong association with booze. And obviously nobody in their right mind would support a lifestyle that culminated in that sort of premature death. But George always lived his life his own way. He had no regard for authority. He was such a free spirit that the ordinary rules did not apply to him. I can't imagine he stayed in at night working out a new pension plan for his old age, nor do I suppose he did a daily check on his vitamin or calorie intake. If he didn't feel like doing something, he didn't do it. He wasn't selfish, he just decided that he had one life and there was no point in wasting it on things other people wanted him to do.

I knew George over more than two decades. I can only tell you about the George Best I knew, and he was a conundrum. For instance, for all that you will have read of him and his wild exploits over the years, I am being completely honest when I say that in those 25 years or so I never once saw him drunk.

My first introduction to the raven-haired genius was a complete surprise. I signed full professional forms for Ipswich just before their FA Cup victory in 1978. The morning after the game I was despatched on loan for the summer to Detroit Express. I had a marvellous time in America and grew up very fast. I had a car, my own flat and more money in my pocket than I had ever had. The lifestyle was brilliant for me, and there was another great advantage. The North American Soccer League had only recently been formed and it had become a magnet for some of the world's greatest players at the end of their careers. Pele was the most spectacular import, followed by 'The Kaiser', Franz Beckenbauer. But the one player I hoped I would play against was George Best. He was in his fourth season in America. He'd spent the previous three years with the Los Angeles Aztecs, and now he was starring with the Fort Lauderdale Strikers.

The American leagues have play-offs in every competition so that all the teams have multiple chances of winning something, thereby ensuring that the interest of the fans who fund the game is maintained right to the end of the season. I was thrilled when I discovered that Detroit had been drawn against George's team in a quarter-final play-off. It was to take place at our ground, the Pontiac Silverdome.

I am not one to be easily impressed in life, but to me, this was a life-changing event. Communications were not instant in those days. There was no e-mail and you couldn't speak to somebody on the other side of the world by flicking open your mobile phone. So I ran up a huge bill phoning my family and all my mates in Scotland and England to tell them I was playing against George Best. It was such an amazing thing to happen that some of them didn't believe me. They did when I sent all the pictures home a couple of weeks later.

When the day of the game came I was amazed to learn that the great Manchester United star was only 32 years old. He seemed to have been around for at least twenty years, but then a quick look at his record revealed that he won his first league championship when he was just nineteen and the European Cup when he was 22. I was nineteen, and it was thrilling to be on the same pitch as this British legend. What more motivation could a player need?

It was a packed house of 40,000 fans, and George opened the scoring for the Strikers. I equalised, but we lost the penalty shoot-out and went out of the play-offs. The game wasn't the highlight of my day, though. All the players met up afterwards in the Silverdome cocktail lounge and had a few drinks. The minute I walked into the room George came over and congratulated me on my performance. He was very complimentary. 'You've obviously got a great future in the game,' he told me, 'and you're with a great manager in Bobby Robson. Everybody I speak to in the game rates him.

'Don't take too much notice of what coaches tell you,' he added. 'Rely on the best of your skills. You've got a great left foot and you've got pace and you can beat men. You'll come up against better defenders than you'll play against in America, but never be afraid to take them on. That's the one thing that is guaranteed to give any defence a problem – if a player is running at them. You can duck and dive. Concentrate on that. You don't have to go back and defend, but when you lose the ball in the attacking half always chase your man back and try to get it back off him. He won't expect you, and you can catch him by surprise.'

George went on to tell me that he loved living and playing in America. England had become a huge goldfish bowl for him and the pressures were starting to drive him mad, and turned him to the drink. Every time he returned to the States for a new season he saw it as a new beginning. He trained hard for their relatively short seasons and he never had the inclination to drink like he had in Britain. He told me he feared he could easily be sucked into losing control of the boozing so he saw the chance to escape to Los Angeles and Fort Lauderdale as a lifeline.

I'm certain that the next time I played for Detroit I was a better player. Ten minutes' conversation with a legend and I felt that I had learnt more than anything I had ever been told by a youth coach in Glasgow.

The following year I actually played with George rather than against him. There was a testimonial game for Bobby Robson at Ipswich, and George played with me in the Ipswich eleven. Some people might ask, 'Why was George Best there? He never played for Ipswich.' The answer is that from the moment it was announced in the local paper, the Evening Star, that George was going to play, there was a stampede for tickets. It was typical of the Belfast boy to agree to appear. As I got to know him over the years I was constantly amazed by his generosity. I've seen him give away all sorts of possessions, even a watch, if he thought he could help somebody less fortunate than himself.

The night of that testimonial was memorable for all sorts of reasons, and one of them was the football. I can't remember which side won. All I know is that George cut through three defenders with his trademark twists and turns and slotted a ball through to me. More than any other goal I hoped I was about to score, I remember thinking to myself, 'For Christ's sake, don't miss this – it may never happen again.' Happily, I did score, and I danced a jig around the field with one of the true legends of modern football.

After the game we went to the players' lounge and had a few beers. Once again George was entirely relaxed. I have never met a man who exuded so much charm. He had piercing coral-blue eyes and a lilting Irish accent that made him sound like he was humming rather than speaking. I also noticed that, despite the fact that he was one of the world's leading heart-throbs at the time, he was almost shy in the company of women. He was terribly respectful to them, and they swooned in front of him.

We were in the lounge for about an hour, and all the time I could hear screaming noises from outside the ground. It wasn't like normal noise. In years to come I enjoyed some spectacular night games – like that one in which I scored five goals against Southampton, or the evening we got through to the final of the UEFA Cup – and there would always be fans outside roaring their approval and clamouring for autographs or just a sight of those they regarded as their heroes. But the noise this night was much higher-pitched. It reminded me of the sound that emanated from the Boys' Pen, when grounds used to have special areas for kids so young that their voices hadn't broken.

I looked out of the window and saw that the ground was surrounded by young girls, shouting and screaming and begging George to come out, or at least give them a wave. Worryingly for me, some of them were carrying knives. When I asked him about it, the Ulsterman laughed. 'They're not knives, they're scissors,' he explained. 'They try to cut locks of my hair off, which I don't really mind except when they cut my ear.' George had to be smuggled out of the ground.

Three days later the local papers were still carrying stories about the effect he'd had on Ipswich, still a fairly remote town in footballing terms. One young fan claimed that as George's car had arrived, one of the wheels had run over her little handbag as the crowd of fans surged behind her. She wasn't in the least concerned about it, but she was pictured proudly holding up her bag with a tyre mark on it. She said she was going to keep it in a glass case. In another story an old woman who had been sitting in the front row of the ground claimed that Best's genius was so dazzling it had helped ease the rheumatic pains she'd had for ten years. This was the sort of madness that surrounded George.

For a few years, when we both worked for Sky TV, we met up on a regular basis on a Saturday afternoon. We would stare at a screen and then give updates to the viewers, who because of broadcasting rules were not able to see the action for themselves. It was a pioneering programme, and we had lots of laughs trying to explain the action. George was a great communicator and could easily have turned his attention to TV and radio punditry if he had been so inclined.

After the show we would go either to the rugby club across the road from the studios in west London or, in the summer, down to the banks of the Thames and sit outside a lovely riverside pub. If you had never heard of George Best, on the evidence of those Saturday-night sessions you would describe him as a moderate drinker. A few beers, a few glasses of wine maybe, and then we'd all drift off home. I can't relate any shocking tales about falling in the river or being thrown out of pubs, or pub-crawls that went on until two in the morning, because they didn't happen. I never saw the chaotic or tormented side of George, though if the stories are anything to go by – being chased around by policemen for various reasons; girlfriends claiming he had stolen their property; well-documented bibulous benders – it undoubtedly existed.

George was always full of mischief, though. I once met him on a train down to Cardiff. He was going to make a personal appearance and, coincidentally, I was going to watch him. But we had no idea we'd be going on the same train.

I was going because earlier that year, 1991, I had been over in Longchamp for the Prix de l'Arc de Triomphe. All the Brits there were backing the Derby winner, Generous, to win on French soil (he didn't). While I was out there I met a big football fan called Sean who ran a pub called the Bank in the Welsh capital. He invited me to go down and stay for the rugby, Scotland against Wales at Cardiff Arms Park. What I didn't know when I set off was that he had hired George to do a roadshow in his pub the night before the game.

My pal and I walked into the first-class compartment of the train at London's Paddington station and there was George with the current woman in his life, a lovely lady called Mary Shatila. We sat down at the same table so that George was sitting next to me and opposite Mary, who was sitting next to my pal.

There was a bit of a strange atmosphere because George had had one or two recent public spats involving drink. The most notorious one was when he appeared on Wogan, one of Britain's most popular chat shows, on the BBC. After being introduced by the other amiable Irishman, Terry Wogan, George fell into his seat. It was clear he was the worse for wear. The ensuing live interview was sensational for all the wrong reasons. When Wogan asked him about the various women in his life, George said, 'I like screwing, all right?' When Wogan tried to move off the subject and asked about what he did the rest of the time, Best said again, 'I like screwing.' The interview was cut short at that point.

But when George was telling me about it later he made the point that he had been entertained for three hours in the guest suite at the studios before the interview. For once in his life he had turned up not just on time but early, and he was shown into the 'green room', where guests can make themselves comfortable until they are called for their slot. There was a huge, well-stocked cocktail cabinet there, and George just whiled away the rather boring hours pouring himself a couple of glasses and reading the papers. By the time he got his call he didn't realise how much he'd had to drink.

Mary, the lady with him on the train, was trying to bring some order into George's life at a time when he had difficulties with the taxman and all sorts of other financial problems. (Believe me, it's a nightmare. I have been there.) So, as penance for recent misbehaviour, Mary had put George on the wagon. The only thing he was drinking at the start of the journey was Coke. I asked if it was all right for my mate and me to have a glass of wine, and not only did George encourage us, he sent some helpful individual nearby off to the buffet car to get us a couple of bottles.

It was a glorious day with a clear blue sky, and the wonderful English countryside was hurtling by. My mate and I were enjoying a glass of Sauvignon, George was drinking Coke and Mary was drinking water. I wondered if Mary had some sort of a problem because George was refilling her glass from the bottle after every couple of sips. We were all having a laugh and a shout when we came to the first tunnel. Whooosh. The train hurtled into the tunnel, and although there are lights in the carriages, they are quite dim, and when your eyes are deprived of the bright natural sunlight you find yourself blinded for a couple of seconds. And then, as you come out of the tunnel and into the brightness again, the same process happens.

We continued talking, but when I reached for my glass I noticed that it was empty. 'That's funny,' I thought. 'I must be getting plastered because I could have sworn I topped it up a few minutes ago.' I filled it up again. George continued to sip at his Coke and to replenish Mary's water.

Whooosh. Another tunnel, and more echoing and clattering noises and squinting of eyes as we emerged again.

What the hell was going on? My glass was empty again. I don't like being made to look like a fool and I thought I was being set up for some sort of elaborate hoax. I stared at my pal and Mary opposite but there wasn't a flicker of recognition in their eyes. Then I looked to my left at George and detected that twinkle in the Irishman's eye.

Just then, Mary said she had to go to the loo. It suddenly dawned on me. George was drinking my glass of wine as we were going in and out of the tunnels, snatching it, downing it in one and putting it back before anybody noticed. And he was filling Mary's glass up every few seconds so that she would have to go to the loo on a regular basis.

'Sorry, lads,' he said, 'but she gets awfully upset if she thinks I'm on the booze. Keep filling her glass with water, will you? And keep filling your own, Al, because I'll need it every time we go through a tunnel. She's not clocked it yet.'

I laughed in admiration. That was worthy of a trick of my own when my wife, Jill, was giving me the third degree about the booze. George went on to perform brilliantly that night. He dazzled the audience with his wit and a host of great stories about his playing days and off-the-field antics.

George, of course, died in November 2005, clearly as a result of an excess of alcohol. Though I personally never saw him at his lowest ebb, it seems to me that as he got older he became less inclined to go through periods of abstinence. It was the issue of George's liver transplant that lost him some sympathy towards the end of his life. He had obviously been responsible for the destruction of his first liver through decades of non-stop boozing. It was assumed that when he was given the chance of life over death with a new organ he would give up the bottle for ever.

George was a self-confessed alcoholic, which means he was addicted to alcohol, so it would have been sensible for him never to drink again. But as I understand it he would sometimes go weeks without a drink. If that was the case, I reasoned, he could presumably have a few drinks once or twice a week without harming himself because he had a new healthy liver. Some of you may feel I must be mad even to consider letting a man who has nearly drunk himself to death to ingest even one drop of alcohol ever again, but I'm just trying to be realistic. I know there was outrage in some quarters when George started drinking again. The cry went up that he had wasted his gift from God of another chance at life. I don't quite understand that. If doctors knew that this world-famous soccer star was an alcoholic – as most of the rest of the world did – then why did they give the go-ahead for the transplant? Isn't alcoholism incurable? I'm not trying to question the miraculous work doctors do to save the lives of people like George, but surely there was a realistic chance he would relapse. He had shown precious little discipline or regard for his health for most of his adult life, after all.

When I read in his newspaper column that George had started experimenting with spritzers – white wine and soda – I took it that he would start drinking again full time. Indeed that happened, and stories started appearing in the papers that George was getting involved in drunken rows. Porky lives in Surrey, very near to where George made his home with his second wife, Alex Pursey. I started getting reports of sightings of my footballer mate.

On one occasion Porky was sitting with a group of friends at a table in front of a lovely country pub. A mini-cab pulled up, but there didn't seem to be anybody in the passenger seats. Then the front near-side door opened and George slid out on to the road. People got up to try to help him but he shrugged them off and went inside. He looked terribly dishevelled and disorientated. After a few minutes Porky went inside to get some drinks. George was by this time surrounded by a group of hangers-on. It's pretty well known that Porky is a talkSPORT broadcaster, and as he was waiting at the bar to be served one of the sycophants who had attached himself to George suddenly marched over. In very coarse language he told Porky to disappear, quickly, that it was people like him who were responsible for the condition in which George found himself.

Fortunately, Porky gets a lot of abuse when he's out and about so he was able to brush it off, but it illustrates the sort of thing George had to put up with most of his life. In my experience, whenever the Belfast boy walked into a pub he never had to buy a drink. Even on the days when he was intending to stay only for a couple of glasses of beer there would be maybe ten drinks lined up on the bar. Part of the adoration people had for George was their desire to buy him a drink. I can quite understand it. Grown men can't really be seen to be asking their heroes for an autograph, but they can go home and tell their wife or their mates the next day that they bought George Best a drink. Inevitably, George would drink the lot.

I read in a column after he died that by talking to his doctors he had worked out that if he took up drinking again after his transplant, he would certainly be dead within five years. He reckoned that was a good deal. He apparently had the choice of perhaps 25 years of sobriety or five years of living like he did when he was younger, boozing day and night and generally enjoying the craic that accompanies drink and the pursuit of it. I can understand his decision, but at George's age – he was thirteen years older than me, and only 59 when he died – I would definitely not do the same thing.

He gave his five-year theory to Jimmy Greaves. Jimmy is one of the British footballers still alive today who got as close as anybody to Best's brilliance. The great Spurs star, who was more famous for a game he missed rather than one he played in – the 1966 World Cup final – was a legendary heavy drinker, even in his playing days. Apparently it was quite common in the sixties for top stars to relax in the afternoons in the closed back-room of a club near the ground with an ultra-friendly landlord. When he retired from football, Jimmy slipped into the veritable hell of alcoholism. As a kid I read his life-story, and the way he described the nightmare of addiction shocked the life out of me. Your life is focused on one thing and one thing only: I need another drink. He wrote about burying bottles of spirits in his back garden to fool his family, and how his body had become so conditioned to absorbing alcohol that he could drink tumblers full of vodka, pretending to people that it was water, and never show the effects.

Miraculously, because I have no idea where he could have found the strength to kick the whole thing into touch, he hasn't had a drink for well over twenty years. I don't know if his life is one long agonising trial of denial or whether he has simply found the mental and physical courage to get on with his life with the booze as a distant and very unpleasant memory. All I know is that I could not do it. I will never drink the sort of quantities that George Best consumed, but neither will I ever consider abstinence. I think it's unnatural.

Booze is a very pleasurable part of my life. I like the taste of champagne, wine and beer, I love the effect it has on me, and I adore some of the places you have to go to get it. It means you are usually in great company with people who think like you do and who want to talk about what you want to talk about.

In the summer I like to be on a beach with a bottle of bubbly, or in a beautiful country pub in rural Suffolk. There are pubs on the estuary of the River Orwell near to where I live which I would describe as the nearest thing to heaven on earth. How can you finish eighteen holes of golf on a glorious July day without a few glasses of fizz? What would the Derby at Epsom be without a jug of Pimms, or Newmarket races of a Friday night without wine chilling in the cold box as you picnicked on the lawn? Do people really fly across the Atlantic drinking coffee, or take an east coast train from Edinburgh to London while savouring a mineral water? And what about the winter months? Is there anything more inviting than being huddled around the hearth in front of a roaring fire in a country pub? Also, the slopes without a bottle of bubbly are unthinkable. As I get older, the active skiing holidays I have enjoyed for years are now tending to be replaced by 'après-ski' holidays.

I like having a drink when I'm travelling, too. I don't know what people do when they are travelling, particularly long-haul, if they aren't having a drink. I don't like flying at night. It's dull and depressing. But a daytime flight with a clear blue sky on the other side of the window is a glorious experience. And clutching a glass of eternal champagne makes it all the better. I've been lucky enough to have flown mostly business or first-class on my trips to America, Australia and the Far East. I can understand a little bit why people get their heads down on their flat-beds at night, but why on earth would you want to do that during the day? I've seen people stretched out for hours on a daytime flight to Chicago. What a waste. The flight is to be enjoyed. There is an endless supply of booze. There are films, pretty hostesses to look after you, and usually some interesting people to talk to.

I drink very steadily on planes. It's not like you have to race along with a group of pals in a bar. I've never fallen asleep with a glass in my hand. In fact, far from making me sleepy on flights, I find that a lovely chilled glass of champagne actually wakes me up.

I have never experienced jet-lag in my life. I'm not sure it actually exists. If you fly to the east coast of America, you lose five hours. It's a journey I love. Once I flew on a ten a.m. flight from Heathrow to New York. I was going to the races at Saratoga and I was with a group of mates. The timing is perfect. The flight takes about seven hours, but with the five-hour time difference it means you land at midday. By the time we got ourselves into Manhattan and into a restaurant on 2nd Avenue to meet up with some other pals it was still only two o'clock. It was one of those great long lunches in a traditional establishment where everything was either polished wood or polished brass.

At seven p.m. we moved on downtown to South Street, and then on to Greenwich Village where we went to an English pub called the Red Lion. By midnight some of the lads were struggling. It never once occurred to me that it was actually five a.m. on my body clock. Everybody else voted to go back to the hotel, but I felt as fit as a fiddle.

They went off, and I made my way back up to 42nd Street – famous because of the legendary musical. Porky had lived and worked in New York in the eighties and early nineties and he'd been back to the city for most of his Christmases and New Years ever since. He'd told me to try an Irish bar that never closed that had been a haunt of English journalists for decades. When I got there it looked like it was all locked up, but on closer examination I spotted life inside. I stayed there until dawn, then strolled back to my hotel. Remarkably, I was the liveliest member of our group when we assembled in the hotel bar later that morning to make our way to the track. And I never felt the effects of the five hours I 'stole' and spent in the Irish pub.

And that wasn't even my biggest 'theft' of waking hours. Years earlier, when I was still forging a new life after being forced out of football by back injury, I went on a crazy trip that surprises even me when I look back on it.

One evening I was in a casino in London when I was approached by a former Yugoslavian footballer called Popovich. He asked me to go to Australia and play for a team called Wollongong. It sounded like an Aborigine name to me, but as everybody had had a lot to drink I thought it was just pub talk, so I said, 'OK,' and then forgot all about it.

I must have given him my phone number because a few days later, at 2.30 in the morning, the phone rang and there was a Greek Cypriot on the other end called Harry Michaels. He explained that he owned this team, Wollongong Wolves, located in a town just outside Sydney, and he wanted me to play for them for four games because he was close to clinching the Australian title. He offered me large sums of money so I agreed to ring him back the following day. I then discovered he was the businessman who owns Oz Aerobics, the organisation that beams pictures around the world of young, very good-looking ladies who work out on mats in exotic locations. It's a very simple formula. Maybe women watch it and exercise along with the girls, but in my experience it is more appealing to men.

My two oldest girls were only little then and I did not want to leave my family for a month, especially with my domestic football career having just ended, and all the uncertainty that surrounds that. Harry agreed when I said I would have to travel with Jill and the girls, and within days we were sitting in business-class seats aboard a Malaysian Airlines plane.

The flight was marvellous. At a stop-over in Kuala Lumpur the British manager of the local Hilton Hotel was waiting to greet us. He was a big Ipswich fan and he had seen my name on the flight lists. He gave us a suite in his hotel for four hours, and you have no idea how welcome that is when you are travelling around the world with two little girls.

We got to Australia without any problems, and I didn't have a single alcoholic drink on the journey. I've always behaved differently with my family. And in those days I was still living my life like an athlete and wasn't really inclined.

We had a lovely stay. I played four games. I scored in three of them, which we won, and I hit the bar twice in the last one, which we drew. Harry, who had become a good friend, was delighted – he very kindly told me that I had been his secret weapon – and believed that the team had done enough to clinch the title with just a few games to go. He happily handed over the big bonuses that were part of my contract. The only game Harry was really worried about was against arch rivals Sydney Olympic, but he believed he had a big enough lead over them now and a good enough team to carry him through. By that time Jill wanted to get home, so we said our goodbyes.

A week after we got home, the phone rang again at 2.30 a.m. Just like the first time, Jill and I were alarmed. Calls in the night usually mean trouble. Had something happened to somebody in the family? It never occurred to me it could be Harry again. But it was. Only this time it was not the calm, composed businessman I had come to know. The man on the end of this phone was panic-stricken.

'Alan, Alan, I've got a big problem,' he spluttered down the phone in his rare accent which was a blend of Australian and East European. 'You've got to help me.'

What on earth could have happened? Had his business collapsed or something?

'Calm down, Harry,' I said. 'It's the middle of the night here.'

He then explained the life-threatening 'tragedy'. In fact what had happened was that his centre-forward had broken his leg and his right-winger had been struck down with a virus. He was begging me to return to Australia. On Saturday the team were playing the dreaded Sydney Olympic.

My brain was scrambled. I couldn't even remember what day it was. I didn't really fancy this at all. I didn't even think I could make it in time. Then Harry mentioned an enormous sum of money, and as I was technically unemployed at the time, I couldn't refuse it.

I'm pretty certain he was weeping when he said, 'Alan, you have saved my life.'

'I haven't yet,' I said. 'But we'll do what we can.'

I was already starting to rise to the challenge of my round-the-world rescue mission. The only problem was that Harry had implored me to find a winger to take with me. And I had to fly within two days. I didn't know where I was going to start. I was only 27 so it wasn't as if I had a load of contemporary mates who were free to fly to Australia to play a one-off match at a few hours' notice. Most of my former team-mates were still playing.

It was impossible to sleep for the rest of that night, and I had to talk Jill through the positives. I would, after all, be away only for about a week and we couldn't really turn the money down.

The fog started to clear in my mind, and I suddenly remembered an old pal I had met in a pub a couple of months earlier for the first time in a year. His name was 'Bruiser' Keys. I've never known his first name; I've always known him as Bruiser. He was a roofer who had been on Luton's books but never made the grade; he'd eventually drifted out of the game to join the family firm. When I had to quit football in the First Division I played in local leagues and for a short while we were team-mates at Bury St Edmunds.

I went to the pub in a little village outside Ipswich where I knew I would find him. He couldn't at first believe what I was telling him, but I didn't have time to convince him gently. I told him that if he didn't jump in his roofing van right there and then and head for the Australian Embassy in London to acquire a visa, he would miss the opportunity of a lifetime.

Twenty-four hours later we were at the Malaysian Airlines desk at Heathrow picking up our tickets. The whole project nearly stalled there and then. I didn't realise that Bruiser had never actually flown before. I'd wondered why he was asking me strange questions on the journey to the airport, like 'Which way do the seats face on a plane?' But I thought he was trying to have a laugh. When we picked up our tickets, I had been given a business-class seat but he had been put in economy. I couldn't have that. The poor guy was going to be on his first flight, which was going to last over 24 hours, sitting isolated at the back of the plane. I had to get the airline to contact Harry, and after explaining that if Bruiser didn't go then neither did I, we both ended up in row nine at the front of the plane in the same seats I had occupied on my first trip.

We were both exhilarated at the speed and the drama of events, and we gratefully accepted a few glasses of champagne. Then we accepted a few more. The cabin crew must have thought we were medically dependent on bubbly because the bottles just kept coming. The plane landed and took off again three times before we eventually reached Sydney. Each time we were directed to the business lounge, and each time it revived us just as we were flagging.

In Kuala Lumpur, the second stop after Dubai, I was determined that we should take advantage of the four-hour stop-over by getting our heads down as we had now been up 24 hours. But as we entered the arrivals lounge, there was the manager of the Hilton Hotel. He'd clocked my arrival again, and he was in no mood to let me sleep. He had gathered a few pals together and he wanted a sing-song in his hotel. After token resistance I fell in with his plans, and the four hours disappeared in a blur.

Back on the plane. More champagne.

The final stop before Sydney was Melbourne. I'd forgotten that I had been in Australia only a month earlier, and when we entered the airport at Melbourne I was instantly recognised. What could I do but accept the hospitality of a group of enthusiastic ex-pats?

After that, Bruiser and I staggered back on to the plane. It was just an hour now to Sydney, and I worked out in my befuddled brain that I had been awake for the last 40 hours and that I'd only had about eight hours' sleep since Harry rang me. 'Never mind,' I thought, 'the game isn't until tomorrow so I can get a great night's sleep tonight. I might as well have another couple of glasses with Bruiser, even though he looks as though he's gone five rounds with George Foreman.'

At last, we entered the arrivals hall in Sydney. I was full of smiles as I spotted Harry and his entourage of club officials. But I sensed immediately that there was something wrong. The Wollongong boss looked shell-shocked. Perhaps he had lost another key player. Or maybe he wasn't impressed with his first look at Bruiser.

Harry had a look of horror on his face as he said, 'Alan, are you all right?'

'I'm fine,' I replied, wondering what he was getting at.

'You look dreadful. Have you been ill? Your eyes are all red.'

I looked at myself for the first time. Sure, there were a few champagne stains down my shirt, and the cuff of my shirt had got torn when I caught it in the door of the loo on the last leg of the flight. But I didn't know what he meant about my eyes. I looked at Bruiser. He looked a terrible mess, and he smelt like a brewery. I introduced him quickly and ran off to the nearest bathroom. When I had a good look in the mirror I realised why Harry had been aghast. I was unshaven and there were huge bags under my eyes, which looked strangely unfocused and resembled the planet Saturn, surrounded by red rings. My hair looked like the mess that sits on the head of the boxing promoter Don King.

I did what I could to clean myself up and made my way back. I still wasn't worried. In 24 hours' time I'd be fighting fit again. But Harry was still looking terribly worried. And Bruiser, the nifty winger I'd selected who was going to tear Sydney Olympic apart, had fallen asleep on top of his case.

'We'll have to stop somewhere on the way so that you can tidy up,' he said.

'On the way to where?' I asked.

'The ground, of course.'

'Why are we going to the ground, Harry? I need to get to my hotel and get some rest.'

He looked at me strangely. He was clearly puzzled.

'We kick off in five hours, Alan. You've got to do radio and TV interviews and have a massage.'

It was as though a bolt of lightning had gone down my spine. Had I heard him right? We were kicking off in five hours? Somehow I had lost a day by travelling around the world (I've always been hopeless with time zones). I was in no fit state to play football. I was in no fit state for anything except a very long sleep, preferably under sedation. And Bruiser? When he woke up he wouldn't even know which country we were in, let alone that he was supposed to be playing football.

What was I going to do? I'd already realised that I'd lost my boots somewhere. Throughout my career I'd always travelled with my boots at my side, and I had a vague memory of giving them away to the manager of the hotel in Kuala Lumpur. I had only one choice. It didn't matter how I felt now, I had to pull myself together and get on with the job.

'OK,' I said, 'let's go. Somebody had better pick up Bruiser.'

'Alan ...' pleaded Harry.

'Harry, don't worry about it. We've come to do a job for you. We'll do it. It's been a long journey and we're a bit knackered, but we've got big reserves of adrenalin. Don't worry about Bruiser. He's not used to travelling. He's got jet-lag, but he'll snap out of it.'

I'd talked myself into a positive frame of mind. Faced with a crisis, I suddenly felt bright and alert. I was up for the challenge. As we were waiting for the convoy of cars to arrive outside the airport, I dropped to the pavement and started doing press-ups. As I breathed deeply I could feel the strength returning to my frame.

We went to a stadium I had not played at before. It was brand new and stood right next to the legendary SCG, the Sydney Cricket Ground. It reminded me of the magnificence of Hampden Park. I stood outside the main entrance to this Australian shrine and took inspiration from the sporting feats that had taken place there. I wasn't too big on cricket but I knew that legends such as Compton, Hobbs and Sobers must have played there, and it gave me a warm feeling.

There were already fans floating around. I definitely didn't want to be seen in the state I was in, so I rushed in, dragging Bruiser with me. We headed for the changing room and spent at least an hour in the showers, me wearing the new pair of boots I had been given. As the hot and then cold water cascaded over us I led Bruiser in a series of loosening-up exercises. By the time I appeared in front of a radio microphone and local TV cameras I was feeling a bit like a footballer again.

Harry was desperate not to let anybody know that we had just stepped off the plane. I learnt later that he had a very big bet riding on the game, plus the bragging rights. Harry, being a Greek Cypriot, wanted to put one over on the mainland Greeks.

Soon we were in the tunnel, and I could hear the crowd. I was really pumped up. It reminded me of my European debut in Barcelona's Nou Camp, when I was playing for Ipswich. 'Come on boys!' I was shouting. 'Come on, we can do this lot! They're frightened of us!' My words echoed off the walls as I looked up and down our line – a motley collection of Greeks, Turks, ex-pats and, of course, Bruiser.

When we ran out on to the pitch the adrenalin really started pumping. After five minutes I realised that, fortunately, the opposition were not as good as I'd feared. Bruiser was burning up and down the right like a madman. We'd filled him full of energy drinks, and it seemed to be working.

***

Half-time came, and we were holding on to our lead. As I got up to go out for the second half, I felt my legs buckle. I knew I wouldn't be able to do any more running. From then on I used my right leg to stand on and my left foot to drop balls over the defence, or to spray them out left and right. I took all the throw-ins and corners. I have never felt so dead on my feet.

As I was lining up to take one corner I heard a shout from the crowd: 'Pelé! Pelé!' Nobody had called me that for years. It was one of my nicknames at Ipswich, for obvious reasons. I looked up and there was my old pal Alex Jamieson sitting four rows back. He had been an apprentice with me at Ipswich but had never really made the grade. I was so desperate for a physical break that I hopped over the wall and walked up the steps to greet him. I don't know what I was thinking, but I just couldn't go on. The referee came rushing over, feverishly blowing his whistle. He ordered me back on to the pitch, where he booked me.

Fifteen minutes later, the final whistle went. At that moment I knew what a drowning man feels like when he breaks the surface and gulps in a lungful of air. I just collapsed on the pitch. I was trembling; my tongue was stuck to my teeth; I had blurred vision. But we had won, and the whole bench, plus Harry, came catapulting on to the pitch. I was hauled off the turf and found myself joining in a lap of honour.

All I wanted to do was go to bed. As soon as I got back to the dressing room I was going to lie on a bench and I was going to stay there for a couple of days. But I didn't have a chance. As soon as I got into the dressing room the corks started popping. Somebody poured a whole bottle of champagne over my head. As it dripped down my face I started to taste it on my lips. Delicious. I was caught in the bubbly trap again.

Showering and changing was all a blur. When Bruiser and I got outside there was a convoy of cars ready to take us out on the town. It was the last thing we needed. Harry and I were in the leading limo; the cars behind us were full of the other players and the girls who take part in the Oz Aerobics. And while I have always been very happily married, the company of a group of pretty girls beats hairy-arsed footballers any day of the week.

We went to The Rocks, which is the most exclusive part of Sydney Harbour. I remember being in a restaurant and to my right was the Sydney Opera House. I had rarely seen such a magnificent example of modern architecture. As the light faded it became illuminated. It was so close I felt I could reach out and touch it. Unsurprisingly, it is my abiding image of Australia.

I didn't get back to my hotel until the early hours. I don't know how the human body works, but I felt so good that I went to the bar with my old pal Alex, who had joined us during the evening. I reckoned that by the time I got to bed I had gone 60 hours without sleep. And by two o'clock the following afternoon I was enjoying more bubbly at a barbecue in somebody's back garden.

The outcome of that victory over Sydney was that I was

persuaded to stay for the rest of the season. Jill was happy enough because the money was important to us and she was settled at home looking after the children.

I was determined at some point to have a reunion drink with Alex Jamieson. There is often an empathy between those footballers who graduate out of the youth ranks and become the real thing and those who fall by the wayside. The feeling from my point of view is 'There but for the grace of God go I'. I've never even considered what I would have done if I had not made the grade as a pro. Fortunately it was something I never had to consider. Lots of young lads returned to 'civvie street', and they just had to get on with their lives.

Alex and I got together one lunchtime – you couldn't do anything socially in the early evening because in Australia you have to train at six p.m. because of the intense daytime heat – and I have to confess that I swallowed a couple of beers and a glass or two of champagne, but genuinely in moderation before going off to a very light training session involving a game of five-a-side. We agreed to reconvene at ten, after I had finished at the club, though I wasn't sure that Alex would still be around by then. I had been measured in my intake in the afternoon, but Alex had drunk for Britain. He'd started off with a few beers but had then got into the champagne. He wasn't a regular champagne drinker and it knocked him sideways. He was soon slurring his speech, and at one point his head fell to one side as though he had broken his neck. As a precaution I booked a room for him in my hotel and told the head waiter that when the moment was right he should get somebody to steer Alex to his bed.

Sure enough, when I got back there was no sign of my pal.

'Everything OK?' I asked the head waiter. 'Did you put my mate to bed?'

He just shook his head. Then a horrifying story spilt out. Alex had tried to drink some more champagne but he'd tipped his seat backwards and collided with a light. Two of the waiters took him up to his room. Half an hour later there was a call from the room next to him. The guests in that room reported that he had been swigging red wine on the balcony before falling to his knees and vomiting all over the floor. He had then attempted to crawl back into his room through what had become a red-wine lake, taking all the mess with him.

Waiters rushed up to the room to be met with a terrifying sight. Alex had even used a curtain as a towel to wipe his hands and face. He was found curled up in the bath. Apparently this sort of thing is quite common in Australia and the housekeeper decided the best thing to do was to leave things as they were and they would sort it out in the morning.

After breakfast the next day I went up to Alex's room with trepidation. I'd already told the hotel I would foot the bill for any damage. But the man who opened the door wasn't a shambling drunk. He was bright-eyed and full of life. He urged me into the room and I held my breath because I imagined that the place was going to smell rather unpleasant. But it didn't. It smelt like a flower shop. Where were the stained carpets and bedclothes, the desecrated curtains and vomit-covered walls?

'Have they changed your room for you?' I asked, puzzled.

'No,' Alex replied. 'Don't worry. There was a bit of a problem last night but I've sorted it all out. See this?' He lifted up a large leather bag, the sort you might see being carried by a doctor. 'I never leave home without it.' He sounded like the American Express advert.

He yanked it open, and it was full of bottles of fluid.

At first I was puzzled. Then I remembered he had told me he ran a cleaning business. I thought he had meant a sort of office-cleaning operation, but his company produced the sort of chemical cleaning fluids that you see on the shelves of supermarkets, and more sophisticated ones for industry. He always had a supply of them in his car.

I laughed. 'You came prepared then.'

'It happens every time,' he said. 'I just can't drink, but I love the taste so I always clean up after myself. This room is in better nick now than it was before I threw up all over it.'

I have often wondered whether one of these days I will get hit by a sleep deficit. Since that missed night's sleep in America and nearly three nights in Sydney there have been many times when I have not got to bed, or maybe survived on an hour or two. I don't miss it. Maybe I built up reserves of stamina as a professional footballer which keep me going to this day.

And it's not all about drink. It is about preferring to be awake. I once read this horrifying statistic that some people spend 40 per cent of their lives in bed. What a terrible waste. You can't do anything with your life when you're asleep. You can't play golf or go to the theatre. Stick those sorts of activities into your daylight hours and your evenings and it means you're pushing back your dining and drinking hours. And sometimes you push them back so far they meet tomorrow morning's commitments.

I contend that I am a responsible drinker with the odd blip. For seven years now I have been doing the breakfast show on talkSPORT. For five of those years I did it with Porky before he suffered his own illness, when his heart packed up on him (more on that later). When Porky and I worked together we did it six days a week. I was getting up at four o'clock in the morning and driving for an hour and a half to work. Of course I've had the odd problem. The saga of Cheltenham which led to me being temporarily sacked is well documented. But in all that time I have presented some 2,000 shows and missed no more than six from the effects of partying too hard the night before. And one of those was when I was implored to attend the office Christmas party.

I have read half a dozen reports about the enormous cost to industry of workers who don't turn up as a result of hangovers. Not many people get up as early as me and I would plead that my absence record for 'sickness' is a lot better than the vast majority of the working population. The difference is that when I am absent it is a very public absence. Most other people's absences are largely anonymous.

I don't want to encourage people into irresponsible drinking. And of course you've got to look after yourself physically. I have big responsibilities to other people, most notably my wife Jill and our three gorgeous daughters. If I thought I was putting myself at risk I'd change things tomorrow. But how can any of us gauge how long we are going to live? After all, we're only here for a visit.

CHAPTER TWO

PUTTING THE BOOT IN

*'I didn't go looking for trouble, but if I'd
ignored it I would have been a different
person to the one I am now.'*

THERE WAS A SHOCKING ATMOSPHERE in the dressing room. Silence, except for the clattering of boots being thrown on to the tiled floor as a dozen Manchester United footballers vented their rage at throwing away a three-goal lead. Then the shouting started. 'What the hell was all that about?' was the general cry from more than one of the lads.

In pursuit of the First Division title we had built ourselves a three-goal lead at Nottingham Forest, recently double European champions. I'd started well, bearing down on the keeper for what I thought was going to be a certain goal until I was up-ended in the area. We scored from the penalty and added another two, only to completely lose our concentration and allow them right back into the game. Stupidly, we found ourselves sharing the points in a 3-3 draw.

At times like that warfare can erupt in a dressing room. Recriminations bounce off the wall. It always reminded me of the book Lord of the Flies. The normal rules of society go out of the window. Everybody is looking for somebody to blame.

The manager, Ron Atkinson, was trying to be as measured as he could, though you could see the suppressed anger in every line on his face. He must have thought that our keeper, the

South African Gary Bailey, could have done a lot better. As we sat around, disgusted with ourselves and pulling our shirts and socks off, he fired a question at the blond-haired Bailey.

'Tell me about that second goal,' he demanded in a none too friendly fashion.

'I'm sorry, boss, I just couldn't keep it out,' Bailey replied.

Atkinson, clearly unhappy with this answer, raised his voice and snapped, 'Well what about the third? Why the hell didn't you come out for the cross?'

Sometimes you can feel sorry for goalkeepers. Their game comes under the microscope all the time because they're between the posts. But in the aftermath of this battle there wasn't much sympathy floating around in that dressing room. We were all trying to find an answer for what we regarded as our failure that afternoon.

Before Bailey could answer the question, our centre-half, Gordon McQueen, cut in with a vicious barb: 'Because he's a bleeding coward.'

Bailey came off his bench like a marble out of a catapult. But he wasn't quick enough for McQueen, my Scottish international team-mate. Gordon thumped him in the face, and bedlam broke out. Bryan Robson, Captain Fantastic to the footballing world, launched himself between the two of them as the rest of the boys piled in. I had my arm around Gordon's neck, but he was bigger than me and full of anger, and he tried to pull away.

Bailey was hell-bent on revenge. Being a goalkeeper, he was big and strong. He pretended to give up, but then he wriggled free and launched himself at Gordon again, this time head-first. Bad mistake. Footballers do most of their work with their feet, and McQueen had no hesitation. He couldn't use his arms because I had them pinned to his side, so he 'volleyed' his team-mate full in the face with his right foot. There was a resounding smack. Bailey's nose burst and blood spattered all over the white-tiled walls, and some of the players.

Now it was chaos. We all dived in again, everybody shouting, swearing and screaming. Dressing rooms echo a lot because they are like the inside of a swimming-pool, and anger and vile intent was bouncing off the walls and ceiling. Somebody was banging on the door and trying to get in, but Ron had locked it ahead of the inquest he was going to conduct into how we had squandered our lead. Ron then reasserted his authority and ordered us all to change as quickly as possible and get on to the team bus. The journey home was tense and miserable. Hardly anybody spoke.

The reason I tell this story is to illustrate exactly how high passions can rise in football. When they do, it often results in physical confrontation. That's the nature of what footballers do. I'm not excusing it, but I am getting increasingly alarmed about society's attitude to footballers. I am worried that players are becoming whipping boys for many of our communities' ills.

One particular case has led me to wonder whether there is a backlash against footballers, who are widely portrayed as overpaid prima donnas who receive a disproportionately high reward from life for what they do. But remember, the multi-millionaires who are on our TV screens every week are the elite of the game, and for every young professional earning phenomenal sums at the top clubs there are ten others who live in semi-detached houses and drive around in Ford Mondeos.

One of the players in that category is 24-year-old James Cotterill. You've probably never heard of him. Neither had anybody else until he got involved in an incident with a young Bristol Rovers striker during an FA Cup first-round tie. At the time of writing, Mr Cotterill is serving a four-month prison sentence for walloping his opponent, Rovers striker Sean Rigg, in the face and breaking his jaw in two places. It was a nasty business. The punch came from behind, and Mr Rigg will have a metal plate in his face for the rest of his life to remind him of the encounter.

But this happened on a football pitch, not on the streets. Of course Rigg, aged just eighteen, didn't deserve to have his face fractured, but at the time he was playing in a highly competitive FA Cup tie. Cotterill was a part-time player in a Conference North team, Barrow, who turned out that day against league opposition in the greatest domestic competition in the world. And the father of one, also an apprentice table-joiner, could not have been more remorseful. It was said in court that 'He is thoroughly ashamed for his family, his club and his profession. It was an act of folly that took place in the heat of the moment.' Cotterill had already told police that his opponent had barged into him earlier in the game and that he had been caught painfully on the back of the foot. He said he thought his opponent was coming after him again, so he struck out to keep him away. But he knew that his behaviour was 'unacceptable' and he told the officers that he immediately regretted it. In fact, he was so mortified by his actions that he wrote to both Rigg and Bristol Rovers Football Club to apologise. The court also heard that he had never before been involved in anything similar. Judge Robert Brown at Preston

Crown Court said, 'I accept that this incident was completely out of character as far as you are concerned.'

He then added, 'The courts have made it absolutely clear for a long time now that this sort of violence on the field of play cannot and will not be tolerated. And for this kind of off-the-ball incident a custodial sentence is inevitable.' I don't get that at all. I am not aware of any recent similar incidents in football, apart from the very high-profile case of Manchester City's Ben Thatcher, who gave Portsmouth's Pedro Mendes a forearm smash in the face that has not been seen on telly since the days of Jackie Pallo. Mendes ended up in hospital and Thatcher ended up with a ban and the wholesale condemnation of his own manager; but, far from going to jail, his career as a £20,000-a-week Premiership footballer is flourishing.

In Cotterill's case, the football authorities had already reacted in the right way: they banned the player for four months and fined him. In my view that should have been the end of the matter. The incident happened on a football pitch, and the Football Association handed out the punishment. So why did it end up in the courts? Almost certainly because the incident appeared on BBC's Match of the Day, which has millions of viewers. Any member of the public can make a complaint, and suddenly the police are involved.

I think it's madness that the case ended up in the courts. A 24-year-old man with a young child goes down for four months. Cotterill also lost his job, despite the fact that the court was told he would if he was absent for more than twenty days. This should make any responsible member of our society angry about the way we treat offenders in our society, and the relationship between punishment and crime.

But what has really infuriated me to the point where I feel like setting off in a boat in search of a new world called Sanity is that just over a fortnight after the footballer was banged up, this country started letting paedophiles go free. Monsters who are a threat to our children were suddenly allowed back into society because we had run out of places in prison in which to house them. One pervert who was facing fourteen years had to be released on bail because there was nowhere to send him or hold him. He'd admitted a string of vile attacks on youngsters, and he had a history of abusing children going back 26 years.

I'm not going to ask the obvious question of who most of us think should be in jail, a footballer who raised his fists to an opponent in a controlled environment or a self-confessed child-attacker. And don't tell me that the judge in the footballer's case was not to know that the jails were about to get full. What is the use of the vast army of civil servants that populate this country if they can't work out that we are running out of jail space? We've got to send more real law-breakers and fewer footballers to jail in this country otherwise the decent majority will increasingly start to take the law into their own hands. How sick are we all getting of reading stories about 'have-a-go heroes' being prosecuted rather than the lawless characters they are trying to reprimand or apprehend?

I do not agree with those who would tell me that we already send more people to jail in Britain than in any other western country. That is because all major institutions of authority have been eroded here by successive governments since the 1960s. The UK has become a sort of Eden Project for social engineering experiments. During the course of this massive reversal of our basic values all those who used to be the pillars of our very civilised society have been neutered. Teenagers now laugh at the police and take pride in their anti-social and law-breaking activities. A day out at court is a good opportunity to meet up with their mates. They don't care how much they get fined because they have no intention of paying. And if they did pay it would be taxpayers' money because so many of these feckless and feral youths have never worked. Many teachers now live in fear of their pupils. Parents have to be careful that they don't exercise too much discipline over their own children in case they breach their human rights.

I sincerely believe that society has turned on its head over the last twenty years to the extent that young footballers can now set an example to most other areas of society. In many instances young trainee footballers are setting standards of behaviour which, if copied by millions of others, would improve our towns and cities and make Britain a much more pleasant place to live. For a lad of fifteen even to be considered for training with a professional club means that he must have focus and dedication if he wants to achieve his dream. He knows he cannot run with his mates. He mustn't smoke, and he certainly mustn't take drugs. The environment of a football club instils discipline and a sense of worth. If every headmaster or headmistress in this country were able to show the strength and resolve of a youth-team coach and therefore safeguard those in their care, juvenile delinquency would be eliminated.

Please don't get me wrong. I know there are tens of thousands of dedicated teachers out there, but in my view they are constantly undermined by central government and a clique of so-called child psychologists and misguided 'do-gooders' who do not show them the support they deserve. Children have lost respect for teachers because successive governments have deliberately eroded the authority of those who should be setting the standards in our society. When you have the Prime Minister's wife banging on about 'children's rights' there is little hope of bringing any meaningful focus to a child's existence. A child cannot always make the right decisions about his or her life. Wisdom has a direct relationship with age, and it is the job of adults to guide young people, and often to save them from themselves.

Sometimes I despair when I see the stranglehold into which our teachers have been placed. Do you know what would happen if an ignorant, out-of-control father turned up at a football club's training ground and attempted to assault a coach because of a supposed slight to his son? He would get beaten up. It would be legitimate self-defence, and the yobbish father would never go near the place again. Neither would his son. To those who would accuse me of advocating violence, I would ask in reply, 'What should teachers do when threatened with brutality?' They should be allowed to defend themselves, but often the loutish parent will be 22 stones of couch-potato lard who would easily overwhelm a teacher who had probably never raised a hand in anger in his or her life.

So often I read of cases of teachers being attacked and months or even years later the assailant eventually receives an ASBO or some sort of other meaningless punishment. The teacher, meanwhile, may have been forced out of the profession through trauma or physical incapacity. Which of these two people should society be trying to protect, a teacher who is a force for good in life, or a useless, violent deadbeat?

You don't very often get a second chance at a football club. That's the way it should be. It is a tremendous privilege for a boy to be given the chance to develop a football career. Why can't all young people see what a privilege it is to be brought up in a country that offers them the possibility of a good education? If a scheming school pupil is responsible for a situation that results in violence against a teacher, then that child should be removed from the educational system. The individual should be put into some sort of vocational training to try to find a way of channelling the energy he puts into his disruptive behaviour.

But enough of that. Back to the world of football and why the law should leave it alone.

People who try to involve themselves in the world of football but who have never been part of that world are not qualified to interfere. The rules of engagement are different to the rest of society. If you want to become a surveyor or a lawyer or a doctor there are plenty of jobs to go for (or at least there were until we started putting record amounts of money into the NHS and then closing chunks of it down). But in football there are only so many jobs because while each town has plenty of surveyor and legal practices, there is usually only one professional football club, sometimes two. And that means that competition for those jobs is very fierce. Football is a physical game, hence the battle to become a footballer involves not only determination and skill, but the physical ability to overcome your fellow youth. This is evident from a very early age, and that is why I firmly believe that the culture of football and other professional sports is very different from the rest of society.

What I would call the 'chattering classes' do not understand the culture of a sport that has its roots in working-class communities. Most footballers come from council housing estates and have never enjoyed the benefit of a great education at a private or public school.

The 'chattering classes', on the other hand, have mostly benefited from a comparatively elitist upbringing. They have enjoyed the privilege of parental wealth and an education at a top academic establishment. They have never had to fight their way out of a playground against a mob of aggressors. The sports into which the 'chattering classes' move are cricket and rugby. Many of England's eminent cricketers over the years have come from the playing fields of Oxford and Cambridge. And there is nothing wrong with that.

I'd never picked up a cricket bat until I was in my early forties. I was doing a breakfast show for talkSPORT at The Oval, and I had to take part in an exhibition batting session. I faced up to a delivery from former England captain Mike Gatting. I smacked it high into the air and I felt very comfortable about it. I think that if you've been a professional sportsman then you have ball-to-eye co-ordination. At the moment I whacked the delivery I felt as good as when you hit a golf-ball plumb in the middle of the head of your driver. I wished that I had played cricket as a young man. I think I would have been good at it.

But the point I am making is that, generally speaking, cricketers have not come from backgrounds in which they've scrapped in the streets as part of their growing up. It is not their culture. But it is from within their culture that judges come who then decide to lock up footballers for a dust-up which happens on the pitch.

What about violence in rugby? The way the authorities respond to violence in this game is an even more stark example of the class division within our three major sports. England World Cup-winning captain Martin Johnson has been involved in violent confrontations on a sports field equal to that of Barrow's James Cotterill. But he's never ended up in court, let alone jail. Why is that? Well, one explanation could well be that Johnson, as captain of our rugby team rather than our football team, is seen by our lawmakers as one of them – one of the establishment. We don't send our own boys to jail!

A perfect example of this philosophy occurred in the 2006/07 season. England's rugby team had not been having a particularly great season. They had just been walloped by the Irish in Dublin and were preparing for a crunch match against the French at Twickenham. On the Sunday before the game the England skipper Phil Vickery was smashed in the face while playing for his club, Wasps, against Bristol in a Premiership game. The blow that felled him left him in the sort of state you see a heavyweight boxer in when he tries to stagger to his feet after being on the receiving end of a haymaker. As he tried to get up, his legs buckled; it eventually took five coaches and officials to guide him safely off the pitch. The assailant was Bristol prop Jason Hobson, who was immediately suspended for two weeks by his club. The Rugby Football Union also dealt with the matter.

But Hobson did not end up in jail and have his life and his career damaged by that one act of recklessness. I would contend that in some ways it was a worse offence than that committed by Cotterill, because it appears to have been an almost random assault. Explaining his reaction to the situation, Bristol head coach Richard Hill said, 'Jason has admitted he was involved. You can't afford to clench your fist and swing a punch. Jason feels really terrible about it, as you would expect. Phil is one of his idols and they were both brought up in the same part of Cornwall. Jason hit out in the heat of the moment. He didn't know who the other player was, and when he realised it was Phil he apologised to him. Jason has been with us four years and this is the first time he has been involved in an incident like this. He is distraught about it because he knows he has let himself down. It's a shame but, on the rare occasion when a Bristol player is involved, we don't try to cover it up.'

There are many similarities between the two cases. Neither the footballer nor the rugby player had a history of violence but both committed a dreadful assault. Each case was dealt with severely by their respective sporting bodies. The big difference, of course, is that the footballer went on to be dealt with by the criminal justice system. The courts showed no interest in getting involved in the rugby player's case.

Don't get me wrong. I do not want to see a competitive young rugby player thrown into jail. I have already made the case that there are thousands of scumbags out there who should not be loose on our streets. What I do want to see is society evening up the way it treats members of our community. It is dreadful to focus on football as though members of that profession deserve sterner treatment than others.

***

Like most people, my upbringing shaped my whole attitude to life. I didn't have to fight my way out of a gutter because I was born into a very respectable and solid middle-class home in the safe-and-sound Glasgow neighbourhood of Simshill. My dad was a shopkeeper and my mum was a housewife, when it was still a respectable thing to be. They have always been wonderful parents to me, despite the problems I've often caused them. I wasn't in any way deprived. If all people were lucky enough to have parents like mine there wouldn't be half the strife in the world that there is today.

But in some ways my childhood was too comfortable. I was a young, impressionable kid, I adored Celtic Football Club, and I was very determined that I was going to be a footballer. I felt a bit cosseted, and like many youngsters I was looking for a bit more 'street-cred'. So I was quite excited when I ended up going to Holyrood School in Govanhill on the south side of Glasgow. It was a huge comprehensive, but it had a good academic record. Better still, it had a reputation for turning out footballers, so I settled in very easily to this new environment.

I learnt very quickly that you had to stand up for yourself. It wasn't exactly a jungle, but the kids with ginger hair, freckles and National Health glasses definitely had a harder time than the rest. I had a mop of tight curly hair, and on day one an elder boy started mocking me, calling me a 'lassie'. I was big for my age and had already started making my mark on the football world. I kicked him in the bollocks and sprinted off. He couldn't tell his mates in the school that he'd been sorted out by a younger lad, and he never picked on me again.

He was a coward, because he sent his mate after me. This lad was even bigger. He attacked me when I wasn't looking, viciously kicking me on the shins, then stamping on my legs when I went down. I got a bruising, but there was no long-term damage. I know who that boy is; his face is burnt on my memory. If I ever see him on the streets of Glasgow I will give him a thorough pasting. But, unlike when he attacked me, I will approach him from the front, not from behind.

I never wanted to get involved in violence, but unfortunately it was an inherent part of my upbringing. I first realised that when I was ten years old and my brother Mike, seven years older than me, arrived home from school with blood all over his face. His clothes were torn and he had boot marks on his white shirt, and even the imprint of somebody's Doc Marten sole on his forehead. It was a foretaste of things to come.

I didn't go looking for trouble, but if I'd ignored it I would have been a different person to the one I am now. And I would never have become an international footballer. That honour would have gone to the kid who was bullying me at school. I was only mates with those who stood up for themselves. I had no time and no respect for those who didn't.

Tremendous rivalry existed between the schools in Glasgow. It wasn't just Protestant and Catholic, it could be about a football match or a 'territorial' dispute. At the age of fifteen many of the lads would carry a weapon in their bag – maybe a hammer – when they went off to play other youth sides. There was often an eruption of trouble afterwards. Drumchapel was a district I never liked going to. I remember a game we won and there was terrible trouble on the touchline. The supporters, which included parents, were often more worked up than the players and we had to fight even to get back to the dressing room. Then, as we came out, me and about half a dozen of the lads were set upon by a mob of at least 50 people. Again, there were parents among them.

Raiding parties attacked other schools. We could be playing football in the yard one moment and suddenly a gang of twenty youths would rush in and jump on us. A few weeks later we would launch a raid on them and try to batter the hell out of our attackers. It was mostly fists and feet, but it could be iron bars.

Sometimes there were tragic consequences. We used to go ice-skating on a Thursday evening because we were too young to go into pubs. Violence would flare up at the ice-rink. We had a young pal called Joe. We all liked him because he was the smallest member of our 'gang', but he was one of the bravest. He was always first in where the fists were flying and he feared no one. But, like all of us, he had learnt to become a fast runner for the times when we were outnumbered. One evening we were ambushed outside the ice-rink. We split up and sprinted off. Little Joe was being chased by three bigger boys. To this day I am not clear about exactly what happened, but Joe was killed. I had always understood that he ran straight in front of a bus and was knocked down. But another of my friends told me years later that he had been caught and battered over the head with a pair of ice-skates.

We also used to go to night-club dances in St Enoch Square. It was always likely that there was going to be a gang in there from the Gorbals, just south of the River Clyde. Whenever it kicked off, the organisers, and sometimes the police, would rush in. Then you would hear the clattering noise as knives, iron bars and hammers fell to the floor. The boys always got the girls to hide the weapons in their handbags, which never got searched.

We used to hang around a shopping centre at Croftfoot roundabout in south Glasgow. It was right next to the notorious Castlemilk housing estate which was said to be the biggest in Europe. It was known as the murder capital of Scotland. That was where I first came across organised gangs of muggers. They just stopped you and tried to steal all your money. A real turn of speed was needed. However, there must have been something of merit about this fearsome urban sprawl because it produced some really great footballers, such as my talkSPORT colleague Ray Houghton, who became a Liverpool and Ireland legend; Celtic's Arthur Graham, who was my colleague at the Boys' Club; and Leeds United brothers Eddie and Frank Gray, the latter of whom was a Scotland team-mate of mine.

One of the worst incidents I can remember as a kid was when I got trapped on top of a bus with just two other pals while a mob of literally hundreds were trying to get at us up the stairs.

We were on the bus heading in from the south of Glasgow for the snooker club in Mitchell Street, near the city centre. A shiver went down my spine as I heard the distant strains of a band. I would know that sound anywhere. It was a traditional Orangemen's march. I was urging the bus on so that it would clear the high street before the parade turned the corner from a side-road. But the marchers made it first, and the bus had to stop. There were a few other people on the top deck. I remember distinctly the smell of smoke and ash, because you were still allowed to smoke upstairs in those days. The other passengers were leaning towards the windows and cheering the marchers on, but my mates and I just sat there stone-faced.

There were two men who looked like marshals, with white

gloves and batons. They spotted that we weren't joining in. We didn't make any provocative gestures or anything like that. We just couldn't bring ourselves even to smile with the marchers to try to disguise the fact that we were from the other side of the divided community. The men in the white gloves had stopped marching. They were waving their arms around, working up those around them and pointing at us on the bus.

Missiles started to bang off the window. As we moved away, we saw a breakaway group of youths rush towards the entry platform at the back of the bus. We were trapped. There was no point in trying to run because we were surrounded by the marchers. I grabbed my two mates and we took guard at the top of the stairs.

'If any of them get up here, we're dead,' I said. 'Boot them back down the stairs.'

All three of us crushed on to the top stair, and as the first of our would-be assailants came round the corner he got it full in the face. Crack. I felt bone breaking as I swung my foot with all my force into the nose of a boy who was wearing a white shirt. The blood burst out of his nostrils and spattered the wall of the bus. A second youth came up with his head down, trying to steam-roller us, but my mate grabbed the rails on each side of the stairs and launched a two-footed attack on the top of his head with his heels. I thought he might have broken his neck because his head seemed to compact into his body and he let out a terrible cry. He fell back on to his mates behind him and prevented anybody else from ascending.

Women passengers upstairs discarded their still-lit cigarettes and started to scream and shout for help as they banged on the windows. By now the parade had broken up in disarray and all the marchers were surrounding the bus. The huge vehicle was rocking from side to side. We were still kicking out at the attackers as they tried to get up the stairs but I thought the bus was going to go over. In a fleeting moment I hoped that it might because that would scatter the mob and maybe give us a chance to get away. I had never been so frightened in my life. I thought we were going to be pummelled to death. We couldn't fight them off for ever.

The women were screaming for us to let them off, but we couldn't move from the top of the stairs. If we did, even for a second, one of our attackers would have had us.

After what seemed like an eternity, the police burst through the throng below and scattered our attackers. We were still very reluctant to give up our defensive position because we didn't know what would be waiting for us. But when police reinforcements arrived, they surrounded us and frog-marched us to safety in a nearby shop as we ducked the missiles that were being hurled at us from the other side of the road. We never got to play snooker that afternoon.

When I think back now, it was crazy. Religion. Is it worth it?

I do not want to glorify violence, nor do I want to glory in it. But it was around during my upbringing and you had to meet it head-on. I think there is something tribal in all of us. I don't know if it is more pronounced among the Celtic countries, but it has been a basic instinct of man to fight for what he wants since the start of time. It's in the genes, and it exists to this day. One of my favourite films is *Gangs of New York*. It's a long way from mid nineteenth-century New York to late twentieth-century Glasgow, but when I watch that film I feel like I am looking at the life-story of my ancestors. For me, the gang I was in was not a pro-active bunch of trouble-makers. It was strength in numbers, for protection against other groups of people who wanted to do me harm. The experience certainly taught me that when under threat the best form of defence is attack.

It prepared me well for becoming a professional footballer. And I don't just mean out there on the pitch during a game. As I mentioned, every young boy in his teens wants to become a footballer. Sometimes talent alone will not get you there. You have got to be mentally tough. If you get worn down by the intimidation and cruelty of the other young boys at your club, you will go under. If you show weakness, it will be preyed upon. If fellow footballers can make your life a misery, they will. Your failure means that they have a greater chance of success.

I had one long-term injury as a youth player just after I arrived at Ipswich. I often felt despair and wondered about going back to Scotland. It's so lonely watching the other lads in those developing years taking another stride every week towards their professional career while you are laid up. But eventually I got fit again, and I fought my way back into the squad and then into the first team. Others didn't make it. I saw one lad come back from a long lay-off and almost immediately we went on a youth team tour. He had a dreadful time. His 'team-mates' kept reminding him that he had fallen down the pecking order and it shattered his confidence. When we got back he was called in to see one of the youth managers. He came out of his office clutching an envelope and he was in tears. He'd been booted out of the club, but there was little sympathy. That's the football business.

Every minute of being a youth footballer is aggressive because of the nature of the business and the pot of gold that is there for you if you succeed. As an apprentice in my day, your duties included cleaning the first-team players' boots and working around the stadium, on the terraces and in the dressing rooms. On Fridays we had to make sure the stadium was spick and span, particularly if the first team were playing there the next day. Two separate groups were allocated to the home and away dressing rooms. We were all anxious to get away early because we wanted to go to the bookie's. We weren't allowed out on Fridays because we would be playing the next day, so we had to get our fun during the afternoon. One day one of our group, Ian Phillips, an Ayrshire boy, was on floor duty. He had to use the buffing machine until you could see your own face in the floor. But when he went to get it he found it had gone. An east London lad had jumped the queue and was using it to do the corridors. The Londoner was a very big lad, and Ian was slight and wiry. He asked for the machine but the Eastender just laughed at him. Ian went and pulled the plug out. The Londoner approached him menacingly, but Ian leapt forward and gave him a classic Glasgow kiss, right in the middle of the forehead. The bigger boy collapsed like a tent that had just had its ropes cut. I don't remember ever seeing him again.

David Geddis, who survived that car crash with Peter Canavan, was another aggressive youngster. He was regarded as very good-looking and had a swathe of blond hair. He would constantly taunt the guys that he was going to take their girlfriends. We were playing five-a-side one day and he laid into a younger Terry Butcher. In those days, believe it or not, Butch was shy and unassuming. The coaching staff would goad him to get stuck in. Geddis threw a punch. Butch ducked it easily and booted him so hard through his midriff that he nearly disembowelled him. Another time, John Wark squared up to Geddis in the gym. There was a fight twice a week, usually involving somebody calling somebody else a cheat.

Though violence was never far away and I was never afraid to meet it, if necessary, it was always better, of course, if you could get away without having to resort to it. Particularly if you thought you might come off worse. That has happened to me on a few occasions, and the one I remember most vividly still sends a shiver down my spine.

I had been playing for Scotland at Hampden Park and I had gone with a group of the lads to a club on Clydeside for a few beers after the game. Generally speaking, when you were wearing the shirt of Scotland you became a neutral in the eyes of most people, rather than a 'Ger (Rangers) or a Hoop (Celtic). In those days a big contingent of the squad was drawn from the two Glasgow giants, unlike today. I was with some Scotland team-mates as well as old school-friends Arthur, Tommy and Neil, for whom I'd got tickets for the game. I was signing autographs and posing for pictures, oblivious as to whether I was talking to Rangers fans or Celtic fans. There was a lot of bonhomie around, except for one individual, a real brute of a man, who suddenly appeared on the scene.

He was a huge, menacing figure, at least six feet four inches tall, I figured. He had a large bulbous head and a crew-cut. He could have been an American army PE instructor, but it was soon clear that he was very Scottish. I don't know why he was in the VIP area with us, but from the moment he appeared the whole atmosphere changed. He was very drunk and he kept going on about a Rangers versus Celtic game that had resulted in a victory for his side, the 'Gers, of whom he was clearly a fanatical follower. I couldn't understand what he was going on about because there hadn't been a recent Old Firm game. I don't know if he knew who I was or even that I was a footballer. He was making plenty of anti-Celtic remarks but that would have been quite normal for as rabid a Rangers fan as this guy. I was trying to be polite but he wasn't making any sense and I became a bit dismissive of him.

A bouncer came over to me and said quietly, 'Alan, watch yourself. That guy's called The Bullet, and he's dangerous. He's going on about an Old Firm reserve game which the Rangers won.'

I laughed. I couldn't believe that anybody could get so worked up about a reserve team game, though I learnt later that it had attracted an astonishing crowd of 27,000 fans.

The Bullet was only a few feet away when he saw me chuckling. He gave me a very dirty look. To try and ease what had now become a tense situation, I said good-naturedly, 'You go to all the big games, do you?'

The Bullet snarled, 'Do you want to go to hospital tonight, son?'

I thought he was joking so I laughed again, but almost immediately I started to feel very uneasy. I moved away and asked the bouncers if they could get rid of this guy. They seemed very uneasy about the prospect of asking him to go, but within a few minutes he had thankfully disappeared.

An hour later we were all ready to go. I nipped into the loo. There were two or three people in there and I was washing my hands when the door burst open and The Bullet was standing there. He ordered everybody else out, and they went without hesitation. 'Now you are going to hospital,' he said in a manner that left me in little doubt that he had every intention of doing me serious harm. He took his jacket off, threw it in one of the sinks and started rolling up his sleeves. He never took his eyes off me.

I tried to stay calm and continued drying my hands. I was trying to work out whether to fight him fairly, try to dance around him, or just volley him as hard as I could in the midriff. Then, thankfully, the door opened and a bouncer appeared. The Bullet still didn't take his eyes off me. He just barked out an instruction: 'Get out or you'll be next.' Meekly, the bouncer retreated and the door closed again.

The Bullet started advancing on me.

'Just what is your problem?' I said to him, trying to hide my fear.

Then the door burst open and my Ipswich and Scotland team-mate Johnny Wark flew into the bathroom. Warky was a fearsome-looking character with a shock of dark hair and a Mexican bandit-type moustache. Like me and my prospective assailant he was a Glasgow boy and not to be messed with. The Bullet was distracted by the speed and aggression of Johnny's entrance. As he reeled from this unexpected intrusion I bolted past him. I had absolutely no desire to whack him on the way out. I'd just played for my country and there were photographers around. Johnny and I left the club at speed.

Amazingly, and by the most bizarre coincidence, I met The Bullet again eighteen months later, with a completely different outcome. I was on honeymoon in Marbella with my lovely wife

Jill. It was the closed season, the weather was glorious, and I was congratulating myself on having made the best move of my life by marrying the woman who has now been my wife for 25 years. We were in Andalucia Plaza, opposite Puerto Banus, walking down to the port using the underpass beneath the road known notoriously as 'The Highway of Death'.

Just as we turned into the tunnel we spotted a couple walking towards us. It was gloomy, and at first I didn't take any notice, but as we got closer my heart skipped a beat.

The man in the couple heading straight for us was The Bullet. I didn't know what to do. I had fears that this was going to become 'The Underpass of Death'. Should I turn around? No, I wasn't going to be chased about by my former aggressor; but I had my wife of four days with me and I didn't want her to witness me being taken apart by this gorilla. I pulled Jill to the safe side of me and clenched both fists. My heart was beating incredibly fast. I tried to see if there was anything like a brick or something I could grab to defend myself.

Then, to my astonishment, as The Bullet drew level his face broke into a broad smile. He patted me on the shoulder, shook my hand and said, 'How are you, son? Still doing the business for your country, heh?' He introduced his female companion and I introduced Jill. I didn't know his real name so I just said 'an old pal from Glasgow'. He coughed out his real name but I never caught it because I was still in a state of shock at his amiable nature. After a few minutes Jill and I walked on. I was the most relieved man in Spain.

I've never seen him since.

CHAPTER THREE

THE ROAD TO NOWHERE

'If politicians had to sit in traffic jams, they would know the frustration of wasting hours of our lives that we could be spending with our families or looking after our businesses.'

THE COUPLE got on at York. He was a City type in a pinstripe suit, young and handsome and very smooth. She was a cracker. A dark outfit with a pencil-type skirt, long legs, high heels and a swathe of gorgeous black hair.

They were obviously not man and wife. Smoothie guided her to her seat in the first-class dining compartment and before he would allow her to sit down he flapped at the upholstery with a white serviette. I don't know anybody who does that for his wife once the marriage has got past the three-month mark. From the ring on his finger, he was married all right, but not to her. She had no ring on her finger, but she did have a confidence of control over her male companion which gave the game away.

She was his mistress. Mind you, she wasn't just his secretary or his PA. This woman was class. Everything told you that – the immaculate clothes, the hairstyle, the leather briefcase.

He picked up the menu off the table and suggested a glass of white wine. She readily agreed. The waiter arrived and he asked for a bottle of Pinot Grigio. The waiter, a boy from north of the border, probably a native of Edinburgh, to where our train was heading, was very apologetic. 'I'm very sorry, sir, I'm afraid all the Pinot Grigio has gone.'

'Ah, I see,' said Smoothie, clearly unhappy that he should be turned down by a humble waiter in front of his posh bird. He settled for the New Zealand Chardonnay.

'I'm terribly sorry, sir, I'm afraid we don't have any of that left either,' said the waiter.

Smoothie was getting agitated now. He didn't want to start to lose control in front of this lovely woman but he clearly wasn't used to being turned down, let alone twice in a row. With a sigh of resentment he settled for a Sauvignon Blanc, snapped the menu shut and went to dismiss the waiter. But before he could the Scots boy delivered further painful information.

'I'm so sorry, sir, we don't have a bottle of that left.'

Smoothie exploded. 'What? What kind of a bloody service are you running here? I thought this was a restaurant car, not a bloody tea shop. Have you got any wines at all?'

'Only half bottles of Beaujolais,' the waiter replied.

'Half bottles of Beaujolais? I don't want bloody Beaujolais. Beaujolais is red – did you know that?'

Smoothie was now losing control of himself. Here was the poor fella on a train with his mistress. The English countryside was whooshing by and all he wanted to do was sit there and stare into her eyes over a nice glass of white wine – but there wasn't any.

Once again the waiter said, 'I'm very sorry, sir.'

'Well, sorry isn't good enough. Where has all the wine gone?'

The Scots boy turned in the direction of where Porky and I were sitting, and pointed. Our table was heaving with the weight of two silver buckets which contained a total of eight upturned wine bottles.

Unbeknown to us, we had drunk the train dry. We hadn't meant to, but a couple of pals from Glasgow had joined us earlier and we didn't know that the train only carried a maximum of two bottles of each of its four selections of wine at this time of day. Apparently it carried more in the evenings, when the dining-car was full.

Smoothie was incensed when he saw all the empty bottles. He got up from his seat and came down the carriage towards us.

'Have you drunk all the wine?' he demanded.

'I don't know,' I said. 'I'm not sure how much wine they've got.'

'If you two have drunk the contents of all those bottles,' he continued, 'I suggest you get to a hospital immediately. You must be suffering from alcoholic poisoning by now.'

This guy was starting to annoy me.

'Why don't you calm down and go back and sit down with that lovely woman who is clearly not your wife,' I suggested.

Only one other table was occupied in the dining-car and the elderly couple sitting there suddenly started to take an interest.

'How dare you,' said Smoothie. 'How dare you.'

'How dare I what?' I said, losing my patience. 'Why don't you push off back to your table, sit down and shut up, and if you behave yourself my friend here will go and get you a brown ale from the buffet.'

Smoothie recoiled in shock. He was clearly the boss of something and probably wasn't used to being spoken to like this.

'Have you got a first-class ticket?' he snapped at me.

I started laughing. It reminded me of following my team Celtic around Scotland all those years ago and ducking and diving on and off trains to avoid the guards. My mates and I never had any money to buy tickets so we used to hide in the goods wagon among bags of mail. Only my ability to out-sprint every railway guard in the country prevented my capture on several occasions.

I got out of my seat and put my face very close to Smoothie's. 'Look, pal, if I hear another word from you, I will take a few of those bottles out of that ice-bucket and shove them where the sun don't shine. Now, unless you want to embarrass yourself in front of your floozie, just get lost.'

He raised his hand to me but I grabbed his fingers and bent them back. He yelped. Porky leapt out of his seat, but the waiter had already jumped in.

'I'm going to have to ask you to leave the dining-car, sir,' he told Smoothie. 'I'm sorry, but I can't allow this sort of harassment of other diners.'

'Harassment? Harassment? He's just assaulted me!'

'I'm sorry, sir, but you started this trouble. Before you came in, Mr Brazil and his friend were just having a quiet drink.'

With that, the waiter steered Smoothie down the train while the poor, embarrassed lady he'd been trying to impress followed him with her face hidden behind her case.

'Bloody trouble-making toffs,' I said too loudly as he disappeared through the door, still ranting and spluttering.

That hasn't been my only problem on trains over the last few years, of course. I've travelled tens of thousands of miles to all sorts of events, and at least on the old rattler you can sit back, relax and have a drink. I often prefer the independence of driving, but the roads in Britain are now so congested that it is a painful experience to try to get anywhere in a car. Unfortunately, on trains you have to deal with officialdom, as seems increasingly to be the case in our country, in all walks of life. And if there is one thing that really gets my goat it is pompous, pumped-up people who think they can attract respect from others in life simply because they are wearing a uniform – even if that uniform is only that of a ticket inspector.

Porky and I were once on the way back from a game in Manchester and were enjoying a glass of bubbly in our first-class seats when the guard came round to check the tickets. For some reason mine was second-class, but that wasn't a problem because we offered to upgrade it. I always travel first-class on trains simply because it's much more comfortable on long journeys, and less crowded. As we were going through this process, another guard came along and told his colleague that the passengers in the next carriage, which was second-class, were being moved into ours because their air-conditioning had broken down.

Normally I'm accused of not being very good at looking after talkSPORT's money, but it seemed obvious to me that if a group of second-class passengers were being moved into our compartment then the carriage was being downgraded. I said to the guard, 'If everybody from the next carriage is coming in here, then I shouldn't be paying for a first-class upgrade, should I?'

The guard went mad. 'I'll have you off at Rugby,' he threatened.

I couldn't understand what he was talking about. He was a big, overweight chap and very effeminate. He started ranting and raving – 'I'm not putting up with trouble-makers like you two' – and then screamed into his radio, 'Help, help, I need back-up urgently! Help, I've got a real problem here!'

'What the hell are you doing?' I said.

He ignored me and carried on pleading with the person on the other end of his radio. 'Where are you? Help me, help me! Call the Transport Police! We'll have to stop at Rugby and have two troublesome passengers arrested!'

I was speechless. Porky, for 25 years a newshound in Fleet Street, permanently sees the world as a series of newspaper headlines. I could see the wheels turning in his head as he pictured lurid ones about us being arrested after being hauled off a train.

He shot out of his seat. 'What on earth is your problem, you fool? My friend merely asked you why we are paying for upgraded tickets when you are downgrading the carriage.'

'Stay away from me!' screamed the guard, who now took on the mantle of the most camp human being I had seen since Larry Grayson. 'I'm having you arrested!'

At that moment a supervisor and another guard arrived. The Billy Bunter character said, 'Oh, thank God, you've arrived,' and threw himself into their arms. The only problem was that he was so heavy that they couldn't bear his weight, and they collapsed under his bulk.

'Pull the communication cord, somebody!' screamed fat-boy. 'Stop the train!'

The supervisor hauled herself back to her feet and demanded to know what was going on. Everybody started talking at once. Eventually we got it sorted out, and the overweight instigator of all the trouble was led away, trembling and perspiring.

We received only a half-hearted apology, and on our breakfast show the next morning we told our millions of listeners the story. We tell them many things that go on in our lives. Unfortunately, during advertisement breaks we could not hear, the very same train operator was running a big promotion with us so the listeners were getting mixed messages, to say the least. Another row.

As I said, I prefer to drive when I am travelling around, to various jobs, football grounds or racecourses. But it has become so difficult to drive in this country and I am now feeling outraged, like many millions of motorists, at the prospect of being fleeced even further by so-called road-pricing.

I prefer to call it tax. It is motivated by the politics of envy, and is so misguided that I believe all it will do is penalise poorer people in our society and probably wreck the economy. The amount of tax motorists pay is already excessive. The multinational oil companies are constantly criticised for the vast profits they make – often running into tens of billions of pounds – but the real robber barons are the government ministers. They take the lion's share of the price of a litre of petrol to satisfy their outrageous spending whims.

I don't have a problem with paying my taxes. I have a problem with the people who spend them. I mean politicians. In that well-known book the ABCDE – the Alan Brazil Concise Dictionary of Eejuts – a 'politician' is defined as 'A person who has never had a proper job or lived in the real world; who is under the impression that everybody else's money belongs to them; and who then spends it on hopelessly wasteful projects in the hope that a lot of people vote for them'. My contempt for politicians knows absolutely no bounds. They are a million miles away from being the paradigms of virtue they would like us to believe they are. The last Tory government was bounced out of power on a number of issues including the fact that it was infested with sleaze. It was replaced by a Labour government that turned out to be just as bad, if not worse.

Porky has a few old pals in the House of Commons, and one year he invited me along to a party to celebrate 'end of term'. I had no idea what this was, but it turned out to be an all-afternoon celebration on the last day of the parliamentary session. The House of Commons is a magnificent historic building, and after lunch we were out on the Terrace overlooking the River Thames. It was a wonderfully sunny day and all the MPs in attendance were getting sloshed on champagne (subsidised by the taxpayer) and shouting out insults at tourists on the passing riverboats. They were raucous, singing bawdy songs and flirting with the young female Commons researchers, of whom there seemed to be dozens. It is the only occasion on which I've felt any respect for those who seek to lead us.

Most of the time our MPs live in a closeted world. If they didn't, they would use the massive motoring taxes they take off us to build a decent road system. Instead of that they use the money to set up mad schemes that make driving your car in Britain an absolute misery. Instead of widening roads, they narrow them. Instead of providing more tarmac for the ever-increasing number of cars, they provide less by turning miles and miles of highway into single-lane tracks reminiscent of the seventeenth century. They tell us that buses need their own roads, like the inside lane of the motorway that takes traffic from London, one of the world's biggest cities, to Heathrow, the busiest international airport in the world. They say they do this to encourage us all to get out of our cars and take public transport.

Why? All they have to do is build more roads with the billions of pounds they 'steal' off the motorist. Roads take up very little space. If you take a train in a north-south direction in this country you will see that although the south-east of England is crowded there are vast swathes of greenery almost everywhere else. You wouldn't upset anybody if you built a new motorway parallel to the current M1. In areas where it would be impossible to build new carriageways, build them on top. Yes, double-decker roads.

I don't accept that this country cannot afford such ambitious plans. At the time of writing I am reading a story that a computer that should link every element of the National Health Service is four years late in being put into operation, and nobody knows when it will be ready, or that it will ever work. The cost? A staggering £20 billion. For that amount of money you could virtually rebuild the whole of Britain's motorway system. Instead, every motorist is left fuming and in traffic jams for hours on end, which clearly affects the mental health of all of us. But it's no good seeking medical help: as the computer doesn't work, you'll probably be treated by mistake for irritable bowel syndrome.

I was watching an episode of Doctor Who recently with my youngest, Steffie. I swear the plot was a vision of what is going to happen to Britain's roads. The Doctor lands in a Britain of the future. Before long, his assistant is kidnapped. The Doctor goes in pursuit and eventually learns that she has been taken by two travellers who are driving the futuristic equivalent of one of those Volkswagen Dormobiles that hippies used to drive around in during the flower-power sixties. The kidnappers don't mean her any harm, they just need a third person in their vehicle so that they can gain access to 'the fast lane'. When asked by the Doctor how long they have been on the road, they reply, 'Sixty years.' They want to speed up their journey, and they can only do that by acquiring another passenger. You are not allowed in the fast lane if you have only two people in your vehicle.

The traffic doesn't just move in straight-line dimensions, it is also stacked about 30 high. The vehicles are actually floating. To get to the vehicle where his assistant is being held the Doctor has to exit through the floor of a Dormobile, then jump through the skylight of the one below, and so on. What you have is a three-dimensional version of the M25 which is high enough to touch the clouds, and traffic moves at the rate of a few feet a day. Now, every time I close my eyes I can see this nightmare becoming reality. Don't laugh. People once mocked Leonardo Da Vinci for saying that one day people would be able to fly.

If politicians had to sit in traffic jams, they would know the frustration of wasting hours of our lives that we could be spending with our families or looking after our businesses. The cost to the economy must be enormous.

Take my own company, talkSPORT. Geographically, our world was severely disrupted in the year 2000 when Wembley Stadium closed down. It meant that the hub of English club football was now in Cardiff at the Welsh national stadium, the Millennium, while the national side became a travelling circus.

Just to digress for a moment, Porky and I were at Wembley on Saturday, 7 October 2000 for the last game before the bulldozers moved in. It was against Germany in a World Cup qualifier. I didn't really want to go because I'm not an Englishman, but Porky was adamant that it was an unmissable event. As it happened, he was right. Not so much because of the fact that England got beaten 1-0, but because immediately after the game the England manager Kevin Keegan quit his post. Porky was in a terrible froth, running around barking instructions down the phone to the talkSPORT office in the Banqueting Hall, and generally going into meltdown.

Earlier, I had had to suffer the indignity of watching my broad-casting colleague once again grovelling to the famous people around us. Sir Steve Redgrave is a very amiable bloke. Whenever I have met the five-times Olympic gold medallist he's always been great company. But on this occasion I sensed there might be a little tension because a few weeks earlier Porky had made the ridiculous assertion that if he had spent sixteen years sitting in a boat on the River Thames he could have won gold medals himself. He reckoned Sir Steve should have had a 'proper job' and not spent all his time training abroad. A brainless idea, considering the glory Redgrave has brought to this country.

In a marquee attached to Wembley we were standing around with a glass in our hands prior to the pre-match banquet when a huge figure of a man came ambling towards us. It was Sir Steve, and he's even bigger in the flesh than he is on TV. Porky saw him first and ducked behind a pillar. I wondered what he was doing, then the Olympic hero was next to me. We shook hands. Sir Steve was all smiles and bonhomie.

'Where is he, Alan?' said the six-foot-five-inch champion oarsman.

Feeling absolutely no sense of loyalty to my radio pal because of his pathetic vanishing act, I reached around the pillar and hauled him into view.

'Here he is, Steve. He's been so looking forward to meeting you.'

Porky looked wan. The colour had drained out of his face and he was simpering, nodding his head, wondering whether he was about to receive a right-hander. Instead, of course, Sir Steve extended a giant palm and shook hands with Porky so vigorously it looked like he might tear his arm off in the process.

'Now then, Mr Parry, I understand you want to come and do a bit of rowing with us,' he said.

Porky nodded his head in a fashion that reminded me of the way *Till Death Us Do Part* character Alf Garnett grovelled when he met his football hero Bobby Moore for the first time. 'Well ...' he ventured.

'Now, don't be shy,' said Steve. 'We'll get you down on the river at Henley and we'll do a couple of hours of light workout.'

In the shape Porky was in at the time I doubted very much he would survive such a tough physical assault on his bloated frame. 'Yeah, and then we can have a burial at sea,' I added. Steve and I burst out laughing, leaving Porky opening and closing his mouth like a fish.

'Any time,' the Olympic hero continued. 'Don't worry, we've got a boat with your name on it.'

He threw his head back with laughter one last time, then

moved on to greet somebody a lot more important than the Porkmeister.

Before the match started we were introduced to another Olympic champion, the heptathlete Denise Lewis. Cue more embarrassment. Porky insisted he wanted to have his picture taken with her. He produced one of those throwaway cameras and thrust it into my hand. Denise, who is a picture of female elegance, clearly didn't want to be pictured with a fat, ginger-bearded little man like Porky, but he insisted, and welded himself to her. I was so embarrassed I gave the camera to the bloke standing next to me, who unlike me didn't realise that my pal had virtually kidnapped one of the country's leading athletes. I never saw the subsequent picture, though I have asked Porky to show it to me several times. I reckon it will depict Denise Lewis looking like she would rather be anywhere else in the world than in the frame with this dope.

As the post-match farewell party broke up I reflected on the fact that a football would never be kicked inside the stadium again. I walked down to the royal box and looked out over the pitch. It was where I had played my last international for Scotland. I remember it vividly. It was the first day of June 1983, a night game, and we were beaten 2-0. It was also the day of the Epsom Derby, and I had refused to let the manager Jock Stein in on my bet on the winning horse. I peered down at the subs' bench where I started the game. I never played for Scotland again, and I've always wondered whether it was because of that bet. But that was all pretty much forgotten by 2000. One thing I will never forget, though, is that it was like being at Hampden that night at Wembley. You could only hear and see the Scottish fans. The colours, the flags, the tartan, the chanting – it was all Scottish. I can remember thinking at the time, 'What's wrong with the English that they let a tiny nation like Scotland completely take them over?'

But, back to travel problems. As I said, for the next few years the major domestic footballing events would be held in Cardiff while the England team would travel around the country. The lack of transport facilities in this country has never been better highlighted than when a mass of English people tried to travel 150 miles across their own country and back again a few hours later. I would never have believed it could be such a difficult operation, but it is actually horrendous.

Take the last final to be played at Cardiff before the opening of the new Wembley, the Carling Cup final in February 2007. It was a worst-case scenario because it pitted Arsenal against Chelsea, two London teams. The game was on a Sunday. For some reason in this country there is a mind-set that the Sabbath is still a day of rest and we don't need any trains; or, what is worse, we can have a few trains but they won't go anywhere because engineering works mean that whole stretches of railway track will be closed down all over the place.

As soon as our show opened up on Monday morning the calls started coming in, as expected, about the horrendous travelling experiences of the fans. One listener told us about having to drive to Gatwick airport at three o'clock in the morning to rescue his very distressed wife and her friend who had set off for Cardiff 21 hours earlier. They had pre-booked their journey from Brighton two weeks beforehand and had allocated seats on all their connections. But they never sat down for the whole horrendous journey. They suffered delays of two hours at a time when the train just didn't move, and nobody gave them any information about what was happening. On the return journey, as the night wore on, they eventually made it as far as Gatwick, halfway between London and Brighton, and that was as far as they could get.

What enraged our caller, quite rightly, was that when they eventually arrived in Cardiff the passengers were told that there wouldn't be as many trains going back as had arrived. Which idiot worked that one out? If you know that 20,000 people have arrived on trains and you only lay on enough trains to take 15,000 people back home, what do you expect to happen to the other 5,000?

Other horror stories came flooding in. One train took two hours to move from Newport to Cardiff, a distance of twenty miles; and trains coming in from London were taking twice as long as normal. Many fans missed the kick-off. That morning I understood how Mussolini managed to take over Italy before the Second World War with the mantra 'I will make the trains run on time'.

The most laughable element of the confused transport policy in this country is that it is supposed to be encouraging us to leave our cars at home and take trains. But then, the roads are just as bad. Again using Cardiff as an example, it has often taken our team of reporters, presenters and technicians up to eight hours to get home after a game. Waiting for an off-course boomerang to come back, with all the misery that must entail, is preferable to sitting on the M4 at midnight going absolutely nowhere. One of the results of massive road and rail congestion is that companies like mine have to put teams of people into hotels overnight in order to guarantee that they are in the right place when the action starts. This must collectively add hundreds of millions of pounds to business costs. That affects a company's profits, which in turn affects the amount of tax the Treasury takes, which then impacts on expenditure, including the building of roads.

And it's not just motorways that cause despair in this country. I contend that it is now impossible to make any road journey without building in a 'jam' factor. When you least expect it you can suddenly find yourself immersed in traffic, as though it has been swept into your path like a tide turning in a bay. And usually, in my experience, it's due to some sort of 'road routing' or 'traffic scheme' dreamt up by a bureaucrat.

Once I was covering a match in Blackburn on a Sunday afternoon. It was a vital end-of-season affair which Manchester City had to win to stay in the Premiership. I set off from my home in Suffolk with hours to spare and stopped about half an hour away from the ground for a cup of coffee because I had so much time in hand. But I hadn't catered for the build-up of traffic, even though there were two hours to go to the kick-off. I ended up crawling along in a jam. Eventually nothing was moving, and the minutes were ticking by.

To make matters worse, I was stuck on a main artery on the way to the ground and Manchester City fans were starting to recognise me. As a former Manchester United player, I was coming in for some abuse. And it wasn't good-natured banter, it was vile stuff, clearly fuelled by the fact that the fans had been in the pub for a couple of hours before moving on to the match. They were banging on my bonnet and thumping the windows. One guy spat on my windscreen. I thought about getting out to sort him out. I was in a desperate situation. I was running out of time, and I was about to become immersed in a mob confrontation. When a fan booted the door of my car, I knew I had to get out of there.

I put my headlights on, moved out of the traffic, burnt up the other side of the road and shot off down a residential road. I had no idea where I was going. I found myself in a cul-de-sac in a private development. Now I had nowhere else to go. I parked the car and jumped out to be confronted by a NO PARKING EXCEPT FOR RESIDENTS sign. But there was nothing I could do. I locked the car and sprinted off just as the local busybody appeared at the door of his house shouting, 'You can't park there!'

I made my way back to the main road and hid behind a wall until I spotted a group of normal-looking middle-aged Blackburn fans. 'Fellas, can I come with you?' I said as I emerged from behind the wall. 'I'm doing the game for Sky and the City fans are giving me terrible stick.' Fortunately they recognised me, so I hid myself among them as legions of pale blue supporters poured by.

My shield was effective for only a few minutes. A City fan spotted me, and the abuse started up again. The Blackburn fans were now getting it. Though I don't always believe that the decent thing is the right thing to do, I couldn't bring the focus on these people who had tried to help me, so I jogged off. But some of the more virulent City fans were determined not to let it go and they came jogging after me. At one stage I was having a running battle with a drunken yobbo who was trying to hit me with what looked like the exhaust pipe of a car. Only the remnants of my professional athlete's frame allowed me to get to the ground ahead of him.

As I rushed through the press entrance I could hear the

teams being announced over the Tannoy. I panted my way up four flights of stairs and bustled my way out on to the gantry. The game was about to kick off. There was one flight of stairs left, going down to my broadcasting seat. I grabbed the rail and slid down them, crash-landing in my seat just as the whistle went. Rob Hawthorne, the commentator, greeted my sudden arrival – as if I had just burst in through the roof – with total aplomb: 'And let me say a very big welcome this afternoon to my co-commentator, Alan Brazil.' I was so out of breath I could hardly speak. I mumbled something about being down in the tunnel and looking in the players' eyes as they ran out.

After the game I had to wait an hour for the fans to disperse before I dared venture out to find my car. When I got to it, the busybody was waiting for me. He told me that if I ever parked there again he would have my car clamped. I told him a clamp would be better used on his mouth, and that if he ever touched a vehicle belonging to me I would burst him like a tyre.

I blame all that stress on the traffic. But I can't blame congestion for one of the most horrendous driving experiences I have ever had.

During their teen years, my two oldest girls skied for Scotland and for Britain. One time Michelle was in a competition in the Nevis Range of hills and I loaded up the car and took her up there on a Friday for practice. It was a very long journey, north of Glasgow, right along the banks of Loch Lomond and right up to Glencoe; then I had to turn around and go back down to Barnsley in Yorkshire where I was co-commentating on the Friday-night Sky game. But at least the journey – a total of 800 miles after starting in Ipswich – was to be done in daylight.

After the game I headed off back up to Scotland to be there

for the competition on Saturday morning. By two a.m. I had cleared Loch Lomond and was heading into the Glencoe Pass. It was pitch black, and a slight drizzle suddenly turned into heavy rain, and then sleet and snow. I was going slower and slower, and suddenly I saw a dozen bright piercing lights in front of me and stopped with a jolt. The effect was that the back of the car slid around, and I knew that just a few feet away from me on the left was a perilous sheer drop into a canyon below.

The car stopped. Everything seemed to be steady. I was about to get out to try to find my bearings when the lights that had first alarmed me started moving towards me. The fear of the unknown flickered in my heart for a few moments until the lights got right up alongside the car and I realised they were the eyes of a herd of deer and stags. At least there was some other form of life in what had turned into a Godforsaken hell-hole.

But my relief was soon tempered by renewed fear. The mighty beasts with their antlers surrounded my vehicle and began to bang against it. I was terrified that they were going to tip it over the edge of the precipice. I thought about sounding the horn, but if that alarmed them they might bolt in the wrong direction and the car, with me inside it, might go. I lowered one of the windows, but the snow and sleet was driving down so fiercely that I closed it again immediately.

I pushed open the door and got out. In twenty years of skiing in all sorts of conditions I had never encountered such bad weather. The snow seemed to be coming at me horizontally, and somewhere the fierce wind was whipping through some telephone lines making a terrible, eerie wailing noise. I'd never realised how big a stag was until that moment. I stood there in the middle of a herd of them, and my head came up to the nose of the beast closest to me and the car. Despite the fear that was running through me I was in awe of the magnificence of these animals, who stood like oak trees against the tormenting weather.

For some reason I started to say, 'Whoa, Rudolph. Easy boy.' I didn't want to alarm them. I didn't raise my hands, but I needed them to move because I was trapped. Then I realised that it wasn't just stags and deer that were surrounding me but cattle and sheep as well. They had obviously come down on to the road because the fields were turning into oceans of snow.

I edged around the back of the car. The wheels were still on the road, but only just. I shuddered as I looked out across the yawning expanse below me. I had no option but to get back in the car and drive, otherwise I was going to be snowed in.

***

As I started the engine and revved it, the herd of animals moved away. Thank goodness for that. But now I had to try to make my way along the last twenty miles of road to Fort William with an encroaching snowdrift on my right and a sheer drop on my left. It was the most heart-stopping journey of my life. The most I ever got up to was 20mph, and two or three times I thought I felt the road disappearing beneath me. Once I even opened the door thinking I might have to throw myself out.

After three agonising hours of this I saw the lights of Fort William. I knew then how it felt for a man dying of thirst to see an oasis in the desert. It was five o'clock in the morning and I nearly collapsed with exhaustion when I got to my hotel. I vowed never to make such a journey again.

It wasn't unusual for me to make mammoth journeys to help my girls with their skiing though. I was very proud that they were international class and I would do anything to make sure they got to competitions. On one occasion we got a call on a Thursday lunchtime for Michelle to go and join the team in the Alps as a late replacement for another girl who had been injured. After looking at all the options, I decided that the best way to do it would be to load up the Volvo estate with all her gear and drive to Tignes, which nestles in a valley on the borders of France, Italy and Switzerland. Even though I was due to be working on a Sky match on the Friday evening I had no qualms about making the trip. French roads are superb compared to the roads in this country, and the weather forecast was good.

It took us thirteen hours to get to the resort. We went down to Dover and put the car on the ferry, and upon arriving in France headed south-east. We stopped only once. After it got dark Michelle slept for the remainder of the journey, but I just powered on through the night.

On arriving at Tignes in the early hours we got Michelle into her hotel. I had one cup of coffee and then set off back to England. I didn't stop once, and considering I had had to retire from football with a crippling back injury, that was probably not the wisest thing to do. It took almost exactly the same amount of time to get back – thirteen hours. Jill thought I was mad, and she had been going frantic. There were no mobile phones in those days and I wasn't inclined to stop to ring home. She knew that we had both got there safely, but she only knew I had got back safely when I trundled up the road on Friday afternoon. I had a quick shower and then set off for the Midlands to co-commentate on the match.

I find driving on the Continent a doddle compared to this country. There are plenty of things I do not like about European life and culture, but they certainly appreciate the value of good roads. I don't mind paying tolls if an excellent service is being provided, as is the case on the Continent. In this country we have the M6 toll road which is absolute bliss. It has clearly eased congestion on the Midlands section of the motorway – truly the road to hell. So, if it has been such a success, why have more not been built?

Instead, the government have tried to pursue this policy of 'road-pricing'. As I said, what that really means is yet another tax on anybody who has a car – and these days that is most of us. To me, this is an absolute confidence trick. It is a disgusting method of extorting money from drivers so that politicians can waste it on another set of massively expensive projects that never seem to work. We are the highest-taxed nation in Europe. You would think that everything worked in Britain. But hospitals are being closed down, there aren't enough jails in which to put our criminals, you can no longer get dental treatment without paying a huge bill, and young people come out of university with huge amounts of debt to start their working lives. So where do the politicians spend all our money?

Certainly not on roads. In any shire county like the one I live in, Suffolk, the roads are a disgrace. Many people in my area end up suing the county council for damage to their cars caused by huge holes in the road. But the council say they are starved of grants from central government because all the money goes to inner-city areas. If we succumb to another mass taxation ploy, road-pricing, how can we have any confidence that anything will change? I've always wondered why we don't rise up and revolt against this injustice imposed upon us by those who choose to rule us.

So I was delighted when objectors launched a 'Stop Road Pricing' petition, and I was very happy to sign it. But, naturally, the fact that within a few weeks of its launch the petition had attracted two million signatures did nothing to sway government minds. Tony Blair himself, then the Prime Minister, said in response to the huge No vote for this crazy policy, 'All the evidence shows that improving public transport and targeting bottlenecks will not by themselves prevent congestion getting worse. Charging motorists per mile is the only practical way of managing soaring congestion levels.' He talked about 'improving public transport' as though there were a history in this country of making trains and buses more efficient. There isn't. They get worse every year. And as for 'charging motorists' being the only solution, no it's not. Build more roads!

Isn't it fairly typical that though the government refused to yield to a mass protest, they suddenly changed their tune when one celebrity took them on? The Top Gear presenter Richard Hammond told Mr Blair face to face that nearly two million people were protesting against his proposed scheme. His response was this: 'If the public says "We are not having this" then no politician of any sense will try to force it through.'

However, I suspect that this is a clear case of pandering

to celebrity. Politicians are notorious for it. England win the Ashes. Great! Invite them all round to Downing Street and give them all gongs. New pop group tops the charts. Super! Let's have a party at Number 10, allow a few rock stars to address the PM as 'Tone', and demand lager to drink instead of champagne. Richard Hammond is one of the biggest TV stars in the country. Already popular for his role in the motoring show, he shot to stardom after being nearly killed in pursuit of a land speed record. He crashed at nearly 300mph and only just made it. A huge wave of compassion accompanied his survival and no politician, certainly not one as bright as Mr Blair, would have turned the Hamster down.

But watch this space. When politicians say they are going to drop an unpopular policy it normally means that they have been beaten this time but they will go away and devise a method of introducing it through the back door. Look what happened to the European Constitution. Defeated in country after country; eventually even the referendum was scrapped in this country. But slowly and surely the politicians, many of whom in Europe are unelected, are trying to bring it back.

On the subjects of Europe and travelling, let me just say that there is one form of transport I actually adore: the Shuttle. It is one of the best ways of getting around I have experienced anywhere in the world. Sitting back in one of the armchairs in a first-class compartment, cradling a glass of bubbly and watching the French countryside whizz by, is a sheer joy. It usually means I am either going to or coming from Longchamp, the HQ of French racing, and I am probably anticipating or reflecting on the l'Arc de Triomphe meeting. There was one occasion, however, when my journey nearly ended in despair, and I have an English policeman to blame for the trouble and a French waiter to thank for rescuing me.

It was a Sunday evening. We were coming back from the race meeting and I was already thinking about Monday morning's breakfast show. The train was absolutely packed, and we were standing in the corridor of a drinks and dining carriage. As we came out of the tunnel into Kent I was chatting to an English policeman who told me he had once been a youth player at Portsmouth. We chatted about football for about ten minutes, and then he drifted off. Then I heard some noise further down the carriage. A bit of argy-bargy appeared to have broken out and policemen pushed past us to sort it out.

I thought nothing more of it, and we soon arrived at Waterloo. But as I stepped off the train I was approached by two other policeman. They told me I was being detained for smoking on board. I laughed out loud. I've never smoked a cigarette in my life. They maintained that people smoking on board had been the cause of the disturbance I'd heard and that I had been identified as one of the main culprits.

'By who?' I asked in astonishment.

'By this officer,' they answered, pointing to the lad I'd been talking to on the train.

'You're mad,' I said. 'I was talking football to him. He said he was a fan. Search me; you won't find any cigarettes on me. Do I smell of smoke?'

'We have another witness,' said the senior officer.

'Well, he must be blind. Who is he?'

They called inside the train and the maître d' of the dining-car suddenly appeared. He was not a typical Frenchman. He was a big bloke, as if he might have been a former member of the French Foreign Legion or something. He had a blond crew-cut, like an American Marine. He was a very imposing figure. He wore an immaculate burgundy tuxedo with bright red lapels. If he had been on the door at Stringfellows I would not have argued with him. I knew his name was Daniel because he'd been serving us Bollinger all the way back and we'd been serenading him with endless verses of 'Danny Boy' as we spent a few thousand euros with him.

He jumped on to the platform. I was flabbergasted. I thought I was going to be the victim of some sort of stitch-up.

The sergeant barked at him, 'Is this the man who was smoking?'

Daniel burst out laughing. 'No, no, no,' he said. 'This is Meester Brazeel. He ees from Scotland. He ees big footballer. He ees friend of Dalgleesh. He likes champagne.'

He stepped forward and vigorously shook my hand. I put my arm on his shoulder and glared at the English cop who had 'fingered' me.

'Call yourself a cop?' I asked dismissively. 'Did they model Clouseau on you, you tosser?'

Put that officer back on the beat.

CHAPTER FOUR

WHERE HAVE ALL THE POLICEMEN GONE?

'The protective shield of the law we once took for granted in this country is gone. I fear this means that people will start to take the law into their own hands.'

THE TWO huge black limousines with blacked-out windows rolled to a stop a few feet away from me as I sat cradling a glass of bubbly in the wine bar. 'Who on earth would come to lunch in such an ostentatious fashion?' I thought to myself. This was either pop star or football money. No respectable businessman would gad about town in a manner that attracted so much attention.

The back doors of the second car flew open and two burly men emerged. They looked like a couple of bouncers from outside Stringfellows. Black coats, dark glasses and ear-pieces. It looked just like a scene on the TV news from Washington DC when the President arrives. Were these guys from the US secret service? Were they escorting the US ambassador perhaps? The American Embassy in London's Grosvenor Square was only around the corner.

The two goons came into the wine bar. A waiter directed them to two tables at the back of the room. They peered at everyone in the bar. Two more men, similarly dressed, then entered. They went straight downstairs to where the loos were. They reappeared a few moments later and then, standing just inside the entrance, they signalled to the car. Another two men in the same attire jumped out of the front of the first limo and opened the doors to the back of the car.

A squat little man emerged. He reminded me of the actor Danny De Vito. He was short with dark, balding hair, and had a pugilist's face. From the other side of the car came one of the most beautiful women I had seen that day. She was taller than her male companion and she was dressed immaculately. Her hair blew in the wind.

The couple were escorted into the bar by what were obviously their two bodyguards. One of them sat at the table with them while three of the other five sat at the adjoining table. One man waited outside, and the other got back into the driving seat of the lead car. I presumed that was the getaway vehicle in case of an emergency.

Every time a drink was ordered to the table, one of the bodyguards stood over the waiter as he poured it. When either the boss man or his lady wanted to use the loo, they were escorted by one of the goons.

After an hour, the entourage left as flamboyantly as they had arrived.

The Danny De Vito character turned out to be Boris Berezovsky, one of the Russian oligarchs who have moved with their billions of pounds from Moscow to London. I had wondered why somebody who was so clearly concerned about his safety would venture out to a wine bar in the West End of London at its busiest time. The answer to why he was so public became clearer to me over the next few weeks as an international crisis situation developed around the man who had sat just a few tables away from me.

The difference between Mr Berezovsky and other former

Soviet bloc billionaires such as Chelsea FC owner Roman Abramovich is that he has been granted political asylum in Britain. Mr Abramovich is free to move in and out of Russia, where he has regional political responsibilities, at will. The situation is a pretty good indication that Mr Berezovsky has fallen out with the Russian leader Vladimir Putin.

Falling out with Putin, a former KGB officer, is clearly bad for your health. Huge publicity surrounded the death in London in November 2006 of Russian dissident Alexander Litvinenko. I shiver when I recall the searing image of him with orange skin as he lay dying in his hospital bed. His story could have come out of a Cold War spy thriller written by John Le Carré. Litvinenko, a former KGB officer himself, fell foul of the Putin government and was jailed in Russia. When he got out he fled to this country and sought asylum. From what he thought was a safe distance he launched a critical tirade against Putin's government, accusing the Russian leader of manufacturing a war against Chechen separatists. He was poisoned in London, in either a hotel or a restaurant. The substance used to kill him was polonium-210, a rare radioactive isotope. A millionth of a gram of the substance, obtainable only in countries such as Russia which have a nuclear arms arsenal, is enough to destroy all the body's organs.

Just before he died, Litvinenko accused Putin of being responsible for his death. There is no evidence of that, but an alarming number of people who oppose Putin appear to end up being assassinated or, in the case of another billionaire oligarch, Mikhail Khodorkovsky, being flung into jail for 'tax evasion'. The link between this saga of international spy games and Berezovsky is that Litvinenko also alleged that one of the reasons he had to flee Russia was because he was ordered to kill Berezovsky. No wonder the small, burly Russian only moves around in a gaggle of black-coated security men. Not only has he seen a fellow Russian being poisoned in England, he claims he has been sentenced to a similar fate.

Amazingly, this dapper little chap was about to create a serious diplomatic row that strained relations between Russia and Britain.

Berezovsky was initially an ally of Mr Putin, and helped him to become the Russian leader. But in recent years he'd accused him of trying to take the country back towards totalitarianism. Berezovsky now openly admits that he is planning to bring down Putin and his democratically elected government. Speaking from the safety of England, he said, 'We need force to change this regime. It isn't possible to get rid of them through democratic means. There can be no change without pressure.' Mr Berezovsky stated that effectively he wanted to see a revolution and that he was actively funding it from his billion-pound fortune. He added later that he was not advocating a violent struggle. Nevertheless, as a political refugee here it's bad form in diplomatic terms for an exiled businessman to go around trying to overthrow the governments of other sovereign states. Not unnaturally, the Russians took a very dim view of somebody hiding behind a British 'shield' while trying to foment an uprising. Mr Berezovsky's comments came very shortly before street demonstrations took place in Moscow with placard-waving protesters complaining about the rolling back of democratic reforms.

So, it seems the reason the Russian exile appears in West End wine bars is because he believes that the more of a public figure he becomes, the more defence he has against being the subject of an 'accident', or maybe being kidnapped.

This became clear a few months after the Litvinenko incident when a big diplomatic row broke out between Britain and Russia over the former KGB man's murder. The British police had requested the extradition of Andrei Lugovoy, another former KGB officer who they wanted to question over the Litvinenko murder. The Russians refused saying that their constitution did not allow extradition of Russian nationals. But behind the scenes it is believed they wanted Berezovsky in exchange for Lugovoy. Britain expelled four Russian diplomats from London and Moscow retaliated by booting four of our men from the British embassy.

However, sensationally, in the middle of all of this, a story broke that MI5 had smashed a plot to have Berezovsky shot in London, allegedly by a Russian hit-man. Berezovsky threw a very public press conference to denounce the assassination plot, directly blaming the Russian leader, Mr Putin.

What worries me is why this sort of thing is taking place in our country. I know we have a long and proud history of helping asylum seekers who are oppressed in their homelands, but this appears to be a dispute between two major Russian power-brokers, and one of them is sheltering behind us in Britain. That might be quite justifiable – I don't know the full story on either side. But I'm pretty sure that if there was an American here calling for an armed revolution in Washington, there would at least be a full-scale inquiry going on because of our relations with the US. Russia is still a big and very powerful country, even if its power these days rests with oil and gas resources rather than the number of nuclear warheads it possesses.

There have been famous spy cases in the past. I remember about 30 years ago the notorious killing of Bulgarian dissident Georgi Markov on Waterloo Bridge in London: he was stabbed with a poisoned umbrella by a suspected Eastern bloc agent. But that was when the Cold War was going on. We had aircraft constantly patrolling the North Sea in case the Russians decided to launch a nuclear attack. Those days have now gone. Russia is now supposed to be a free country. Its people are free to travel the world. When they come to London, Russians are supposed to enjoy the safety our society has traditionally afforded to its citizens and visitors. But now, after Litvinenko's death, you have to wonder just who controls the streets. How do we know that the next time somebody is targeted for assassination it will not be with guns? A shooting match might break out in a restaurant. I have no evidence that Berezovsky's bodyguards were armed, but I'd be very surprised if at least one of them wasn't. I might have been sitting near a man with a gun in his pocket, which is rather unsettling when you're trying to get your tongue around a forkful of spaghetti bolognese.

Which brings me to one of my main complaints about Britain these days: there is no visible police presence on our streets. I don't care what the figures show, crime is endemic in our society. You have to suspect that it now actually overwhelms the forces of law and order, who are dishing out ridiculous bits of paper called ASBOs while young men are routinely – and that is not an exaggeration – being slain on our streets with knives and guns. The latest pathetic gimmick is to have somebody sitting in front of a bank of cameras with the ability to shout at somebody who, for instance, has dropped a piece of litter. OK, so in a trial run we saw people shocked enough to respond to a command from a voice booming out from a speaker. But that won't happen for long.

Authority has all but disappeared. Many young people have never experienced it anyway. Let me ask you this question. If you were on a train and a hooded youth sitting opposite you had his feet on the seat and mud from the soles of his trainers was marking that seat, would you tell him to put his feet back on the ground? Of course you wouldn't. And you should no longer feel any pangs of guilt or in any way regard yourself as cowardly for saying so. If you did, it is almost a certainty that you will be abused, and there's a distinct possibility that you will be attacked. These days, some young people carry a weapon with them in the same way that I used to carry a football with me.

The protective shield of the law we once took for granted in this country has gone. I fear this means that people will start to take the law into their own hands. It is, after all, a primeval instinct to protect yourself and your loved ones from aggressors. Ever since I was a little boy I have had faith in – indeed respect for, bordering on fear of – our policemen. I can't tell you the number of times I was clipped across the head by a copper when I was a kid. That can't be done today because the policeman would, ridiculously, be accused of assaulting the child. But even if we have to abide by that silly politically correct mantra, the mere presence of policemen on streets would stem the ever-increasing tide of crime.

I very, very rarely see a policeman walking the streets. But the last time I did it illustrated how effective they can be. I was in the courtyard of Canterbury Cathedral looking at that fantastic building the day after I had been to see Elton John in concert on the adjoining site. Without warning, a terrible domestic row erupted between a man and a woman in the street. The man lost control of himself and began roughly trying to drag the woman along the pavement in a direction she didn't want to go. She was screaming, and he was threatening to hit her.

To me, hitting a woman is the lowest thing a man can do. I looked around helplessly to see if there was any sort of authority about who could intervene. There wasn't, so I moved towards the couple, prepared if necessary to engage in a bit of fisticuffs if the bloke got aggressive. I told the man to let the woman go and leave her alone. He told me to get lost with a barrage of swear words.

But before anything else could happen a policeman appeared from around the corner, riding a push-bike. The instant the aggressor saw the uniform he released his grip on the woman and held his hands up. Even before the copper addressed one word to him, the man was apologising to him and to his girl. In a few minutes the situation was sorted out and everybody had calmed down. The man also apologised to me for swearing at me, and then the couple walked off, hand in hand.

I thought this was community policing at its best, and I congratulated the copper. I asked him if it was his force's policy to regularly patrol the streets. Unfortunately, he told me it was a very rare event for him to get out; he spent much of his time behind a desk processing forms.

From all the evidence of living in this country I would have to conclude that the police have largely given up on the idea of tackling crime. Of course you see outstanding policework in high-profile, well-publicised cases of serious crime. Hopefully monsters like the child killer Ian Huntley will always be hunted down. But for the most part, the millions of us who rely on the police for law and order, for which we pay enormous amounts in tax, get a raw deal.

The trouble with the police is that they put their enormous resources into all the wrong things. I travelled down to Surrey once to see Porky. As I got off the train I was greeted by a wall of policemen. Some had dogs with them. There must have been twenty officers there, and outside the station there were four police cars. As I was trying to move through them I joked with what looked like an inspector that they must be hunting a couple of bank robbers.

'No, sir,' he said. 'Thorough ticket-check.'

I thought he was joking, but he wasn't. I then noticed that in the midst of the coppers were a group of ticket clerks issuing tickets and fines.

It's fair enough that people should not try to travel on trains if they are not prepared to pay for their journey, even though the fares in this country are extortionate. But to use twenty policemen, some with dogs, to bring in the muscle against passengers is silly.

We have all seen examples of police resources being used in such a way. One that really makes me furious is the mobile speed-camera unit. Despite the fact that there are thousands of enforcement cameras in this country designed to suck millions of pounds out of drivers' pockets, police forces still feel the need to have mobile units doing the same job. And every time I come across one it's always manned by about eight officers. Shouldn't they be searching for the thousands of criminals who have been let out of prisons because nobody had the foresight a decade ago to realise that when you let hundreds of thousands of new people into the country a percentage of them are going to be villains?

And there are always brand-new police cars parked by the side of the road. The police have far too many cars. The sound of a police siren is now as familiar in this country as the sound of a mobile phone ringing, but I want to know where all these cars are roaring off to. All the time I hear sirens wailing and I see two or three police cars with their blue lights flashing, presumably racing to the scene of a crime. But I never see that crime scene, and I don't know anybody who does. I scan the local paper and listen to the news bulletins to try to locate a 'happening', but I never find out why these police cars are racing about all day. I seriously wonder whether on each shift a policeman and his mate are ordered to spend a set period of minutes racing around with their flashing lights and sirens on in order to remind the public that they are there.

My fears are endorsed by a report I discovered at my local library. According to this document drawn up by the Inspectorate of Constabulary, only one officer in 40 is free to answer 999 calls; the rest are said to be tied up on 'special duties', which include neighbourhood policing. Senior officers refuse to move their men from the designated task of the day to respond to emergency calls and real crimes. Scandalously, this is because such a common-sense move would interfere with their ability to hit government performance targets. And also in line with my suspicions, the report went on to reveal that cars on patrol spend nearly half their time driving around aimlessly with nothing to do. They are not used to target crime hotspots. As a result, a backlog of 999 emergency calls builds up. The individual police forces then have no option but to downgrade the call from an emergency. The result is that householders who may actually have found a burglar in their house are not getting a visit from a police officer until 24 hours later.

The fact that coppers no longer patrol the roads is a particular grievance of mine. I was aghast when I obtained another survey that stated that only one in 58 police officers is out on patrol at any one time. I want to know what the other 57 are doing. I see new police stations being built all over the country. They seem to be bigger than the traditional 'cop-shops' of my youth. Is that because for every one policeman out on the beat there are now 57 sitting at desks pursuing some daft psychobabble policy to protect criminals from the law-abiding? According to this report, a uniformed lower-ranked policeman now spends just 14 per cent of his time walking the streets or patrolling in his car. That equates to no more than an hour in an eight-hour shift. Coppers I have talked to say that the rest of the time is taken up by filling in forms and meeting government targets in providing a 'service to the public'. The best service to the public would, in my view, be done out on the streets, preventing people from being attacked or robbed.

It can't be a coincidence that as the number of bobbies on the beat declines, street-crime is increasing, not only in numbers but in its seriousness. Not very far from where I live in London there has been a spate of killings of very young men. Some of it is gang-on-gang violence, but sometimes the victim is completely innocent and has never had a relationship with his attacker. It doesn't matter. What sort of country are we running when children are being murdered for whatever reason?

A patrolling policeman on the streets of London was once so common that it was a tourist attraction. I bet there aren't many Americans in recent years who have been able to show the folks back home a picture of a British bobby. By contrast, every time I go to New York I see policemen patrolling around Times Square. I now feel much safer on the streets of an American city than I do in Britain.

I want to make clear that I have no problem with rank-and-file police officers. As far as I can see they continue to be trained in a way that instils in them traditional British values. It's the senior officers who I think are changing the fabric of our police service because they have to yield to their political masters. The police used to act more or less independently, though answerable to the Home Office. It now seems to me that they have been politicised and are used as a tool of government to change society.

How many times have we read of people being arrested for trying to detain those who are damaging their property, or for trying to protect themselves against mobs of feral children? One such case which came to my attention was that of councillor and businessman Fred Brown. His horrific story encompasses many of the faults of modern policing outlined above.

Mr Brown, a shop owner and local councillor in the community of Littleport in Cambridgeshire, received a distress call from a fellow trader who could not raise the police. He went to the launderette which had had its windows broken 60 times in five years and found a fourteen-year-old youth sitting on a washer violently battering the machine with his heels. Mr Brown told the yobbo and two other youths to 'clear off'. The gang just went next door to an optician's and started causing more trouble. Mr Brown forced them out of there, but only after the prime trouble-maker had spat at him and made head-butting gestures. Outside, the same individual then lurched at Mr Brown with a clenched fist. Acting in self-defence, the businessman stopped him with one hand and slapped him around the side of the head with the other. When Mr Brown's wife stepped in, the youth also spat at her.

During the course of this exchange, three 999 calls were made to the police. There was no response, except for the community police officer (whatever one of those is supposed to be) who turned up at Mr Brown's house the following morning to tell him that they had received a complaint against him.

***

Mr Brown was charged with assault. Seven months of near suicidal worry passed before the case got to court, and when it did he was acquitted. Witnesses called in his defence said that far from attacking the boy he had been trying to back away from a confrontation. The chairman of the bench at the court in Ely, Hamish Ross, said, 'We find the force he used was indeed reasonable because in the absence of police which he had requested he felt a duty of care to staff in the optician's and to customers.'

This case outrages me on a number of points. Firstly, do we now assume in this country that there is no longer a 999 facility because policemen are being instructed by their superiors to ignore such calls? Secondly, how on earth did this case ever get to court, at vast public expense? If a magistrate – a member of the public – can figure out from the defence evidence that this was a case of self-defence, why couldn't the investigating policeman also realise that? Did he bother to talk to the witness before issuing the assault charge? Thirdly, should there not be a statutory scale of compensation for innocent citizens whose lives are made torturous by incompetent policemen? After all, the cops seem to be terribly anxious to placate career villains with compensation payments if, on occasion, they nick a wrongdoer for one particular offence and fail to prove he committed it.

My fourth point is that I hope Cambridgeshire Police conducted a full investigation into the incompetence and stupidity of the senior officers involved in this case. How can the people of Cambridgeshire have any faith in their police force when the public servants they employ are running around ignoring real, desperate pleas for help from those they are supposed to be serving, because they are too busy trying to prosecute decent, law-abiding citizens who are forced to take the law into their own hands because the police have abandoned them? I'd like to know how many officers involved in this case have been sacked. Not just from the Cambridgeshire force, but from the police service in general in cases like this.

This sort of horrendous story is so common now it no longer surprises any of us. This is the dawn of a mad social experiment in which the government would like us to consider the 'causes' of crime. The causes of crime are the criminals. We now have a situation where ordinary, solid police constables and sergeants who want to act with fairness and common sense on the ground are being taught that this is no longer the right way. It did not surprise me at all to learn that over a three-year period starting in 2004 more than 6,000 police officers left our forces. Most of these were no higher than sergeant in rank, and the majority were constables. A report highlighted that the men and women of the police force no longer feel they are serving the community and are frustrated by having to waste so much time on bureaucracy, red tape and political correctness. According to the report I read, the police officers who quit did so because they were bogged down with paperwork, sometimes having to fill in as many as 50 different forms for one arrest. And all their work was affected by a need to meet 'operational targets' dictated to them by senior officers as a consequence of political influence.

I have friends in the police who agree entirely with this report. A mate of mine who is at inspector rank has told me in confidence that a large body of officers are unavailable to him at any one time because they are away on 'diversity courses'. On these courses his men are taught how to speak properly to different members of the community. But that is something he has already trained his men to do by patrolling with them on the beat. The stupidity of the new way of doing things is that vast amounts of money are being spent taking cops off front-line duty to teach them things they already knew from when they were on front-line duty; and as they now spend so much time behind a desk the skills are useless anyway because they no longer mingle in the community. This is disastrous for our country. Only policemen who mingle with the people they are supposed to serve can react to specific situations. You can't solve some problems by reading a textbook about what you are supposed to do. I've learnt that plenty of times, from situations where nobody intended any real harm but which nevertheless went pear-shaped.

For instance, there was one night when I was out with Porky in Suffolk for a convivial evening in a Chinese restaurant. My pal was his usual exuberant self, and he started telling the only joke he knows, which is about a Chinese philosopher who can't pronounce his words. Most people find it very funny. The joke is not about being cruel or unkind to the Chinese, it's about mocking an Englishman who can't find a girlfriend and who goes to a Chinese philosopher for help. It's the sort of soft joke you might hear on a comedian's variety show in a town like Batley.

Porky wasn't being offensive, and one or two of the waiters were sharing a laugh with us, but when he'd finished and he started telling it again I told him to shut up. Before he did, the manager came over and asked us to leave. I tried to plead Porky's case, but they were adamant. Not wanting to attract any attention, I said, 'OK, no problem. We're sorry you've taken it like that, we'll go somewhere else.'

We left the restaurant, wandered across the road and went into a bar to contemplate Plan B for dining that night.

About a quarter of an hour later we came out of the bar and there were two police cars parked in front of the Chinese restaurant. I wondered what on earth had gone on in the short time since we left. Then a waiter came running out, followed by a police officer, and started shouting, 'This is the thief!'

I immediately bridled. I reached out, grabbed the waiter and asked, 'Hey, who are you calling a thief?'

He recoiled with a look of terror on his face, as though I'd hit him. 'No pay for food,' he said.

A policeman stepped between us.

'This bloke's nuts,' I said. 'We didn't have any food. We were asked to leave before we could have anything to eat because one or two of these guys had a sense of humour failure.'

'Well, sir, this gentleman says that you did in fact order some food and that you were asked to leave because your friend was being disorderly.'

'Well, I'm telling you that we didn't order any food and we weren't being that disorderly.'

At that point I realised that Porky was poking me in the arm.

'We did order food, Al,' he said. 'I ordered some spring rolls and starters and things when you went to the loo. But when they threw us out I just assumed they'd cancel the order.' Porky turned to the Chinese waiter. 'You must have cooked it at breakneck speed. It was only about three minutes between you taking the order and telling us to go. You're trying to set us up.'

The waiter exploded again, but the cop quietened him down. Apparently, when the manager asked us to leave he didn't know that Porky had ordered some food. When he found out he rang the cops and accused us of theft. I didn't know that we'd placed an order when we left. It was true that we left pretty hastily because I didn't want to make a fuss in an area where I am quite well known, but according to this waiter we had done a runner. I was fuming at the injustice of it all.

The cop took control. 'Now look, gentlemen. It seems to me there has been a bit of a misunderstanding here. The best way all round to sort this out is to find a way of settling the bill.'

'We don't owe them any money,' I said, still fuming at their attempt to smear us.

For once, Porky stepped in as the diplomat.

'How much food do you say we ordered?' he asked the waiter.

'Nine pounds and forty pence,' he replied.

I shook my head in disbelief that a commercial business could call out the cops and accuse two of its customers of theft when it was clearly a misunderstanding over less than a tenner. We'd done nothing to warrant being thrown out in the first place. We had certainly committed no crime.

Porky handed the waiter a ten-pound note.

'Right, that's settled,' said the policeman. 'Now we can all go about our business and have a nice evening.'

With that, the two police cars disappeared.

When I read about the way the police carry on these days, with all the crazy PC views that prevail, I wonder how that matter got settled in such a sensible and straightforward fashion. I often reflect on that incident when I hear about some of the nutty situations that arise today. Policemen are being made fools of by their senior officers.

Take the case of the ten-year-old boy from Cheshire who was visited at home by two cops after using the word 'gay' in an e-mail to a class-mate. The little boy explained that he had used 'gay' as an alternative to 'stupid' because that was one of the expressions he and his pals used in the playground. He didn't really understand what 'gay' was in modern society. The police despatched four officers to investigate this 'crime'. Two went to the boy's home and two went to his school. The boy's mother was a magistrate. The lad's father was a company director who said he had never had a 'suitable response' from the police to break-ins at his business. Unsurprisingly, the boy was never treated as an offender. A spokesman for Cheshire Police said at the time, 'We'd be hard pushed to say it was a homophobic crime.' Which police college did that man go to in order to be able to reach that conclusion? Once again, the operational officers were made to look ridiculous by their senior officers, who construct policy.

Maybe I just live in a reasonably sane part of the world in East Anglia, because there was another time when a sensible policeman got me out of a sticky situation that had turned really ugly.

After I was forced to retire from football I bought a pub in Ipswich called the Black Adder. It was a lovely olde-worlde traditional boozer on the edge of the centre of town, and Jill and I had high hopes of making a long-term success of it. One summer's evening near closing time an old pal, an established international footballer, suddenly walked through the door. I knew it wasn't going to be an early night.

Once all the punters had left, we locked the doors and settled down for a session, and some reminiscing. After about an hour my cleaning lady, Kate, came over to say goodnight. She was a fine-looking young lady, very shapely with a great figure and a lovely smile. My pal was immediately smitten and invited her to join us, only to be slightly disappointed a few minutes later when her boyfriend, Bernie, came to pick her up. I could never figure out what Kate saw in Bernie. He was a long-haired, greasy-looking individual who constantly looked as if he needed a bath. He was apparently some sort of rock musician, but it didn't look to me like he'd done a day's work in his life.

We all sat at the table and sank a few drinks, and before long my pal started to regard the boyfriend as invisible. There were one or two other people around and I became lost in the conversations I was having with them, but I suddenly noticed that my pal had disappeared. Alarm bells started ringing in my head. I had seen this routine before in hotels around the world. A few minutes earlier Kate had left the table, saying she was going to the loo. Bernie had been getting cigarettes from the machine.

When he got back he asked where his girlfriend was. Everybody shrugged their shoulders. Then he realised my pal had also disappeared. Jealous and possessive at the best of times, he let off a roar and went hurtling up the stairs. I shouted after him, but to no avail. I was limping at the time because the previous day I had played in a charity five-a-side game and had turned my ankle, so I could only hobble towards the stairs. But it was too late. I heard the smashing of wood and realised that Bernie was kicking down the door of one of the ladies' loos.

I tried to get up the stairs as fast as I could but my ankle was really hurting. When I reached the top my pal came bolting out of the bathroom with blood all over his face. Bernie, a much bigger man, was following in a frenzy. I grabbed him and pinned him to the floor. My pal did not hesitate, and volleyed him in the side of his head.

At that moment Kate emerged from the bathroom. Her jeans were around her ankles and she was rearranging her underwear, and when she saw the commotion in the hallway she screamed, 'Bernie, stop it! We weren't doing anything!' Not immediately aware of how ridiculous she sounded, I told her to get herself dressed and get downstairs. My pal booted her boyfriend again. When he screamed, Kate yelled at him again, 'We weren't doing anything!' and then she started kicking him.

Bernie was like a madman. He wouldn't give up. I had to throw my whole bodyweight across him to contain him. Eventually he calmed down, so I let him up but held him in a bear-hug. I told him, amid all the shouting and screaming, to stay calm or I'd throw him down the stairs. He went limp. Foolishly, I relaxed my grip. As I did so Bernie sprang free, whirled round and punched me in the face. I was thrown backwards towards the wall and Bernie leapt on my pal again. This time he was ready for him. He wellied him between the legs, and as he went down he gave him another volley in the head.

But Bernie was coming at him again. I grabbed him and tried to pull his jacket over his head, shouting to my pal, 'For Christ's sake, just get out of here, will you! This guy's fighting mad and I don't want my pub wrecked!'

He scampered off.

I pulled Bernie to the floor again and lay on him like a deadweight. The poor guy had only come into the pub to pick up his girlfriend after work. Thirty minutes later he had discovered her in a bathroom in a highly compromising position with an international footballer. I couldn't really blame him for getting upset. But at that precise moment I had no time for sympathy. If I hadn't stepped in he could have wrecked my pub. And apart from the cost of the damage, I was still on probation as a newly licensed landlord and couldn't afford to be in control of a disorderly house. Ipswich was still very much a quiet country market town in those days and magistrates took a very dim view of people fighting each other in pubs.

'Now look,' I said to Bernie, 'you either promise me you will behave yourself or I will stay here lying on you all night. I'm sorry about what has happened to you but it's nothing to do with me and if you try taking it out on me again I will break you in two.'

Bernie was clearly feeling very uncomfortable. He was having problems breathing, and he gave me a solemn assurance that he would go home. I didn't know what was going to happen between him and Kate, but I couldn't get involved in that.

I got off him, and he got up. His face was a mess and his clothes were torn. I guided him downstairs, out of the back door and up the alleyway. But as we turned into the street, the worst possible thing happened. Kate was sitting on the kerb opposite, smoking a cigarette. I don't know what she thought she was doing, but the moment Bernie saw her he roared like a lion and went to get her. He even tried to grab a bottle, which I assumed he was going to use to hit her. I knocked it out of his hand and threw him off balance. In the process, his elbow went through one of my side windows. Then he steadied himself and took a running kungfu-style kick at my main plate-glass window. It was a huge leaded construction. I held my breath, because if his foot had gone through it he would have caused thousands of pounds' worth of damage. He might also have sliced his leg off. Luckily, he bounced back into the street.

Now I was raging angry with him, and I booted him with full force between the legs. Unfortunately it was with my damaged foot. I let out a howl. The pain was intense, and I decided Bernie was going to pay for it. I grabbed him in a head-lock. Then with my free hand I clenched my fist and started thumping his face like it was a punch-bag. This time it was me who had lost control. But I'd given this nutter enough warnings, and he was threatening my livelihood.

Just at that moment a police car glided around the corner. That was all I needed. I stopped thumping Bernie and threw him to the pavement. The window of the cop car slid down and a police officer, who fortunately I knew very well, grinned at me. His mate, who was leaning across from the driver's seat, looked more astonished.

'Anything we can do to help, Al?' said the one I knew, surveying my bloody nose, my battered victim and the debris of my pub.

'I suppose a late-night licence is out of the question, officer?' I said, starting to laugh for the first time in a while.

They started laughing too. This was my luckiest break of the night. A couple of friendly cops. If they hadn't seen things my way I might have faced losing my licence. I told the two of them briefly what had happened. They picked Bernie up off the floor and he scampered away in pursuit of Kate. I never heard another word about the incident.

We need more policemen like those two.

***

When you look at our society on the surface, it appears to be one of the most law-abiding in the world. But actually, I believe that criminality in our country is never very far away. It's just that for most of the time, until they are caught, criminals are pretty sophisticated at what they do.

For years I was on conversation terms with a big punter who I bumped into at race-tracks around the country on many occasions. At first I knew him only as 'Brian'; later I learnt that his nickname was 'The Milkman', because he had a reputation for always delivering. I took that to mean on information, or 'the goods' in whichever business he worked. I never bug a man about his business. I think everybody is entitled to conduct their business affairs in whatever manner they want. I just understood Brian Wright to be an entrepreneur who used his money to indulge his passion for gambling. According to legend, he once won £400,000 at one meeting at Royal Ascot.

He was a very charming, immaculately dressed man who was always first to the bar in any company. When we used to chat he made it clear that he thought money was probably the most important thing in the world, and in many ways I agree with him. He had lots of friends, including people of the calibre of my racing mate Mick Channon. He spent a lot of time in Newmarket and was often to be seen at the smart Bedford Lodge Hotel where he appeared to keep a suite of rooms. He always had a tan – I understand he had a place in Marbella. Apart from when he was partying, though, he seemed to be on his own a lot. He was actually fairly typical of a lot of people I mix with: a rich, successful businessman who largely kept himself to himself and was attracted to the glamour of the race-track.

So you can imagine how shocked I was when I picked up the papers one morning to discover that he had been sent down for 30 years after being convicted of running Europe's biggest cocaine smuggling operation. According to the reports he had amassed a fortune of £600 million using armadas of private yachts to sail from South America to mainland Europe. There was so much money at stake in these shipments that the boats, which could be worth £5 million, were allowed to run aground in remote coves and left for a few days to make sure that they were not being tracked. Then gangs would swoop on the vessels in the middle of the night and remove up to £50 million of cocaine, simply abandoning the boat altogether.

Brian was, apparently, an associate of Terry Adams, the notorious head of the Adams crime family whom police allege are linked to 25 gangland murders. Adams himself is now serving a nine-year sentence after being convicted of tax evasion on the huge fortune he had made from 'business'.

I could hardly believe the newspapers were writing about the same mild-mannered man with whom I had often talked racing over a few glasses of champagne. But that was not the first time I had belatedly discovered a criminal background to people who on the surface looked so respectable.

When I was running my pub, a middle-aged chap started coming in and splashing a bit of cash around, usually from mid-morning to lunchtime. His name was Bob, and he was a very affable chap and pleasant enough to have in the bar. He used to stand there drinking pints of bitter and endlessly smoking tiny cigars.

Over the course of a few weeks the story emerged that he was setting up home with a new lady. She had a son who was at a local school and now he wanted to buy a big house so they could all move in together. He also said he was shortly going to finalise a deal that was going to give him 'a substantial amount of money' and that he was planning to invest that in bloodstock. It was another reason why he wanted a house in the area – to be near Newmarket, the home of the racing industry.

OK, so looking back it seemed like a classic conman's cover, but there were no signs then. Bob brought his lady in with him a few times and I couldn't believe that she was involved in anything dodgy with this guy. She was smart and rather sophisticated.

I was very active in the racing world and I was happy to introduce Bob to my friend, Robert Sangster. That is not something I did lightly. Mr Sangster, now sadly deceased, was as big in the racing industry in those days as the Maktoum family are today. For anybody who wanted to seriously invest in the world of racing, there could not have been a finer introduction.

One day Bob asked me to accompany him to see a house he had spotted just outside the beautiful Suffolk village of Lavenham. He wanted a second opinion. Bear in mind that I was very well known in East Anglia, having not long retired from football. He hoped that my presence might sway the deal. I agreed to go in exchange for lunch at the Swan in Lavenham, one of the most beautiful pub restaurants in Britain.

We got to the house, a converted thatched barn typical of that part of the world. It was a magnificent property set in acres of beautifully manicured grounds. The owner came out to greet us, and I was sure I was looking at a man who was not very well. He had clearly once been a tall, strong individual, but he was old now – beyond his years, I thought. He was stooped and his hair was grey, going on white. His skin had a strange greyish pallor. His name was Jeff. When he spoke, I realised he wasn't a local man, probably from London. Jeff was accompanied by a much younger and fine-looking lady. At first I thought she might be his daughter, but from the way they behaved with each other it was soon obvious they were like man and wife. We spent nearly an hour at the house, with Bob asking all the sorts of questions you would expect from a prospective buyer.

A few days later I got a call from Jeff. He asked me to go over and see him. We sat in his conservatory and he poured me quite a few fine glasses of wine as he asked me if I could vouch for Bob. I said he seemed genuine enough. I couldn't really say anything else. Jeff was very courteous and told me, 'I'm not a well man, as you may have noticed, and I want to make sure this deal is for real for the sake of the missus.' I didn't envisage any problems.

Another few days went by, then I got another call to go and see Jeff, and this time to take Bob with me. When we arrived at the house it was clear the atmosphere had changed completely from my previous visit. Instead of the front door we were led in around the back by a young, thickset man I had never seen before. We were taken through the kitchen, down a corridor and into a lounge I had not seen before. It was immaculately furnished. The focal point of the room was a huge antique desk, its top covered in green leather. Jeff was sitting behind it.

Bob opened his mouth to speak and extended his hand, but Jeff waved his arm at the two chairs laid out for us opposite him and barked out aggressively, 'You two, sit down. Sit down and shut up.' There was no courtesy in the old man now. The mild-mannered guy I had been sipping wine with three days earlier was now a snarling, bullying individual. The atmosphere was poisonous.

A number of items in the room caught my eye. They focused the mind rather intently and made matters even more unpleasant. On the desk was a framed picture of the Kray twins. For those not old enough to remember, Ronnie and Reggie Kray were the most notorious gangsters of post-war Britain. They ran a crime empire in east London which involved protection rackets, extortion, prostitution, drug smuggling and extreme violence. They and their henchmen were feared like no other criminals in Britain had ever been. Those who upset them for the slightest reason – a wrong look or a lack of 'respect' – might find themselves being tortured with a hot blade in their eye. They ran a campaign of terror for a decade, protected by a wall of fear-induced silence and lavish bribery.

They would not hesitate to kill opponents with their own hands. George Cornell, who called one of the brothers 'a fat poof', was shot through the head in a packed East End pub, the Blind Beggar. Another East End lowlife called Jack 'The Hat' McVitie was stabbed to death at a party and his body was disposed of in a carpet. The police couldn't find one single person who would come forward as a witness. Eventually, in the late sixties, after years of relentless policework, they were both nailed for the murder and other offences. They were sent to prison and never tasted freedom again.

As Bob and I sat down opposite Jeff, a shock-wave went through my system. It was the 1990s and the Kray twins were still very much alive and said to influence much in the crime-world from behind bars, as they had done when they were on the streets.

Jeff pointed his finger at the picture and said, 'I'm their effing godfather.'

Great. That's all I need. Another fine mess you've got yourself into, Brazil. But the revelation that the man in front of us was the godfather of the most notorious gangsters ever born in Britain was not the worst of it. Leaning against the desk on my right was a double-barrelled shotgun. And on the green leather top next to the protruding barrels were two cartridges. I remember thinking how well the brass casings had been polished.

'Now, Alan, can you two see what is to my left?' Jeff asked.

'I haven't taken my eyes off it since we came in,' I replied.

Jeff stared straight at Bob and addressed him menacingly in very ripe language. 'I think you're bullshitting me. And I don't tolerate that. I don't tolerate it from people I might have cause to fear, and I certainly don't tolerate it from you. Now, I have put that gun and those cartridges there just to remind you how I sort out business when people are trying to mess me around.

'Where do you think I got all this?' he continued, sweeping his arm in the air to indicate his big house and all that was in it. 'It wasn't given to me. I earned it. Sometimes people didn't want to give it to me so I had to work a little bit harder to persuade them. So you had better tell me now, when is the money coming? Or are you, as I suspect, just trying to play with the big boys and therefore wasting my time – something I don't have a great deal of at the moment?'

Bob certainly had a lot of front. Seemingly unimpressed with this show of terror from the old man, he sprang out of his seat and started ranting. 'How dare you even question my integrity. You will have my money in 48 hours if I still decide to go ahead with the deal.'

Jeff came straight back at him. 'You will go ahead with this deal. Even if you don't then as far as I am concerned you owe the asking price for this house. You've said you're going to buy it. That means I am expecting the money. And I will collect.'

Bob started shouting again, but he was backing out of the house at the same time.

We eventually reached the car, and rather dramatically he said, 'Alan, we need to get to Coutts. I'm not backing out of anything.'

Coutts is often known as the Queen's banker. It is, apparently, where the accounts for the royal family are held. That means it is a very upmarket bank. It's not the sort of place where somebody can just walk in off the street and open an account with a hundred pounds. If you have an account there you are worth a lot of money.

I was confused. I didn't know whether Bob had just been showing bravado or whatever in front of the old man. 'Look, we've got to get this sorted out,' I said to him. 'You've got to come clean.'

To try to get to the bottom of things, to solve this problem in which I had managed to immerse myself, I told him we would indeed go straight to Ipswich station and then into London to Coutts. Throughout the journey I half expected him to try to make a run for it. At every station I thought he might just jump off the train. But an hour and a half later we were standing in the Strand on the other side of the road to the bank.

'Right, I'll leave you here, Bob,' I said.

Coutts is a sort of state-of-the-art building with glass panels in its walls. You can see people travelling up the escalator after they have gone in. As Bob crossed the road I ducked into a shop and watched him intently because I still suspected he would do a runner. But he didn't. He went inside and up the escalator. I moved to a restaurant with a vantage point and ordered myself a cup of coffee.

He was in there for an hour before he came out. He then started walking, and I followed him at a distance. He didn't have my suspicious mind because he never turned round once, or even indicated that he thought he was being followed. We walked across town for about half an hour, and then he ducked into a Masonic Lodge in the Holborn area. I just couldn't figure it out. I waited for some time outside the Lodge, but eventually I gave up and went home.

The next day I got another call from Jeff asking me to go back and see him. He had reverted to the charming fellow we had first met. His lady was once more in attendance and I spent an intriguing afternoon in their company being shown pictures and newspaper clippings of his association with not only the Kray twins but just about every other well-known villain of the last 50 years. Some of the pictures had been taken in Marbella, but many more – older ones – showed the rather grim surroundings of the East End of London in the post-war years. We had a few drinks as he wistfully recalled stories about the people he had had dealings with. He never actually spoke of criminal matters. In fact, if you believed him, all his rather dubious pals were 'businessmen', or those who looked after the community when the police couldn't.

He never mentioned Bob. The last thing he asked me was where I was going to be over the next week. I told him I would be at the pub.

Two days later the phone rang. It was Jeff's lady. He'd died in the night. I never found out what was wrong with him.

And I never saw Bob again.

I went to my coat cupboard that afternoon as I was going out. My leather jacket wasn't there. Then I remembered I'd lent it to Bob before we went to see Jeff, the day we went on to Coutts. The last time I'd seen it was when he disappeared into the Masonic Lodge. I honestly wondered whether by now it would be full of bullet holes.

CHAPTER FIVE

VODKA ON
THE MENU

*'My first visit behind the Iron Curtain had a
profound affect on me. Nobody had taught me
in school that there were places like Poland.
I was shocked by the poverty and deprivation
I had seen.'*

THE SMALL CHILDREN who surrounded our coach were pathetic little figures. They looked emaciated. Their skin was grey and they were wrapped in bundles rather than dressed in clothes. They didn't look as though they had a bean between them. Which was probably why they were standing outside our hotel every day with their hands outstretched. And why they always chased the team coach into the hotel compound. Poignantly, it wasn't money they wanted to improve their miserable lives, it was sweets. The little figures that flitted in and out of the shadows wanted to enjoy the simple childhood pleasures of munching a piece of chocolate or sucking on a humbug.

I was barely more than a kid myself at the time, but I was lucky enough to have had a comfortable upbringing. A shiver went through me when I looked at the squalor in which these children lived. The inside of our hotel offered them a glimmer of the comfortable life we lived in the west. Those home comforts included the odd toffee bar in the fridge, or some mint imperials. All the lads and I scooped them up every day and took them out to the youngsters. Beyond that 'tourist' hotel, their world appeared to be one of abject misery.

It was 1980 and Ipswich Town were in the city of Lodz, right in the middle of Poland, for a UEFA Cup tie. It was a bitterly cold December and the temperature never moved above zero throughout our three-day stay. The ground was covered in ice and snow, and apart from training on pitches that were like concrete we hardly ventured out. There was nothing attractive to look at anyway. In fact, I think that at that stage in my life it was the most miserable place I had ever been in.

Communism still had a tyrannical grip on Eastern Europe. I had never been behind the Iron Curtain before and it was a lesson for me about how comfortable, by comparison, we were in the west. Everything was so drab. I had heard about the great architecture of the cities at the heart of the communist empire, but Lodz clearly wasn't one of them. Apart from a smoky industrial landscape there seemed to be nothing but row after row of what we would have described in Glasgow as council flats. The people were miserable and ugly too. Women seemed to have aged before their time. Many of them had black teeth. Men were small and squat with moustaches covered in ice. Their faces were full of fear. As a young footballer I didn't have much of a grasp on the political picture, but it was explained to me by the hotel manager that all the time they lived under the threat of Russian tanks rolling across their borders and into their towns.

Poland was a satellite state of the Warsaw Pact, the military alliance that was completely controlled by the mighty Soviet Union. Countries such as Poland were virtual colonies of the USSR, which ruled over them with an iron fist from the Kremlin in Moscow. But despite the oppression imposed upon them following the carve-up of Europe after the Second World

War, some of the Eastern bloc countries had rebelled against their Soviet masters. Hungary was ruthlessly crushed in 1956 when tanks rolled into Budapest. Similar scenes horrified the world in 1968 when the beautiful city of Prague was re-annexed by the Russians.

Alexander Dubcek had only risen to power in Czechoslovakia a few months earlier. He realised that you could not keep people in captivity for ever and had introduced a series of liberal policies never before seen behind the Iron Curtain. He allowed more freedom of movement for his people. Amazingly, until then, citizens of the Soviet empire were mostly not allowed to travel outside the borders of their own towns. Dubcek accepted the influence of western culture – pop music, clothes, etc. – and people were able to assemble to attend meetings and concerts. But in Moscow this was seen as a threat to the total control the politburos had over their people. Russian tanks moved on to the streets of Prague and the 'rebels' were rounded up and taken away. The brave Mr Dubcek was detained for 're-education'.

It was against this backdrop of tyranny that Poles lived their lives. I couldn't see for the life of me how their appallingly drab lifestyle posed any sort of a challenge to the uniformity demanded by the Russians. I had never come across such a depressing form of human existence. If Poland was deemed to be getting too liberal then God only knows what life must have been like in hardline Russia. It is no exaggeration to say that the living conditions of the Poles were worse than the cramped and condemned tenements in which my father had been brought up in Glasgow's notorious Gorbals 40 years earlier.

It was on that visit to Lodz that I first learnt that communism, far from being an 'everybody is equal' system of rule, was in fact as elitist as George Orwell had described in his book *Animal Farm*. 'All animals are equal, but some animals are more equal than others' was the famous conclusion to this classic tome, and now I understood why. The hotel in which we were staying was apparently run by the Communist Party. On each floor, as you stepped out of the lift, there was a woman sitting at a desk, monitoring the movements of the guests. Other people staying at the hotel clearly had something to do with government. They didn't look like the wretches we saw on the other side of the hotel gates. The men looked like western businessmen, and the ladies with them were all beautiful, well turned out and dressed glamorously. I assumed they were all prostitutes because none of them ever said a word. They just sat there and looked beautiful, in complete contrast to the harridans outside who were overweight and careworn, with scarves wrapped round their heads.

We had taken all our own food to Poland on Bobby Robson's insistence, but in our hotel restaurant you could have been in Mayfair in London. The food seemed to be 'normal' by western standards. It was only when we went to an official reception held by the club, Widzew Lodz, that we realised what ordinary Poles had to endure. They served us a buffet dinner that was remarkable for two things: there was no real meat and no fresh vegetables. The meat, such as it was, was nothing more than gristle. None of us could touch it. And what we took to be vegetables were black and indigestible.

We already had a 5-0 lead from the home leg. It was the season when we went on to win the UEFA Cup, and we were red-hot on that campaign, but frankly, we couldn't wait to finish the job in Poland and get home. We actually lost 1-0 on the night in the coldest temperatures in which I had ever played, and our plane took off just three hours after the end of the game.

My first visit behind the Iron Curtain had a profound effect on me. Nobody had taught me in school that there were places like Poland. I thought people all around Europe grew up like me, and I was shocked by the poverty and deprivation I had seen. It came as no shock to me, therefore, when many years later Polish people started to leave their country en masse. If I had been a young man growing up in such a deprived country I too would have fled at the very moment the borders were opened and the yoke of communist rule was removed.

I'm all for anybody who wants to better themselves in life. If people are ambitious and work hard then they generally have enough energy to be a force for good – that is, a force to provide for themselves and at the same time to contribute to the economy of the country in which they live. I would welcome to this country any Polish person who had a specific contribution to make. My only proviso is that the decision to allow that person to live in Britain should be made by the British people, represented by the British government, voted into Westminster by the people.

But of course it doesn't work like that. Since the enlargement of the European Union in May 2004 we don't seem to have any choice any more about how many people we allow into our country. Through successive governments we are now fully signed up to the European ideal, so we no longer have the ability to open or close the gates. That decision is made for us in Brussels. The gates stay open at all times. That, apparently, is one of the basic rules of the European Economic Community.

However, I have travelled extensively throughout Europe

and I know for sure that other western European countries, such as France, are very much more selective about who they let in and who they don't. The French are very good at bending the rules when it is to their advantage. They are also very good at hitting out at other member states, such as the UK, when we are seen to be less than compliant. And the gutless individuals who sit in Westminster always comply when the pressure is put on by the other Europeans.

One thing we have to get right is that if we accept people from other countries then we have to agree to allow them to benefit from the institutions we have built up over centuries or decades, such as the National Health Service. But the NHS is in a terrible mess. Despite billions of pounds being poured into it I read every day about wards being closed all over the place because of huge debts. Surely if it can't cope with the needs of the current population, how will it cope in the future if immigration remains unbridled? As I said, I believe that in Britain we should put out the welcome mat to those who want to join in. But there has to be some control.

There is a madness in our country that brands as a 'racist' anyone who even questions a policy regarding immigration. Never mind that you want the system to work for everybody, including immigrants. If you try to point out that overloading the system could lead to its collapse, you are shouted down. But no other European country I know of has just opened its doors and waved everybody in. If you were the captain of a ferry that was about to set sail to the promised land and you let an unchecked number of people on board, your vessel would sink and everybody would suffer. You would be very popular for about five minutes as you welcomed each passenger aboard, but ultimately your failure to take proper responsibility and say no to people would result in disaster. This is what I believe has been happening to our immigration policy for decades, and it has definitely speeded up in the past ten years.

My frustration comes from the fact that I have been banging on for the same amount of time about the dangers of open doors. I am not alone. Believe me, in the high streets, the pubs and the wine bars of Britain, millions of people have the same concern. The only problem is that we have never had anybody who will look at our concerns and analyse the argument sensibly. Thirty years ago the huge raft of liberal politics which exists in this country and covers all the parties represented in the House of Commons introduced a vow of silence on the topic. As I said, what they decided was that even to question the immigration policy in this country was unacceptably racist, and anybody who protested that the face of Britain was changing too fast was guilty of racism.

So you can imagine my mixed reaction when I was sitting at home one Sunday morning watching a political programme and the then Home Secretary John Reid suddenly popped up to talk about 'voters' concerns'. Amazingly, he put immigration at the top of the list. A few days earlier the immigration minister Liam Byrne had admitted that the tolerant people of Britain had become 'deeply unsettled' by mass migration. It soon transpired that private polls over the previous six months had started to indicate that people were finally speaking up about immigration. Politicians were going to have to drop the accusation of racism against anybody who showed concern for overcrowding.

And, surprise surprise, shortly after the Home Secretary suddenly started admitting that we have immigration problems, new figures were released to show that 600,000 people had entered the country in the last year.

What really annoys me is that even as recently as the last general election in this country, May 2005, anybody who tried to point out that we couldn't keep allowing people in for ever was just shouted down. This is one reason why I have so little time for politicians. A politician's job is to try to be popular with those who have a vote. That in itself results in a completely flawed political machine.

People want everything for free, not to be told, for instance, that they have to pay for prescriptions. But in the way our society is structured it has been accepted for many years now that you have to pay for prescriptions, otherwise the cost is borne unfairly by all taxpayers. Still, in an astonishing piece of political chicanery there are some people in Britain now who don't pay for their tablets and medicines. People in Wales get them for free. And that is because the principality now has its own assembly, partly independent from the British government in Westminster, and those who sit in power on that assembly want to make sure that they are popular enough to be voted back into power by the grateful populace, so in effect they use taxpayers' money to buy votes.

I use the example of prescriptions to illustrate the cynicism of politics in relation to the immigration question. If you open the door of your rather opulent house (Great Britain) which was lovingly built by your ancestors and invite in to stay, for as long as they like, the poor neighbours from the other side of town (the Poles), the new residents are going to be very happy. Politicians gamble on the fact that immigrants into this country will be so grateful to be admitted that when they become citizens they will vote for the 'good guys' at every future election. The 'good guys' will warn that the 'bad guys' are the opposition who might want to eject them from the house. In this way an incumbent government can sort of import its own fan club, swell the numbers of its supporters ahead of future general elections.

The problem with that theory is that politicians are naively assuming that grateful immigrants will forever be in their debt. The truth is that any immigrant worth his or her salt will very quickly become independent-minded and, once established, will be beholden to nobody. Look, for instance, at the power and wealth established by Asian business people over the last 30 years. They have taken full advantage of the opportunities offered to them in Britain. They now form a huge economic bloc, something which has undoubtedly contributed to this country. Nevertheless, the argument about the economic value of immigration can be put equally forcibly in either direction: it either helps our economy to grow or it drains our resources. It is particularly relevant now because of the rapid acceleration in the inflow of people over the last decade.

What cannot be argued, however, is how the arrival of people from different cultures around the world since the Second World War has changed the face of the United Kingdom. There are now parts of the country which don't look as though they are British at all. And this is where I don't understand the 'integration' and 'diversity' argument that is so often put forward to justify mass immigration.

I travelled recently to Romford Dog Track in Essex where I was attending a function. My car took me through the East End of London, past Brick Lane and through Seven Kings and

Stratford, which is the hub of the 2012 Olympic site. At times I could have been in Asia. People were dressed like Asians, and all the shops were catering to Asian tastes and fashions. There was only a shred of an indication that this was the capital city of the UK. I am not talking about a street here or a street there, I mean whole neighbourhoods, sometimes a busy high street half a mile long, which have taken on all the cultural associations of an Asian city. Many people clearly didn't even speak English because much of the signage was in languages that to me were incomprehensible.

What I saw that day, and what I have seen in other big British cities, doesn't fit either the 'diversity' or 'integration' test. Diversity means that a community should be mixed. I haven't got a problem with Asian people living in Britain. In my experience they are usually independent and hard-working. But what has happened is that poor planning and handling of immigration has resulted in old-established British communities becoming Asian communities. I have heard the complaint many times that people who used to live in traditional East End communities no longer feel that they belong there. It is they and not the relatively new arrivals who have felt pressurised to leave the neighbourhoods in which they grew up. A new and totally alien culture was being forced upon them. The danger is that situations like that become a breeding ground for resentment. And that breaks all the definitions of 'integration'.

From the evidence of my own eyes I can see that Asian people are happiest living with those of their own culture without having to adapt to the traditional British way of life. In towns such as Blackburn and Bradford in the north of

England and Luton in the south, people from different ethnic backgrounds very rarely mix with one another. Is it right that whole communities exist in this country where English is at best the second language, and sometimes it is not spoken at all? Every time the authorities have to provide an interpreter to be present in a court of law, for example, whatever the issue or the dispute, is that an acceptance that you can survive in Britain these days without learning our language? Why don't we stop pretending that 'integration' works and that the vast majority of us are happy with it? The talk on the street is that we are not.

If we started to be honest with ourselves then we could perhaps do away with the ridiculous multi-billion-pound race-relations industry which sees discrimination at every turn. A mate of mine who has been a cricket commentator for years has always referred to the Pakistan cricket team as 'the Pakis' in much the same way as the Australians are 'the Aussies'. It's an abbreviation of each country's name, and they are accepted terms in the game. In conversation, everybody refers to people from Japan as 'the Japs', don't they? So why is it that the racism-is-everywhere brigade insist that only 'Pakis' is a derogatory term?

No, it doesn't seem to me that people from different cultures want to mingle together. Therefore multiculturalism is something that is forced on all sorts of different communities by social engineers. If they didn't have that to do they wouldn't have a job. 'Diversity' is a mythical social trend which should be left to the individual rather than those on the outside who think they know best. If people want to live together they will; if they don't, why should they be forced to by those who want to live their lives for them? When individuals are left to get on with it themselves things, generally speaking, work out much better.

The last time I was in Glasgow I went to a wonderful Indian restaurant called Mr Singh's. It had all the flavour of the mystic east: lovely aromas coming from the kitchen, sitar music drifting gently out of the speakers, and scented candles wafting in the air. We were enjoying a few pre-dinner lagers and studying the menu when a waiter asked me if we were ready to order. I looked up to say that we needed a few more minutes, but I couldn't see the person who had just asked me the question. There was a very attentive young Indian man standing there, but the bloke who'd been talking to me had a thick Scottish accent. I squinted in the dark, looking around.

'I'm sorry, sir, are you looking for someone?'

It was the same Scottish voice, and it suddenly clicked. The man with the local dialect was the Indian.

I laughed. 'Sorry, pal, was that you?'

He laughed too. 'No, it was my parrot,' he replied, in a Strathclyde accent that was stronger than mine. He stepped back to reveal that he was wearing a kilt, complete with a sporran. With his plain white shirt he looked like one of the army of Scottish football fans who had followed the national team in which I played to Spain in 1982. We had an immediate bond. This guy was no longer Indian. He was Scottish. He sounded like a Scotsman and he was dressed like a Scotsman. His ethnic origin was irrelevant.

That would be my definition of integration. Not setting yourself up as an alternative and distinctive culture in the middle of an alien landscape, but merging into that landscape.

Apart from anything else, it's good business. I always go back to Mr Singh's now when I am in Glasgow.

I think that the huge influx of Polish people to our shores presents them with the same challenge. Almost every Polish person I have met I have liked or respected. I don't know where the catering trade in the UK would be today without workers from the Eastern bloc. Every restaurant and bar I go into, anywhere in the country, seems to have Polish barmaids. They are usually bright, efficient and welcoming, and they all speak very good English. They make great efforts to integrate, but through sheer force of numbers I can see Polish communities springing up. Increasingly I see Polish shops opening in big towns, selling only Polish goods. Around Crewe in Cheshire recently I saw a road sign in Polish. When I later asked a local in a bar why they had to have foreign road signs I was told that as much as 5 per cent of the town's population, numbering some 3,000 people, is now made up of Poles.

On further investigation I found that Crewe is by no means the biggest Polish community in Britain. There are 9,000 emigrants from Eastern Europe in and around the Welsh town of Llanelli. Bognor Regis also has a sizeable community. And it is not only Poles who are seeking a new life here. A mate of mine in the Midlands supplies goods to a Lithuanian supermarket in Birmingham. Apparently there is now a community of 5,000 immigrants, and growing, from the Baltic state.

These figures are astonishing. The phenomenon of our culture changing so rapidly has crept up on most of us without anybody noticing. As I said, in my experience, Eastern European immigrants make great efforts to integrate themselves. I find that in restaurants and bars staffed largely by Eastern Europeans, predominantly Poles and Lithuanians, the service is usually efficient and presented with a smile. In those sorts of establishments there has also been a return to the old-fashioned habit of believing that the customer is always right, even when the customer is wrong.

Nevertheless, by their very presence, their distinctive culture is bound to be an influence on the communities in which they have settled. And just as I have a problem with people not being able to speak English in the courts, the same applies to all communities. Once again, I don't think it is right that policemen in these towns should have to go on courses to be taught to speak Polish. In other parts of Britain policemen are being taught Romanian. Surely it's much better for those who want to come and live here from overseas to learn our language? That immediately removes the main barrier to integration. I would urge all immigrants to do just that.

America, the richest and and most vibrant country in the world, was created by mass immigration throughout the first half of the twentieth century. Today it is a veritable kaleidoscope of influences from all over the world. The main ones are Italian and Irish, but you can add to that Scottish, Scandinavian, German, Russian, Cuban, Chinese, Korean, Turkish and many others. It has all moulded together well, and the main reason for that is because the Americans did not feather-bed their immigrants. They always insisted that if they wanted to get on in the United States, they had to do it by speaking English. Through taking a tough, pragmatic approach, America managed to breed loyalty into their immigrants who grew up to understand the value of the opportunities the country could provide to anybody who wanted to work hard.

One of the best examples to me of this 'immigration loyalty' is the story of the Hollywood movie giant Louis B. Mayer, who was taken to America as the baby son of Eastern European refugees. When he went for his first job, as a clerk on a film-lot, at the age of thirteen, he realised he had never known his birth-date. So he gave it as 4 July – Independence Day – to constantly remind himself how lucky he was to be in America.

I was always fascinated by listening to that international Mr Fixit Henry Kissinger, the former Secretary of State for the United States. He was of German origin, and his foreign accent was so strong that I sometimes couldn't make out what he was saying. But he was one of the most powerful men in the world. The actor-turned-politician Arnold Schwarzenegger is another immigrant to America who hit the heights as a mega-Hollywood star and then Governor of California without losing his foreign accent.

What puzzles me is how all the Eastern bloc arrivals in this country manage to find jobs. Who did all those jobs before they got here? The large-scale immigration of the post-war years from the Commonwealth produced a new labour pool which was easily absorbed. The scores of thousands of people who were killed in the war dented not just one generation, but the future generation those victims would have produced. With peace came a big surge in the economy, and there was a labour shortage, which is what started the drive for immigrants in the first place. But when the new wave started coming in the late 1990s the country was pretty close to having full employment. Yet you don't see many unemployed Poles wandering the streets.

You do, however, see hordes of feckless British youths

hanging around, looking as though they are doing nothing in particular. I read one report that estimated that as many as five million adults in Britain are not in occupational work and receive some form of handout from the state. This figure has apparently not been challenged by the government departments concerned.

Sometimes I wonder whether politicians are actually quite proud to be running a system that manages to absorb five million deadbeats who contribute absolutely nothing to the economy, only milk it. I am so suspicious of those who govern us that it wouldn't surprise me if this was seen as some sort of crazy success for the social engineers. And, as I have mentioned already, is that army of spongers – that's the only word you can use to describe them – seen as a secret army of loyal voters? On further examination I discovered that a quarter of the adult population of Manchester and a fifth of the people of Birmingham are on benefits. We now seem to have a new labour market principle: pay a lot of British people to do nothing in order to create vacancies for hundreds of thousands of immigrants.

Evidence of this phenomenon exists everywhere. Go to any working-class area of a town – and I do because I have old mates all over the place – and you'll find pubs full of people of working age who stay there all day. Yet in the same boozer there is a sign in the window saying STAFF WANTED. Has it never occurred to some of these people who sit there ordering pint after pint of beer and smoking expensive cigarettes that they could actually reverse their role? They could be on the other side of the bar, the working side, earning a living, earning respect, instead of being a parasite. Similarly, how many times have you got stuck in a jam behind a bus and read a notice on the back that goes something like 'Want to drive this bus? Then call this number. Drivers urgently required'?

What kind of a system have we got when a reasonably intelligent human being finds life a lot more attractive when he's inactive than when he's got a job? I don't understand it. I just can't fathom how any individual would opt for a life with absolutely no challenge in it whatsoever. Those who don't apply for these vacancies have apparently managed to use the system to get themselves slotted into convenient categories such as 'disabled', because they have managed to convince some overworked doctor that they are suffering from stress or depression. It's the rest of us who should be suffering from depression, having to watch the welfare system being so badly abused. Besides, it is a gross insult to somebody who is in a wheelchair through genuine infirmity.

Once again, I think gutless politicians are happy to let this situation drift along and bury their heads in the sand. Polish immigration hides the fact that millions of people in this country are on unemployment benefit because they don't want to work. They don't appear on the unemployed register because they are listed as 'unavailable' for work, and the vacancies created by the idle staying in bed are filled up by the wave of immigrants.

And not all those who come here from the new member countries of the European Union seem to have the same intention as Polish people to make an honest life for themselves. I once sat in a West End wine bar puzzled to see a scruffy little child running around the tables. Suddenly the child grabbed a mobile phone placed innocently on the table by a diner relaxing over lunch, and before anybody could react, the child was gone. The bar-owner told me the child was Romanian and that the area was plagued with organised gangs that came here from one of Europe's poorest countries. It is not a secret that criminal gangs such as these operate across Britain, and that one of their favourite scams is fiddling money out of people's bank accounts through rigging hole-in-the-wall machines.

It is no surprise to me that with an open-borders policy we have imported career criminals. If you try to rob people in Romania, where there isn't much wealth anyway, you face the prospect of being shot by a trigger-happy policeman. If you don't get shot you might get banged up for ten years for a relatively modest crime in a stinking hovel of a prison, and you'd be lucky to survive. Why should you risk all that when you can easily go to a country where 'conditions' for your business – in this case crime – are much more appealing?

And why is Britain more appealing to these types? Firstly, because our police are permanently engrossed in a battle against the potential threat of terrorism. Some would say that this is because of a misguided policy in Iraq and the Middle East, but that is another argument. Secondly, the priorities for policing in Britain today are confused by 'right-on' political correctness. Police have to decide how to divide their time between chasing gangs of thieves and investigating allegations of homophobia. Thirdly, we haven't built enough jails to keep pace with the increase in crime, so even if these robbery gangs are nailed there might not be anywhere to lock them up. Even if there is a cell or two free, they might be given the key to the door. Amazingly, this policy was advocated recently by those who work in our criminal justice system.

If I was a villain, I know which country I would rather take my chances in.

Of course, these things work both ways. If I'm urging immigrants from overseas to try to embrace our culture and learn our language, I would make a similar plea to people from this country to adopt the same attitude abroad.

I blame the English in a big way for spreading resentment about Britain around the world. For instance, I am appalled when I go to Spain and I happen to wander into one of those towns that look like Blackpool sea-front. The 'real English breakfast' and the 'Watneys Red Barrel on sale here' signs make me feel embarrassed. Why would anybody want to go to a foreign country to experience a cheap imitation of the lifestyle they have left behind for two weeks to get away from it all? I would never go into a place like that. When I'm in Spain I want to go to a great local tapas bar and enjoy some local cuisine, and wine that tastes of the country where I am a guest.

The Spanish authorities must have been mad to allow all those cheap and tacky 'real English pubs' to grow up in places like Benidorm. They attracted the worst elements in Britain, fat, drunken yobbos who travelled to those sorts of places with the express intention of spending a fortnight getting drunk all day, every day. I firmly believe that behaviour of that kind over a period of more than twenty years created a footprint of the young British male that exists to this day. It took the Spanish authorities another twenty years to get rid of those sorts of places. Only now is Spain once again being taken seriously as a holiday destination for those who want a bit of class and culture.

Spain does, however, have one of my favourite towns: Puerto

Banus, just outside Marbella. There is a very big English influence in that part of the world. One of my pals works there, and he is a very good example of how you show respect for local culture. His name is Paul Breen-Turner, and he moved to Spain over a decade ago after his ambition to become a national radio broadcaster in Britain had been continually thwarted. He decided that if he couldn't find a station that wanted him, he would try it the other way round and buy himself into a broadcasting organisation he could then use as a platform for his skills.

Spain is full of independent radio stations. The law on regulations and licences is very vague. In Britain you would be closed down within a few hours if you tried to put an aerial on your roof, push out a few records off a turntable and air a bit of chat. But it seems that on the Costas, anything goes. Paul latched on to a marketplace of ex-pat Brits in and around Marbella who like to listen to English music and keep in touch with the football back home.

We had used Paul a few times as our stringer in Spain, and we found him lively and entertaining. He wanted to do more work for us, and he decided to come over to meet Porky, who was then the programme director as well as my broadcasting partner. To my shame, I pulled a diabolical trick on Paul which completely skewed his relationship with talkSPORT, though to his credit he went on to recover and worked a lot more for us again.

After a midweek breakfast show with Porky he told me, as I was leaving, that he was having a meeting with Paul that day. I thought nothing more of it until I got out of the lift downstairs and saw Paul sitting there.

'Hi Paul,' I said. 'What are you up to?'

'I'm waiting to see Mike upstairs,' he replied.

The devil rose in me. I don't know why, I just decided to be mischievous.

'Oh, haven't you had the message?' I said. 'Mike's been called up to see the chairman. He can't see you until twelve.'

Paul was understandably a bit fazed by this.

'Don't be worrying,' I said. 'I'm going around the corner for a coffee. Come and join me.'

He gladly accepted this goodwill gesture, and we left the office together. Twenty yards up the road I hailed a taxi. I bundled him in and told the driver to take us to the Caxton Wine Vaults in the City of London.

'I thought we were going for a coffee next door, Al,' said Paul.

I told him not to panic, that the Wine Vaults did a fine breakfast which included great coffee.

When we got to the wine bar it was still only twenty past ten, but I was a regular there and the champagne was usually on ice by the time I walked in. I greeted the staff with my usual bonhomie and they poured Paul and me a glass each.

'I can't drink this,' said Paul indignantly. 'I've got a meeting with your boss in an hour or so. I can't go in there stinking of booze.'

'Don't be ridiculous,' I said. 'Do you think Mike won't have had a glass by the time you see him? This is his regular weekly meeting with the boss. They always crack a bottle. I've seen him come out of those meetings seeing double.'

Paul hesitated for a moment, trying to weigh everything up. He knew there was a certain drink culture at talkSPORT.

It was part of our identity.

'Well, OK then,' he said, with the attitude of a man who actually wanted a drink but was having to try to pretend he didn't.

At that moment my mobile phone started ringing. I could see it was Porky's secretary, and I knew what it would be about. I told Paul it was the trainer from my stables and went outside into the courtyard.

'Hi Lauren,' I said, 'how are you doing?'

'Yeah, I'm fine, Al, but Mike's on the warpath. Paul Breen-Turner was supposed to be here to see him this morning but we haven't seen him or heard from him. Have you seen him?'

'Funny you should say that,' I replied. 'I've just had a message from him. He says his plane was delayed and could I get hold of Mike and tell him. I was just about to ring you.'

'Oh, that's great,' she said. 'I'll tell Mike.'

Call finished, I went back into the bar.

'I've just had a call from Mike,' I told Paul. 'He said he's going to clear things at the office and come and join us at about twelve. He's ordered us to get stuck in.'

I topped up Paul's glass with frothing champagne as Paul smiled to himself. He was no doubt enjoying the thought of joining a company that encourages its employees to start tanking it up at eleven o'clock in the morning.

One bottle became two, two became three, and at one o'clock Paul asked me where Porky was. By this stage he was well gone. The rather tense and humourless individual I had met a few hours earlier had given way to a hail-fellow-well-met boozer who couldn't get it down his throat fast enough.

I went outside and rang Porky.

'I've found Breen-Turner for you,' I said. 'I've just walked into the Caxton and he's at the bar, holding court. He's well pissed.'

Porky was speechless, which was just as well because I was so enjoying my joke that I was doubled up with mirth and could hardly speak.

'What the effing hell is he doing in there?' asked my bewildered boss.

'I don't know, pal. He seems to have a few mates with him so maybe somebody told him it was one of our office boozers.'

'Don't let him go anywhere,' said Porky. It was an angry instruction rather than a request. 'I'm on my way over.'

I couldn't wait for this. I went back into the bar and ordered two more bottles, both to go into the bucket.

'Mike's just on his way over, Paul,' I said. 'He's looking forward to seeing you.'

'Great stuff,' said Paul. 'I like the way you guys do business.'

As I raised my glass to my lips and muttered 'cheers', I was picturing Porky slamming down the phone, bolting out of the office, furiously waving down a cab and jumping into the back of the vehicle with steam coming out of his ears. He would now be winding himself up to take on Breen-Turner, who, as far as he was concerned, had blanked a meeting with him to get boozed up with his mates instead. Hell hath no fury like a programme director scorned.

My thoughts were interrupted when the door of the bar burst open and Porky came in like a hurricane. Oblivious to the fury that was boiling inside him, Paul, in total innocence, smiled broadly and proffered his hand towards my irate pal.

'What the effing hell do you think you're playing at, you fat Spanish get?' said Porky.

Paul was completely taken aback.

'So you think you're good enough to drink with the big boys in London do you? Do you? Champagne, eh? Champagne? Why don't you eff off back to your beach and get back on the Rioja, you dozy paella pig!' Porky was in full flow. 'TalkSPORT? You won't be working for talkSPORT. You'll be back on hospital radio in Benidorm, you fat friggin' drunk!'

Breen-Turner had gone white. I had to fight very hard to contain myself. I didn't want to laugh because it would have given the game away, and the joke was too good. Instead, I dramatically stepped between the two men.

'Don't be too hard on him, Mike,' I said. 'His flight was delayed and it looks like he got slaughtered on the plane. He doesn't know what he's doing. I don't think he can even remember why he's here in London.'

Breen-Turner's look of horror now turned to one of total astonishment. He started trying to say something, but all that was coming out of his mouth were splutterings. His face now reflected total incomprehension.

Porky started again. Bellowing now, he demanded, 'What have you got to say for yourself, you fat fraud? Somebody should be sued under the Trades Description Act in describing you as a radio presenter. You're a dip-soak wino and you'll never work for talkSPORT again. In fact, if I have my way you'll never work in radio again.'

I had poured Porky a glass of bubbly. Now, unthinkingly, in his anger, he snatched it out of my hand and started drinking it.

Paul remained totally bemused, looking around as if to find somebody to speak up for him.

After a few seconds Porky suddenly snapped again. Leaning into Paul's face, he said, 'What am I doing drinking this? I didn't come here to drink, I came here to boot you off back to Spain!'

Breen-Turner had now regained some of his composure.

'But you've already been drinking,' he said.

'What?' said Porky, with great indignation. 'What the hell are you talking about? Have you completely lost your marbles?'

I couldn't take this any longer. I burst out laughing. If I hadn't been leaning on the bar I would have fallen on the floor. Now both of them were looking at me with a mystified expression on their faces. Something stirred in Porky's eyes. The first glimmers of understanding. He turned back to Paul.

'How did you get here?' he asked.

'Al brought me, of course. He told me …'

He didn't get the chance to say anything else. Porky launched into me with a string of shocking expletives. Then he started laughing. He knew he'd been had. It was just like watching somebody being caught on television on Jeremy Beadle's show. Then Paul, who has a real chest-heaving, barrel-rolling sort of a laugh, erupted and put his head in his hands. He then gave me a volley of similar expletives. But we were all laughing now and slapping each other on the back. Porky felt terrible for giving Paul such a hard time and Paul felt pretty foolish. I just thought it was a great wind-up.

An hour later we all felt great. The champagne was going down like an elixir and we decided to go off to a great Chinese restaurant to eat. By six o'clock we were well fed as well as watered. For some strange reason we then decided to head back in the direction of the office. It's a strict rule of business that you never go anywhere near the office if you're full of booze, but I think Porky just wanted to show Paul the office wine bar and introduce him to a few of the lads. He was compensating for the hard time he'd given him at the start of the day.

But you can never tell what sort of state you're in when you've been on the sauce all afternoon. In hindsight, we should never have gone.

As soon as we walked in I realised we had made a mistake. In the corner was a table of talkSPORT bigwigs. We should have beaten a rapid retreat without opening our mouths, but Porky decided to go the other way. He marched straight up to the table and introduced Paul as our new Spanish correspondent. As Porky pushed him forward, the execs looked him up and down. They were staring at a man whose shirt was open down to his waist. His hair was dishevelled. He was clearly inebriated too, as we all were. They must have been wondering what was going on.

Then it got worse. As Paul moved forward, presumably to try to shake somebody's hand, he tripped on the leg of a chair and went hurtling forward. The execs recoiled in horror as this man they had never met, and who wasn't dissimilar in appearance to a whale, crashed on to their table. Everything went flying, and Paul lay on the floor looking dazed and confused. Porky and I grabbed him, hauled him off the floor and headed for the door without once acknowledging the outraged protests.

Paul sobered up pretty quickly after that. He was horrified at the thought of the first impression he'd made on the staff of talkSPORT. He thought he would be black-balled for ever. It was only fair that the next morning I should go to the bosses and explain the cruel trick I had played on him. Fortunately, it didn't blight his career in any way. He deservedly became our Spanish correspondent and actually spent a whole season hosting our drive-time show with Rodney Marsh.

Several times Porky and I went over to Spain to do various shows and I always admired the way Paul had integrated himself into the Spanish way of life. Unlike many English people over there, he wasn't an arrogant Englishman. He spoke fluent Spanish, he owned a bar which employed Spanish people, and he had a share in a radio station where the other partners were also Spanish. He had a coterie of ex-pats for friends, of course, and among them was Sir John Hall, the former chairman and then life president of Newcastle United Football Club.

For some weird reason Sir John fell out with Porky when we were doing a show on the beach. He took an instant dislike to him – though believe me, it's not that unusual. We were doing the show on the decking behind a restaurant, and when we got a break at the top of the hour Porky would go off and have a paddle in the water. He had his trousers rolled up, and when he wasn't in the water he remained bare-footed. Sir John arrived, and as Porky approached him with a microphone he suddenly roared, 'Get away from me. How dare you approach me without your shoes on. I can smell your feet from here.' Porky thought he was having a laugh because everybody else around us – the production crew and a few guests in the restaurant – were barefooted too. Sir John, however, was wearing a sort of pair of pumps.

Porky smiled and kept going. But Sir John thrust his arms out in front of him and screamed at him, 'I'm telling you, get away from me. Your feet smell. Get some shoes on.' Porky realised now that Sir John wasn't joking and that he wasn't going to talk to him unless he put some shoes on. But all he had was his standard black leather shoes from England, which were in the car. He had no choice but to put them on, and he looked ridiculous on the beach with shorts, no shirt and these clumpy black leather shoes which were getting soaked as the waves lapped over them.

It was on that day that I hit one of the lowest moments of my life in racing.

After the show on this particular morning we went into the restaurant, Silks By The Sea, from where we had been broadcasting to have lunch with the proprietor Richard Scott. It was a beautiful setting, and I was delighted to have my two oldest girls, Michelle and Lucy, with me. They were holidaying nearby, while my other girl, my 'little one', Steffie, was back home in Suffolk with her mum. Richard was big into racing back in England, and that was all we talked about over lunch. But I was uncomfortable talking about horses on this of all days. I explained in my previous book how I went to Chicago for the Breeders' Cup meeting and when I got back I found that I had been outvoted by my two co-owners to sell what I thought was our outstanding horse, Indian Haven. Well, that day Indian Haven was running in the Irish 2,000 Guineas, a top race, under the control of its new owners.

I assumed that the race would be inaccessible on television in Spain, though I have to admit that I wasn't planning to make any great effort to find out. In terms of losing that horse, my wounds were still very raw. But after I mentioned it Paul said without hesitation that he could take us to a bar where we could watch the race. It was in fact Vinnie Samways' bar in Puerto Banus, almost next door to the legendary Sinatra's where many years before I had spent the night drowning my sorrows with thousands of Scotsmen after we went out of the World Cup. I wasn't keen, but Porky urged me on. (Apart from anything else, Vinnie Samways had played for Everton, Porky's club, and I suspect he wanted to grovel to one of his heroes.) I resisted, until the girls started having a go. They knew the animal well: they used to go to the stables to pat it and watch it exercise on the gallops. Eventually I agreed that we should go and watch the race.

We rushed over in a convoy of cars and got settled in our seats in front of a giant screen just as the horses went into the stalls. I looked at my horse and pain shot through me. The jockey wasn't wearing my colours. It hurt. I think I was more nervous than I would have been if I had still owned it.

Clang. The gates opened and the horses leapt forward. Indian Haven made a good start. It didn't go straight to the front but sat on the shoulder of two pacemakers. Then, as the race got to the halfway point, it made its move. Slowly, gently, it floated forwards. Then a burst, and it was out in front. It looked strong. It looked good. I could read the horse's mind from having stood on the freezing gallops on Newmarket Heath on many a winter morning watching it being put through its paces. I knew it was going to win.

It did. The lads around me, Porky and Paul, didn't know how to react. I didn't know how to react. I hadn't uttered a word. The thoughts going through my head were so confused. I was so proud of the horse, but so sorry it was no longer mine. I hated my partners for selling it, and cursed them for not recognising great bloodstock when they saw it. The beautiful beast was now worth well over a million pounds after winning this Classic, and I hadn't even benefited by a penny because I couldn't bring myself to put a bet on.

I was dumbstruck. Porky told me later that I went as white as a sheet. The only thing I integrated with that night were half a dozen bottles of champagne.

CHAPTER SIX

THE FAIRWAY TO HEAVEN

*'Golf and Porky just don't go together.
It's a good job my scheme to open up courses
to youngsters was not around in his day.
He would have ended up a disturbed child.'*

MY ELDEST and youngest daughters are eight years apart. But in terms of how they spent their youths, they could be a century away from each other.

Michelle spent her entire teenage years out in the open. She loved outdoor sports and had a finely developed sense of competition. She was the only girl in the school hockey team, and her teachers pushed her into cross-country running. And because we went to Switzerland after I retired from football in this country, she became an international skier. When she wasn't on the slopes she was training by running up and down mountains.

Steffie has grown up in a different era. Though she is very sporty too, she is a child of the computer age. In her early teens she might have been out riding her horse; she is now more likely to be found at home on her computer. She is more academic than my other two girls and I'm sure she will go on to higher education. But she also spends time on her machine 'chattering' to her friends on websites. It is what youngsters of her age do.

(In between, incidentally, there's Lucy. Could any father ever have been blessed with three such wonderful daughters?)

I am not the only parent who has noticed this big change in youngsters' behaviour. When I get together with parents of other children our conversation is always the same: how can we get our kids to close down their computers and get out on to a field to exercise and play some 'proper' games? My mother and father could never keep me in the house. All I ever wanted to do was go out to play football. I suppose we knew nothing else. I didn't have my own telly in my room like kids have today. Even if I'd had one, there'd have been nothing to watch on it. I wouldn't have recognised a computer if one had parked itself on my school desk.

For years now this country has been guilty of withdrawing outdoor facilities which provided areas for children to play. Local authorities have been guilty of selling off communal and school playing fields in the misguided belief that it will benefit the community. What short-term thinking. Politicians of all persuasions are useless at maximising value out of assets. Businessmen do that. So when a crafty property developer comes along and offers what seems like a fortune for a scrubby bit of grassland, the councillors all pat themselves on the back and assure themselves that they have done a fantastic deal for the taxpayer. They have, maybe, reeled in a few million pounds for the council's coffers. But we all know that money will then be wasted. It will be spent on some worthless project which eventually benefits no one, like hiring a few dozen more compliance officers to make sure that everybody puts their plastic bottles in the right bin. What it will not do is spare any of us from a hefty increase in next year's tax bills. And it will deprive us of an open space for children where they could have played football or rounders, run around and got their lungs full of fresh air. If youngsters have nowhere to go, they will end up back in their bedrooms in front of a computer.

Quite apart from anything else, a doctor warned me recently that all human beings, particularly those who are still growing, need Vitamin D for their skin. This is mostly provided by the sun's rays. Obviously too much sunshine can be harmful, but if you don't get enough you will suffer deficiencies. According to my medical pal there is a serious danger that we are producing a generation of youths who are growing up indoors, to the detriment of their health. Just as is the case with smokers, it will come back and smack them around the face when they are older.

There is another issue here, and that is that children in competitive situations develop life skills that should equip them for adulthood. Take this simple example: if a youngster is surging forward with a ball at his feet, he can either pass to the left or right, or go through on his own to try to score a goal, but he has to make a decision. Life is all about making decisions, and you don't make many decisions when you are on a keyboard for hours at a time conversing with your pals. Moreover, when you make that decision on the football field, you are also taking a risk. Risk-taking is an essential part of growing up. It is the staple diet of the businessmen who make our economy tick. If people don't know how to calculate risk then society will grind to a halt.

When Rupert Murdoch introduced pay television into Britain in the late 1980s, it was a calculated risk. He knew that the massive profits of his newspaper empire would not last for ever and he had to risk getting into some other form of media business to open up new avenues for revenues. He launched

Sky TV. In its first few years it nearly collapsed and dragged the Murdoch empire under. But through sheer resilience and the brilliant coup of obtaining the rights to Premiership football he rode out the storm and went off to build one of the largest media groups in the world.

Figures show that modern children are not taking as many risks as they used to. This conclusion comes from a study of hospital admissions which showed that the number of children treated for minor injuries after falling out of a tree has gone down by one third in recent years. Climbing trees, for me, was a staple of childhood. I loved climbing trees. I always wanted to climb higher than anybody else. I wanted to scramble up to the thinnest, uppermost branch so that I could stick my head out of the top of the tree. It combined the excitement of exploration with the thrill of adventure as you got higher and higher off the ground and freed yourself from the shackles of gravity. And it was risky. Whenever I looked down my tummy turned as I realised how high up I had got. But I felt safe, immersed in a web of immovable branches and boughs. The tree always felt like the strongest thing on earth. I did sometimes fall, and that was usually when I was trying to scramble down. But I never really hurt myself. Even if I did, the pain and grief were easily outweighed by a sense of conquest and achievement.

The report that showed that kids don't take to trees much any more also revealed that there has been a big increase in repetitive strain injuries from constant finger-tapping on computer keyboards. Now, I haven't got much time for most of the quango-type pseudo-government agencies that intrude into all areas of our life, but I have to say I like the style of the

Royal Society for the Prevention of Accidents. They said this in the report's conclusion: 'Climbing trees and falling out of them is all part of growing up, and having small injuries helps children learn about risks. We take the view that it's a good thing to try and equip children and young people and help them to make informed decisions about the risks they take. We would prefer children to climb trees in playgrounds rather than [play in] building sites, factories and other potentially dangerous locations.'

It's too late now to try to reclaim those fields that have been scandalously sold off, where, no doubt, trees were unearthed and disposed of. Nevertheless, we should not give up on trying to reverse the trend of our children spending all their leisure hours in a bedroom in front of a computer rather than out in the fresh air.

***

I was at a family lunch recently when I got talking to a group of my pals' children. One young fellow there impressed me when he told me he played golf. Golf is one of my passions. There are few other pursuits (apart from imbibing the odd bottle of bubbly) that interest me and relax me so well.

I asked the lad where he played.

'Anywhere I can,' he replied.

'Like where? Do you go out locally with your mates, or your old fella?'

He looked at me as though I was mad. 'No, I play at home,' he said.

I didn't understand what he was talking about. There

are some pretty wealthy people around me in Suffolk but I couldn't think of any of the houses near mine that had their own golf course. This lad was clearly committed because as he talked he had been practising his drive with a theatrical sweep of his arms.

My daughter nudged me. 'He plays on his computer,' she said.

'What? But he's waving his arms around as though he handles a club. I don't understand.'

It was then explained to me that a computer has been developed which replicates the actions of a golf club, or a tennis racket, in much the same way as they do with the steering of a car on a race-track. I couldn't believe it, but a few days later it was proved to me. You can stand in front of a screen and hold the computer console in your hands like a driver. Then you swing, just as if you have a golf club in your hand, and all of a sudden you are watching your ball, on the screen, disappearing into the distance. You get a read out of length and direction. It's absolutely amazing. But it's also dangerous, because it could easily become a substitute for the real thing. Another generation of children lost to the outdoors.

When I mused on this remarkable piece of technology it set me thinking that golf could in fact be the salvation of those children sitting in front of their computers. It is a wonderful game of skill. It takes place in lovely, sometimes beautiful, locations. It is competitive, and will usually entail walking between three and four miles, which is excellent exercise. We have fantastic national and international role models too, ranging from Tiger Woods to Justin Rose, and it's one of those rare sports that, as a nation, we are good at on the world stage on a consistent basis. Some of the finest courses in the world are here in Britain. You wouldn't expect children to play at Carnoustie, but youngsters should go there to have their ambitions fired. Some of the greatest champions of all time are British, from Henry Cotton to Nick Faldo. It is truly a national sport in this country and we are shamefully poor at recruiting youngsters to it.

I know we are a small island and that the popularity of golf among adults has mushroomed over the last couple of decades, but there is still plenty of scope for youngsters to play. It does not have to be elitist, as it is viewed in many quarters. For instance, whenever I play with Porky, we play on municipal courses. This is for two reasons. Firstly, Porky is so laughably poor at the game that he can't get into a decent club. Secondly, he is such an embarrassment that I would never take him to one of my clubs because I would probably get black-balled merely for introducing such a dreadful hacker to a proper course. Municipal courses, usually owned by the local authority, are invariably deserted during the daytime in the middle of the week. That is the very time when school-kids should be undertaking physical exercise lessons. They only need the same sort of equipment you need to play hockey or tennis. I'm all for girls playing golf because in the early teenage years there is no huge difference in the physiques of the two sexes.

We have tremendous golfing facilities in this country. During the eighties and the nineties new golf clubs were springing up all over the place. There was a golf boom in Britain. Nick Faldo had become the best in the world, and as we all got more prosperous it was anticipated we would all be taking to the fairways. It didn't quite work out like that, though, and a lot of the new courses failed to attract sufficient membership and lay fallow. They should now be revived. Local authorities that no longer have facilities such as playing fields to offer to the community should turn their attentions to golf instead. It fits all the requirements of what young people should be doing during their developing years.

Considering that the game was invented within our shores, that British golf has such a huge following around the world, and that Britons have been consistently successful in the sport, I am astonished it does not form a greater part of our developing lives. It's not like, for instance, tennis. In that sport we have the greatest tournament in the world with the most iconic name, Wimbledon, yet you have to go back to before the war to find a male British champion. The girls have done a bit better, but the last winner, Virginia Wade, did the business a fair few years ago now. It doesn't surprise me that a Scotsman, Andy Murray, is now our best hope of a Wimbledon champion. (Andy will, of course, become 'British' the minute he becomes a big winner as the English try to adopt him as their own.) At least in golf we back up our heritage with regular victories in the big tournaments both here and around the world.

Golf has given me a million pleasures, mostly during the playing of it, but more recently while commentating on it. Naturally, of course, like most things in my life, it has not always gone completely smoothly.

I was taken on by talkSPORT because of my football background, but when I discovered the company had the commentary rights for the Open I was thrilled. The first one we covered was in 1996 at Royal Lytham St Annes, just outside

Blackpool. I've been on golf courses all my adult life, but I've never been in the sort of location you get when you cover a tournament. The first time I saw it my stomach actually turned. We were going to be working from a studio on a platform about 200 feet above the eighteenth hole, positioned right on the edge of the green above the rows of seating put in for the competition. Just getting up there was a nerve-racking experience. The stairs were just wooden planks slotted between scaffolding. The higher I got the queasier I felt, but once at the top the view was so magnificent that all the fear dissipated. We could see right around the course, and then out into the Irish Sea. The wind was fierce, literally rocking the studio and whipping the flags on the scaffolding so that they sounded like whips being cracked all around us, but it was glorious, particularly at five o'clock in the morning, watching the course wake up.

The caddies who serve the biggest names in the sport are a fascinating bunch of people. Every morning you would see them pacing out the fairways and examining the locations of the pins so that they could report back to the pros and give them the best possible briefing on how the course was lying that day. I'm amazed that they all made it out there at dawn because I've spent plenty of nights in the company of caddies, many of whom show tremendous tenacity with the booze. At the same time, the traders who run the burger bars would move into place, along with the ice-cream vans. Some competitors would already be out on the practice tees. And, most importantly of all as far as I am concerned, the refill lorry would arrive outside the Bollinger tent to ship in the day's supply of bubbly. All the way through the four-hour breakfast show the pennant-like Bollinger flags flapped in the wind, a constant reminder of my first destination at 10 a.m.

The problem was that on the first day of the competition I had agreed to go out on to the course after the show and do some outside broadcasting. Somebody had caught me in a generous mood. Never mind, I thought, the champagne would taste even better when I eventually got to the tent at lunchtime.

As we came off air, I strapped the OB unit to my belt and set off with headphones and microphone to tour some of the crucial holes. Crikey, I hadn't appreciated how hard it was trudging around a golf course when you're not playing. When I got to the fourteenth I was feeling very tired. I'd had a big evening the night before, having met up with some old pals from the world of football. And I'd had my usual very early start that morning.

Looking around me, I suddenly realised that I was very close to the house where I was staying. In fact, it was only about a hundred yards away. There was a railway line to negotiate, but that wouldn't be too much of a problem. I'd had enough, and the Bollinger tent was calling. All I needed to do was hop over the fence, grab a quick shower and head for the bubbly.

A few minutes later I was emerging from the shower in our rented house. There was a lot of noise coming out of my OB pack. I could distinctly hear Porky's voice, shouting and screaming. He was effing and blinding and having a terrible row with somebody back at base. I often reflected on the fact that Porky shouldn't take life so seriously and that one day he would have a heart attack. In fact he was, in years to come, nearly finished off by a much more serious complaint than a heart attack, but he insists it was a genetic problem. I have my doubts, because he was always thumping tables and rowing with people.

Within half an hour of leaving the course I was safely ensconced in the Bollinger tent, and I switched my phone on for the first time (you're not allowed even to display them on the course). There were a series of maniacal messages from Porky, who was then the boss of the station, directing operations from our control truck. He seemed to think I had gone missing, which of course was ridiculous. I gave him a bell and asked him if he was coming over for a glass. He was spluttering with rage.

'Where are you?' he demanded.

'In the Bollinger tent, where you should be, you numpty. Now get your arse over here.'

He started trying to say something else but I just hit the off button. Ten minutes later he appeared in the tent. His face was red with anger, his hair was standing on end and he was waving his arms about, shouting and cursing.

'Calm down,' I told him.

'You should be on the fourteenth hole,' he said. 'It's on your list.'

'What list? I did everything I was asked to do and I've been up since four-thirty, so just shut it and get that down your throat.'

I handed him a glass of champagne. He reacted as if I'd just given him hemlock.

'Champagne?' he screamed, throwing it out of the glass on to the floor. He was seriously out of control. What was wrong with the boy? 'Do you know what you have just put me through?'

He then spilt out the story, and I started laughing, as did everybody else around the table, all full of fizz except Porky. When I left the course I hadn't switched off the OB equipment, mainly because I wasn't sure how it worked. So the producer kept trying to get hold of me thinking I was still on station. When he continued to get no response from me he told Porky that he thought I had gone out of range of our aerial. This sent Porky mad because at great cost and to the considerable doubt of the bosses at talkSPORT he had authorised the hiring of a gigantic telescopic mast which would cover the whole course. He went storming into the offices of the people who had supplied the equipment and told them their equipment was useless, that they were all incompetent halfwits and he wanted a new mast. The suppliers were adamant that there was nothing wrong with the equipment but Porky demanded that somebody must climb up the mast to find out where it was broken. And if they didn't find somebody to scale the 130-foot-high structure, he would do it himself. He was attempting to get up the mast when a field engineer walked in and casually mentioned that he'd just seen me entering the Bollinger tent. This deflated Porky and he left, muttering apologies and feeling like the dope he was.

And now here he was in front of me, boiling with rage, throwing champagne all over the floor and threatening to send me home.

I know my broadcasting buddy pretty well and I sorted out my tactics to get him to regain control of himself. The first drop of alcohol on his tongue would defuse the situation. I called one of the lovely promotional girls over. She was a darling, shapely with a mane of blonde hair and wearing a short black dress and a big yellow sash. I introduced her to Porky and told her, 'Mr Parry is having a very stressful day and he needs a large glass of champagne to de-stress himself.'

'Oh, absolutely, no problem,' she said, and within seconds Porky was being handed a glass the size of a plant-pot, full of sizzling, fizzing champagne. The hand that was proffering it to him had long slender fingers on the end of which were beautifully manicured ruby-red nails. Instant anger-management. Porky smiled at the girl like a little puppy-dog that had just been given a bone. And as the first splash of bubbly hit the back of his throat the hint of a smile spread across his face. He tried to suppress it, but within five minutes he was in the bosom of our company and attacking the champagne like a man on a mission.

Most of the people in the Bollinger tent at the Open look as if they have some sort of connection with the sport, or at least with business. Some wear suits with open-necked shirts, others wear golfing slacks with a Pringle jumper or casual jacket. Then one man approached our table dressed in jeans and a flat cap. He wasn't particularly scruffy, he just didn't look 'golfish'. Porky was in full flow now, trying to impress the promotional girls with tales of derring-do from when he was a reporter in war zones in the Middle East, and didn't notice our new friend.

Suddenly, the chap said, 'Gouranga.'

Everybody stopped talking. We assumed our visitor was a foreigner. He then started speaking in English and produced some sort of identity card from his pocket. On his card there was a picture of him in orange robes. I looked at it and immediately it reminded me of one of those Hare Krishna guys in the film *Airplane* who get beaten up by the captain of the plane in Los Angeles airport. Then I looked at the writing on the card. Some of it was in English, some of it was in a language that was unfathomable. It stated that this guy was a holy man. He actually was a member of the Hare Krishna movement.

He was collecting money for some sort of religious school he ran in, of all places, Dundee. He had quite an interesting story. His name was Adrian and he was an English graduate. During his years at university he came across the writings of the Hindu faith. He studied them and eventually decided that was how he wanted to lead his life. From being a normal beer-swilling student, he gave up all his worldly possessions and studied for years to become a Hindu priest. Part of that process, apparently, involved being a member of the Hare Krishna sect, and part of his work had been to go out on the streets with a drum and spread the faith. But his main job now was as a fund-raiser for this institution in Scotland. He drove around in a Volkswagen camper-van which was his home while he was on the road, sometimes for months on end.

When I asked him why he had turned up at the golf, he was searingly honest. 'I go to lots of sporting locations because that's where you find people in a good mood,' he said. 'When people are enjoying themselves, particularly when they have had a drink, they become very generous, and my job is to maximise what I can raise for my school.' In other words he was saying that in every beer and champagne tent at every sporting event in the country you will find a gullible mug who will hand over a load of dosh.

I decided to put his theory immediately to the test.

'See that guy there with the ginger hair?' I said, pointing at Porky. 'He's a foolishly generous man. Go and tell him about your fund-raising work.'

Adrian went and positioned himself next to Porky. The boy was clearly very good at what he did because it only took him about five minutes to extract £50 from my pal's pocket. In exchange, Porky got a badge which read GOURANGA, the very phrase with which Adrian had greeted us earlier. We discovered it meant 'Be Happy'. I soon wished the priest had never turned up because over the next four days Porky kept parroting 'Gouranga' every time he opened his mouth. More than once I vowed that if he said it one more time he would be hospitalised, never mind be happy.

Adrian came to visit us in the Bollinger tent every day. And every day Porky handed over a bundle of notes. He struck up a form of friendship with the priest and was sort of using him for spiritual guidance. I think my pal liked the idea of having a kind of 'guru' at hand. He had always been a huge Beatles fan, and he constantly reminded me during that Open at Lytham that George Harrison's life had been mapped out by the Hare Krishna movement. I reminded Porky that he was not a multi-millionaire pop star who had been part of the most famous group of all time, but a rather more mundane broadcaster who needed to be able to tell a putter from a wedge, something he often had trouble with.

Over the next few years we met Adrian at other sporting events, including, every year, the Open. He was an extremely plausible bloke. There wasn't the slightest hint of the conman about him. As Porky got to know him better a picture of his life emerged. He basically travelled all the time, collecting money and living a Spartan existence free of the pleasures most people associate with life. When he wasn't on the road he was in his robes back at his school, which sounded more like a monastery, where he spent his time reading the scriptures of his faith. I liked him. I admired his way of life, even though I could never, in three lifetimes, contemplate going through the self-denial and dedication to faith that were the mainstays of his existence.

I don't know if Porky had foreseen the future when he struck up his generous friendship with Adrian, but some sort of God was clearly looking after him on the afternoon of the third day of the competition at Lytham. It was the one time in his life when my buddy needed a priest to be praying for him.

It was mid-afternoon when we emerged from the champagne tent and we were all in top form and full of bubbles as we headed over to the eighteenth. Every time we approached those stairs to our aerial studio a shiver went down my spine because they went up so high and they were very steep. Also, being on the coast, as the Open always is because it is played on a links course, meant that it got very windy as you went higher up. Porky saw the apprehension in my face and started taking the mickey.

'Come on Al,' he said, 'I'll race you to the top.'

With that he started sprinting up the stairs, weaving from side to side with the obvious effects of the champagne. When he got halfway up to a break platform he stopped, turned around and started trying to mock me again. The trouble was that he was so out of breath that he couldn't speak. I was still on the lower steps, and I saw Porky trying to suck in air, then stumble backwards and roll over the scaffolding hand-rail.

'Christ,' I thought, 'he's going to fall.' I sprinted up the stairs towards him and saw that he was hanging on with one arm hooked around a bracket under the steps. I reached through the rail and grabbed him. All I could do was hang on to him. I couldn't possibly pull him back up as he was a deadweight being blown from side to side in the wind. And he was slipping as his crooked arm started unfolding. 'Hang on, hang on!' I shouted, even though I knew there was nothing for him to hang on to. I was panicking. The ground looked an awful long way down and I knew that if he fell he was going to do himself some serious damage.

My face was only a few inches from Porky's, and his eyes were completely blank. Far from appearing to be frightened, he seemed to have forgotten altogether where he was. He just kept mumbling, 'Are you all right, Al? Don't panic, mate. I'm OK. There's nothing you can do about it. Adrian told me.' Adrian had told him what? That at the very least he was going to break both legs that afternoon; or maybe that he was going to fall off the stairs and an angel would swoop down and carry him to safety?

If it was the second scenario we could certainly have done with the angel right there and then. I estimated we were about 20 feet up, and though it was grass below us it was the height of summer and the ground was like concrete. I felt utterly helpless as Porky inched away from my grasp. A startled crowd, aware of the drama, had gathered below and some of them were rushing around trying to find something to cushion Porky's fall. Then I noticed a line of plastic wheely bins about twenty yards away. I didn't know what was in them, but we needed them.

'The bins!' I screamed. 'Get the wheely bins!' Nobody could hear me above the roar of the wind, so I tried again. 'Get the wheely bins!'

Fortunately, somebody had run up the stairs behind me and he caught what I was saying. He rushed down again and started waving his arms around. Everybody went after the bins.

'Please be quick,' I was mumbling to myself. My arm was now nearly coming out of its socket and I couldn't keep a grip on the underside of Porky's arm for much longer. I had his jacket around my fingers but it had pulled so tight it was cutting into my fingers like string. It was agony.

At the moment Porky fell I didn't even know if the bins were in place. But within a split-second I heard a tremendous bang followed by a crashing noise and then what sounded like a round of applause. I looked over the steps. Porky wasn't where I expected him to be. He was about twenty feet away. Apparently he had bounced off the bins, which were all splintered and smashed below me, and been catapulted into the crowd, who were now holding him up and pouring drink down his throat. He was celebrating as if he'd just won the Open and the crowd were applauding him as though he was an acrobat who had just been entertaining them. I looked at my hand. It was cut and bleeding. I was more injured than he was.

Golf and Porky just don't go together. It's a good job my scheme to open up courses all over the country to youngsters was not around in his day. He would have ended up as a disturbed child. He is easily the most hopeless golfer I have ever met. Hopeless, as I said, to the point of embarrassing. I refuse to play with him any more. We once met a couple of mates of mine at the prestigious Vale of Glamorgan course in

Wales, prior to the FA Cup final. It is such a top place that the Arsenal team were staying there. Porky was a disgrace. He took four air swings before he even got a ball off the first tee. My mates were doubled up in mirth. One of them even had to put a handkerchief in his mouth to stop himself laughing out loud in such august surroundings.

He once put a talkSPORT reporter in hospital. The Open was being played at Sandwich in Kent that year and we had to do some promotional work for our sponsor, Callaway, which manufactures golf clubs and equipment. We were on a simulator, and all we had to do was strike a ball at a net and a computer would figure out how far and in which direction the ball had gone. We had a reporter standing at the side of the tee with a microphone because we were doing a live report on the shoot-out between me and Porky.

My shot was reasonable, and then Porky stepped up to the tee. He took about three minutes to steady himself, bending his knees like an old-fashioned policeman and waggling his driver around as though he knew what he was doing. I had seen him miss the ball completely on so many occasions, yet he was clearly determined here, in front of a large live audience, at least to make sure he struck the ball properly.

At last, he took an almighty swing. He connected with the ball, but in the same split-second as his club followed through there was a piercing scream from the edge of the tee. Porky had sliced his ball at a 90-degree angle straight into the knee of our reporter, who had dropped his microphone and was rolling around on the floor in agony, clutching his leg. The pain was so severe that he was having trouble breathing, and involuntary tears were dripping down his face.

More involuntary tears were rolling down my face, but these were of laughter, not pain. Everybody else was laughing too. Porky did not know what to do. He looked as if he wanted to comfort the reporter, but by doing that he would be admitting he had just hit a ball that would easily get on to the shortlist in the 'worst ever shot' category. In the end, our reporter had to be helped out of the tent by two St John Ambulance people and taken to their tent where he was given a crutch he had to use for the rest of the tournament.

The shot was so bad that when I think about it now I've no idea how anybody could actually execute such a stroke. It would take Tiger Woods five years to perfect the art of sending a ball sideways like that.

Another indication of how poor Porky is at golf is the fact that he's the only person I know who has ever been thrown off the list for a charity event for being so inept. Normally, charity golf matches are a combination of big names and personalities, two or three days of fun and frolics, and a couple of late nights, all culminating in raising wheelbarrows full of money for very worthy causes. There will be a quota of pros in the tournament together with celebrities and lots of former footballers. You only really have to be able to knock a ball in the right direction to qualify to play. Porky was invited to attend the annual Sir Bobby Robson golf tournament, which takes place every June in the Algarve in Portugal. Porky's other broadcasting partner at talkSPORT, Andy Townsend, was also playing, along with me. But when Porky sent the forms back, the organisers rang him to ask about his handicap – a box he had left empty. He had to admit that he didn't actually have a handicap because no club had yet taken him as a member. He tried to bluster his way through, saying that he'd never had the time to join a club, but the truth is he is so hopeless that nobody wants him thrashing around their course.

The biggest laugh about it is that if you saw him approaching the first tee you would be forgiven for thinking he was a first-class player. Porky has a set of clubs most people wouldn't be able to buy. They were made for him by Callaway, in their scientific laboratory near Porky's home in Surrey. We both had a set made at the same time. You stand in the middle of the room, take a club and just practise normal shots. You do it with drivers, irons, a putter and any other club you fancy. While you are doing this thousands of images a second are being taken from every angle on cameras positioned around the laboratory. These images are then transmitted instantly to Calloway's world headquarters in Florida, and fed into their computers. The result is that a few weeks later a set of clubs is shipped to you measured exactly to your height, weight, swing, the width of your shoulders, the size of your feet, the length of your arms and hundreds of other measurements on your body unique to the individual. Porky also has the best shoes and jackets, and he buys the most expensive balls – loads of them, because he loses so many.

If only he had the slightest idea how to play.

My own first experience of golf was an unfortunate one. I had never even picked up a club or been near a golf course when it was first suggested to me that I should take up the game. I didn't have the slightest interest in it, but as the suggestion came from Bobby Robson, my club manager at Ipswich, I thought I'd better seem enthused.

Bobby – Sir Bobby as he is now – has old-school beliefs. I think he liked his players to get married young because he hoped it would keep them out of trouble. And he was constantly railing against the 'bookies and pool-hall culture' which he thought was bad for young footballers. Consequently, when I turned seventeen and signed my first professional contract for the club he suggested I join a golf club. The truth is that I preferred to spend my time in the bookie's. Since arriving in Ipswich I had developed an abiding interest in the racing industry. I hitched a lift whenever I could, with the older players, over to Newmarket. For me, my first professional contract meant that I was going to have enough money in the future to have a proper bet. But Bobby had other plans.

He came in one morning and told us very excitedly that he had fixed up an interview for me in front of the committee at somewhere called Purdis Heath. From the way he was talking you would think he had fixed up an audience with the Pope. His attitude was that he wanted his boys to 'raise their game on and off the pitch'. The boss had also cajoled another young player into taking up the game. Steve Gardner was a very promising footballer. He had been an England Schoolboys star and looked set for a great future. We were all envious of him because even when he was an apprentice he had a car, which was unheard of then. A car was seen as a bird-puller, and we all tried to scrounge lifts off him all the time.

Our interview with the committee was set for a couple of weeks hence. Then suddenly, as so often happens in the profession, Steve left the club. That in itself was no great problem, except for the fact that he was supposed to be driving us to the golf club for our meeting. I didn't have a driving licence then.

I was a very young footballer, and I assumed that if Mr Robson still wanted me to go to the golf club on my own he would get somebody to pick me up. You have to remember that apprentice footballers don't actually ever do anything for themselves. Perhaps clubs became convinced that youngsters are too daft to be able to organise their lives. They fix up where you live, what you eat, how you get to work and back, what to do with your money, and everything else in your life. Even if I thought I should still have gone to Purdis Heath I would not have known how to get there. I didn't have a clue where it was and I'd never ordered a taxi in my life. I half thought about asking somebody at Ipswich for advice, but I couldn't even remember the name of the course. I just assumed that somebody else would sort it all out – a trait that has been with me now for most of my adult life, and which has often got me into trouble. I put it to the back of my mind and forgot about it.

A few days later I was summoned to see Mr Robson. I was still training with the youths and didn't have a lot of dealings with the boss, so it felt good to be summoned. I assumed he wanted to see me because I had put in some impressive performances recently, including games for the reserves. I was certainly scoring plenty of goals. I was soon disabused of the view that this was going to be a friendly chat.

As I entered his outer office it was clear there was a problem. His secretary normally had a cheery smile for the younger players, but she tried to avoid my greeting. I was ushered through to the inner sanctum. Bobby had his head down over his desk. But as I went to take the seat opposite him he suddenly leapt up and said, 'Who told you to sit down?'

'Sorry, boss,' I said sheepishly. I genuinely had no idea what was troubling him.

'Why didn't you turn up for your interview at my golf club yesterday?'

I didn't know it had been scheduled for the day before. I said the first thing that came into my head: 'Sorry, boss. After Steve left I thought it was all off.'

'You've humiliated me in front of the committee of the top club in the east of England. Have you gone mad?'

Bobby was raging. He was red in the face and spitting and spluttering his words. He berated me for my bad manners and lack of organisation, but it soon became clear that what he was really angry about was that he'd clearly had a dreadful dressing-down from the top nobs at the club. Apparently there was a very senior policeman on the committee, and the boss had even been threatened with his own membership. He'd been told that he could never propose another footballer again.

Years later I learnt that the etiquette of British golf clubs can be matched by no other institution in the world. They are almost feudal in the way they are run. Since that day I've played at some of the world's finest clubs, and now, of course, I respect all the rules – bizarre as some of them are – of my hosts.

The etiquette and rules of golf may be predictable, but for me, the game itself is easily the most unpredictable in the world. You can be brilliant one moment and awful the next. There is no way you can tell as you approach the first tee whether you are going to have a great day or a shocking, frustrating, almost suicidal experience.

In football I always knew when I was up for it and when I wasn't. Physically you have to be right, and I would say that most footballers are carrying some sort of twinge or niggle 50 per cent of the time. You can weigh up the opposition to work out who is probably going to be marking you, and you know in advance the strength of what you are up against. But golf is so unpredictable. You're not really playing against another human being; you are playing against the course. It might be too wet or too dry, the grass might be too short or too long, the wind might be too strong or non-existent. And you can have no idea whether your arms and legs and eyes are going to be working properly until you hit that first ball.

This was proved to me in classic fashion when I accepted a challenge to take part in a version of the Ryder Cup. I was running my pub in Ipswich at the time, the Black Adder. An old mate of mine from Glasgow, Brian Doherty, would pop in every now and then and we would reminisce about our schooldays. Brian had done very well for himself. He had moved south, and he worked in the finance and pensions industry. He was a member of Woodbridge, another very fine golf club in Suffolk. Brian had two English pals who were fellow members, and they had proposed a Scotland v. England match: the two of them against Brian and me.

The night before the match Brian came into the pub early. He had one pint, then left with the words, 'Early to bed. Remember, I'm picking you up at a quarter to six.' I assured him that all was well and I had no plans for a late night.

I was about to go to bed at ten o'clock when a group of old pals came in. Some of them were lads who had been apprentices with me but who had never quite made the grade. I always liked to see them because it gave my life a bit of perspective, and I was always in total admiration of these boys who had been rejected by football but who had then managed to make good lives for themselves in other ways. Some had started their own businesses and become a lot more successful, financially, than me. Though I was anxious to be in good shape for the following morning, I couldn't just disappear now. I got a couple of rounds in and before I knew it we had the doors locked and the night was in full swing. We all went out to a Chinese restaurant that stayed open for us, and then, instead of going home, I invited them all back to the pub again for a nightcap.

It was four o'clock before I eventually crawled into bed.

The next thing I recall is Jill trying to wake me. I didn't want to get up. I felt dreadful, and I had forgotten all about the golf. But Brian was waiting on the doorstep downstairs and he was hopping about, worried that we would miss our tee time. I had no option but to get up. I was in and out of the bathroom in record time. I cleaned my teeth under the shower and put my clothes on while I was still wet, and without rinsing the soap out of my chest hair which turned to mass dandruff as the morning wore on.

I felt awful. My head was spinning, and I nearly fell down the stairs. There were cobweb-type blurs over my eyes.

I don't know what I looked like, but as soon as Brian saw me his jaw dropped. He started trying to moan but I wasn't in the mood. I told him everything would be OK. He said that I stank of booze, but I reminded him that he was doing the driving and that as far as I was aware it was not yet a criminal offence to have alcohol on your breath on a golf course. If it was, golf would be extinct.

I was so wet through having not had time to dry myself after my shower that I was squelching in his passenger seat. Car seats were made of foam and a sort of velour-type material in those days, and when I got out of the car I noticed it was damp. Nothing was going right.

As we strode over to meet our playing partners – or crawled over in my case – Brian clearly had the hump with me. There was nothing I could do about it now. I would just have to do my best, even though I was having serious problems co-ordinating my arms and legs to get my golf shoes on.

A few coins were tossed, and unfortunately I was selected to take the first shot. I could have done without that. In a foursome, the first shot often defines how you and your partner are going to perform. I feared I was going to be hopeless.

Even though it was just after dawn the course was already busy and there were half a dozen people waiting at the first tee. It was agreed that we would start at the tenth to ease the congestion. But the tenth was a stroke index one, par four hole, notorious as one of the toughest you could face. Nobody could remember a player even achieving a birdie there.

As I bent down to put my tee in the ground I experienced a sudden bout of dizziness that completely disorientated me. I rocked forward and my head hit the ground like a hammer would hit a nail. I rolled sideways on to the floor. My playing partner literally had his head in his hands as I tried to pull myself together and regain a bit of composure. After that, I couldn't get on with it quick enough. I stuck the tee in the grass, took one step back and whacked a shot fuelled by anger and disappointment down the fairway.

As we set off after our balls I didn't have a clue where mine had gone, and this was one of the longest holes I had ever seen. More by luck than design, it was sitting nicely. All the others played their shots first, then I took out a five-iron and hit what felt like a belter to the green. I was still feeling dizzy. I couldn't see the flag up ahead, and I couldn't see my ball either, so on the way to the green I double-checked that I hadn't come off our fairway on to an adjoining one.

At the green I assumed my luck had run out. I spent about three minutes trying to find my ball around the green, but it was lost. Brian gave me a look of thunder. One of our opponents two-putted and got down in one-over – a very respectable score of five for such a difficult hole. But when his ball rolled into the cup it didn't make that distinctive 'plop' sound that usually indicates you are home. He knelt down at the flag and reached into the hole. His hand emerged clutching two balls. The second one was mine.

It was like a golfing miracle. And it gave me the fillip I needed. I suddenly didn't have the burden of guilt of letting my partner down sitting on my shoulders. From then on I played like a demon. After the first nine holes I was on level par, and Brian and I were easily outplaying our opponents.

Then a strange thing happened. The previous night's booze started to wear off, and as it did so I started to flag. I hung on desperately, determined to prove myself despite the previous night's excesses. On the last green I needed to sink a long putt to score a level par round. I pushed it too far, but it was still the best round of golf I have ever played, by a country mile.

I've used my preparation for that round as a blueprint ever since.

CHAPTER SEVEN

THE HEALTH
OF NATIONS

*'The NHS is a vast, lumbering monolith
which is so inefficient that if it was a
private enterprise it would have gone
bankrupt years ago.'*

ONE OF the scandals of the age in which we live is the way that politicians waste so much of our money. It is tantamount to fraud. We are very proud of our democracy and it has been going on for hundreds of years, but does the system really work when it comes to entrusting our money to incompetents?

Let's make one thing absolutely clear: politicians don't have any money. Politicians, from all parties, are like salesmen. They get your money from your pocket by promising you a good bargain. 'Vote for me and you'll get a great country. It's a bargain!' The deal is that you accept their patter then hand over your money in the form of taxes. Am I the only person in the British Isles who thinks it is a scandal to have to hand over nearly half of my money to foolish, greedy politicians who can then use it with hardly any public accountability? Remember, these people rarely have any expertise in the field in which they are spending your money. A Defence Secretary doesn't know how to drive a tank, a Health Secretary has probably only ever been in a hospital to have his or her piles done, and a Chancellor has never usually worked in the marketplace to be able to understand things such as effort and reward, the benefit of the profit motive, and value for money.

Politicians are in it for themselves, not for you or me. An MP in the United Kingdom now 'earns' about £200,000 a year. OK, so the official salary is only about £60,000 a year, but on top of that come the so-called expenses, most of which, it seems to me, are a rip-off. They pay their wives to work for them in Parliament, for example, or in their constituencies, and the sort of money that is claimed for travelling expenses and postage is quite ridiculous.

When I saw the figures once I worked out that some MPs would have had to send out about 2,000 letters a week to justify the claims. Who's even got time to sign 2,000 letters a week, never mind write them? And some of our honourable members must have to drive to Moscow and back every week to justify the mileage claims. They are not even required to submit receipts for the petrol they buy.

Do I think they are on the fiddle? Undoubtedly.

Local politicians are just as laissez-faire with public money. Ken Livingstone, as the Mayor of London, is the most powerful councillor in the country. But he uses public funds to build big swish offices, create his own empire and pursue his eccentric policies. For instance, the traditional Routemaster London bus was built as a double-decker after the Second World War for a reason: as a way to save space on London's crowded, bomb-damaged streets. Since those days, of course, the streets of London have become much more crowded. So Mr Livingstone decided to scrap the double-decker buses and replace them with bendy-buses which are twice as long and which sometimes take up six times the amount of road space when trying to navigate a tight corner.

Can anybody explain this madness to me?

If there are more cars on the road then my suggestion, as you know, would be to build more roads, or put the age limit for driving up to 21, or build smaller cars. Mr Livingstone thinks we should close down roads.

Near to the talkSPORT studios in London stands a vital artery of the capital, Blackfriars Bridge. By definition there are only a limited number of ways motorists can travel from south London to north London because of the fact that they have to go across the River Thames on a bridge. You can't exactly take a short-cut down a side road because you'll end up with water in your engine. So you would have thought that a vital requirement of the person in charge would be to make sure that these limited number of bridges provide as much road space as possible to keep the traffic flowing. After all, it's basic common sense that a vibrant economy can't run properly without an efficient transport network, the most versatile component of which is roads.

But Mr Livingstone does not see it that way. He is trying to strangle the life out of the capital by doing all he can to restrict mobility on the roads. On Blackfriars Bridge the pavement is now wider than the road. There is a cycle-lane squeezed in as well, meaning that for a motorist it has become a nightmare. What used to be a main route into the east side of the city now has one lane for motorists and a space twice that width for cyclists and pedestrians. The stupidity of that is borne out by the fact that I hardly ever see anybody walking over that bridge. It is a commercial route. It doesn't actually go anywhere. It's not the bridge over to the Houses of Parliament, or the Tower of London, or the shopping mecca of Oxford Street, or the delights of Leicester Square.

And then there is the so-called 'Congestion Charge'. This nefarious local tax is heading to your town or city very soon, believe me. The political explanation for this £8-a-day payment is that traffic has to be kept down or the city will grind to a halt. But the charge hasn't had the effect at all of dramatically reducing traffic-flow. Some people have tried to change to public transport, but trains and buses, and in the bigger cities underground services, are so badly run in Britain that they are intolerable to civilised human beings. No, the real point of the Congestion Charge is to further decongest your wallet of your money.

Politicians have to keep dreaming up wackier ways of stealing your hard-earned dosh. If it's not a tax for driving into a city it's a tax on taking your family on holiday in the guise of a 'carbon tax'. Politicians think all the people are stupid. They honestly believe that if they tell us we can all contribute to saving the world by shelling out anything between £5 and £40 surcharge on an airline ticket, we will believe them. The truth is usually revealed because most of the electorate are brighter than thick-as-plank politicians, who are too stupid to be able to earn a living outside the cosy little club of their parliaments and councils.

One bad trait of the British people is that we don't complain enough. We don't moan about queuing or shoddy service, and when the politicians stick it on us we usually shrug our shoulders and get on with it. But if we think that a politico is really taking the mickey then we tend to get upset. I think the carbon tax is a good example of this. The announcement that flying – like country motoring, one of the great freedoms of the liberated western world – was to be taxed further was slipped out in a pre-budget report. Ludicrously, it was said to be the only way to make people realise that every time they got on a plane they would be contributing to global warming; it forced us to think about whether our journeys were really necessary.

That's if you accept that global warming is caused by man in the first place, of course. I don't know what causes it. I have read compelling arguments from all sides and I have an open mind about every possibility, ranging from the gases that cows emit and sunspot activity to simple cyclical change. I'd like to know how the Romans were able to cultivate vines in Northumberland 2,000 years ago. It must have got colder since then because the north-east is one of the few places in this country where you can be fairly certain of snowfall every winter.

But Mr Brown decided it's all man's fault because it suited his purpose. Then someone pointed out very soon afterwards that Britain is responsible for only two per cent of the world's carbon emissions. Much, much more filth is emitted into the atmosphere by America and the massively expanding economies of China and India. Did Chancellor Brown go knocking on the doors of those countries to try to persuade them that as Britain, the fourth largest economy in the world, was fighting a worthy moral battle, they should join in? I very much doubt it. America never takes a blind bit of notice of what we say anyway, as evidenced by the contemptuous way in which at a summit of world leaders President George Bush said 'Yo, Blair' in that embarrassing piece of footage we all saw. And you get the feeling that China and India are more interested in allowing their tiger economies to expand as rapidly as they can, to improve the lot of their people, rather than shackling their expansion with taxes to provide public money.

It was not explained what the government was going to do with the billions of extra pounds they were taking off holidaymakers and business travellers. Did they announce that they were going to use the money to build some magic machine that would change carbon dioxide into fresh air, or perhaps invent a way of making it rain for 30 extra days every year to fill up our reservoirs? Of course not. We would all have been quite sympathetic to the idea if they did have a grand plan, if they'd asked us to contribute to a properly thought-out scheme to restrain global warming. It became quite clear that all the politicians wanted was more money in their coffers to shore up a deficit in another part of the public spending budget which had lapsed into hopeless debt.

And just in case you think I am being anti-Labour here, as they currently form the government, I am not. I've got just as much contempt for the Conservatives. They, in fact, have announced plans, should they return to power, to load travellers with even more so-called 'green' taxes. Is it any wonder that I have given up voting?

We have an Irishman to thank for largely exposing this ruse. Michael O'Leary is the chief executive of Ryanair, the hugely successful budget airline. He and other entrepreneurs like him – the risk-takers politicians seem to despise because of their intelligence and their energy – have transformed all our lives by making international travel cheap and accessible. Politicians don't realise how much they owe to people like Mr O'Leary and all other successful businessmen. When you start up a business like Ryanair and run it with dynamic energy, everybody benefits. It creates growth in the economy, it slashes fares and therefore contributes massively to keeping the cost of living down, and it creates thousands of jobs, therefore keeping unemployment down and giving people money to stimulate spending.

Mr O'Leary was not prepared to take all the old flannel from the Chancellor. Mr Brown's greed for more taxpayers' money posed a threat to the business he had worked 24 hours a day to build over the previous decade. He took out a series of national newspaper adverts in which he challenged every premise Mr Brown had put forward to justify the new carbon tax. In fact, he called him a liar. And at the time of writing I am not aware of a team of libel lawyers preparing to challenge that claim. Politicians tell lies on a regular basis, and Mr Brown knows that.

People like Mr O'Leary should be running the country, not professional politicians who have had no experience of the real world. It's madness that we are ruled by people who use economic models to make decisions rather than those who have experienced life. Almost every successful football manager – I think Lawrie McMenemy is the only exception – has at some stage of his life played professional football. Not all great players become great managers. In fact, very few really good players become successful bosses. But they do have a lifetime in the game behind them. If I was asked to vote for an MP who had left school at sixteen, worked as a bricklayer and then started his own house-building company to make himself a billionaire, I might go along to a meeting to listen what he has got to say. He would have experience of wealth creation and job creation, of providing for his family through getting cement under his fingernails, and of supplying a market that needs products, i.e. the housing market. I would be more inclined to trust him than somebody who has gone to a public school, on to Oxbridge, and then researched politics until gaining a seat to sit in the House of Commons. What does that person know about life?

The American system is much better. They can appoint people to key positions on the basis of their expertise. Former captains of industry run key government offices because they have demonstrated that they know what they are doing. And just imagine in this country if a big-screen actor suddenly announced he wanted to be the Prime Minister. He would get mocked and derided, and the establishment across the whole political spectrum would work against him. But in America, Ronald Reagan convinced the electorate twice that he was the right man for the job, and he now rates as one of the greatest of the US leaders. When he came to power in 1981 America's role in the world was fading after the hostage crisis that lasted 444 days in Iran. Jimmy Carter, his predecessor, had even been advised to grow a beard to make himself look tougher in the eyes of the world. Reagan not only restored America's role as a superpower, he eventually broke the iron rule of the Soviet bloc in Eastern Europe and Asia – or the 'evil empire' as he billed it. He was successful because people could see that this was an ordinary man from the streets, a former Second World War military photographer who loved his country and its people and wanted to make them both great again.

We should think about replacing politicians with real people. When we give a politician a big title, a huge office with thousands of staff, and a chauffeur-driven car, that individual is often not up to the job. Billions of pounds a year are then spent on so-called advisers. Who are these people who sit around a table with some government mandarin who wants to know, on behalf of a minister, what the government should be doing? Surely we elect and pay our politicians to make decisions which affect our lives? Whole companies employing hundreds of people have been set up in this country in the last ten years to 'advise' government departments. I thought that was what civil servants did. The number of civil servants has increased by 50 per cent – that's two to three millon – over the same period of time, so I want to know what everybody is doing.

One of the most ridiculous aspects of the way we are governed is that when the Prime Minister has a Cabinet reshuffle, the person who has been in charge of Education might suddenly become the Foreign Secretary; or a person who has been working at Health is at a stroke deemed to be expert enough in economics to be appointed Chancellor of the Exchequer. It's absolutely crazy. One of our former generals who has had experience in theatres of war should be our Defence Secretary. Somebody like the haulier Eddie Stobart should be in charge of Transport, because he has first-hand experience of the misery of Britain's congested road system. Education should be run by a former headmaster or headmistress because they would understand about life in a classroom instead of spending weeks dreaming up some silly system to ensure that every child who takes an exam is immune from failure. The Chancellor should be somebody who understands the basic theory of the family budget, which is this:

Income – £100
Expenditure – £99.50p
Result – Happiness

The alternative is this:

Income – £100
Expenditure – £100.50p
Result – Misery

But what usually happens in this country is that we go into massive deficits because of overspending. The person in control of the purse strings obviously hasn't got a clue. Then we move into spending cutbacks, which have a dreadful effect on the economy.

They impact on everybody. You might lose your job due to a squeeze on high-street spending or the public sector being forced to slash jobs. Your mortgage repayments may go up because interest rates have to be raised to cope with inflation, which might have been caused by government spending. It's classic boom and bust. One minute you feel confident and wealthy, the next you can't figure out where all your money has gone and you're fearing for your future.

The area of government waste which most appals me is the National Health Service. Fair enough if I have a health problem as a result of quaffing too much champagne – I only have myself to blame. And if somebody is daft enough to smoke 40 cigarettes a day for 30 years I would not be very sympathetic if they contracted lung cancer. Nevertheless, with more than half of my life gone I have never personally had to rely on the NHS.

All my footballing injuries were dealt with privately. However, I do have great cause to thank this wonderful institution because when my youngest daughter, Steffie, was born she had a problem with her heart and it was sorted out at Guy's Hospital in London. Thankfully it was rectified at the time and, fingers crossed, it has not been a problem ever since.

I mean it when I say that the NHS is a wonderful institution. But, just like my opinions on the police force aired earlier in this book, I think hard-working, dedicated front-line workers are badly let down by their managers.

I looked up the figures for the NHS, and they are truly shocking. Something like one hundred billion pounds has been pumped into the NHS over the last ten years. Despite that, all I ever read about in the papers are massive cuts to services and hospitals shutting down all over the place. Worse still, qualified doctors are coming out of our universities to find that there are no jobs for them, and nurses who do have a job are being laid off. This is an absolute scandal when you consider that there are more managers than there have ever been. I was horrified to discover that the number of people working for the NHS is greater than the number of soldiers in the Soviet Union's Red Army when the USSR was one of the two world superpowers before the Berlin Wall fell. The problem is that only half of them are clinical staff. The other half are managers. That works out at one manager for every nurse. What kind of madness is that? Which incompetent, or successive incompetents, has allowed a situation to arise where half of the money spent in the biggest area of government expenditure doesn't have any direct effect on giving somebody a new kidney or treating heart disease or leukaemia?

When I was a young man bringing up a family you very rarely read anything about the NHS. It was just there. There were hospitals staffed with nurses and doctors where you took your children if they fell off their swing. You didn't have to pay £16 a day to park your car outside that hospital while you sat inside waiting for your wife to give birth. You could ring up and book an appointment with a dentist and have your fillings done for free. Now you can't afford to go to a dentist if you earn the average wage. If you had to take a prescription to a chemist it cost you about the same amount as a pint of beer.

For some reason, it turned from being part of the taken-for-granted British way of life into the hottest political potato. Now, the NHS is a basket case. For about ten years it was used by the government to create tens of thousands of jobs. Some of that was about the provision of more nurses and doctors, but just as many were managerial. Huge new layers of administration were created, such as regional authorities. At every budget, Gordon Brown would boom out in his resonant Scottish tones 'Forty billions extra spending for the NHS' – or was it twenty billions, or thirty? I don't know. There seemed to be so many pledges of money that I lost count. (I also always wondered why he used the expression 'billions', the plural, rather than word 'billion', singular, which most of the rest of us would use.) We all assumed we were going to get a state-of-the-art service that would see us all glide through life safe in the knowledge that should our health let us down, the NHS certainly wouldn't. Where did the plan go wrong, then? Why is it now that the only headlines above stories about health concern how many people are losing their jobs?

According to the Royal College of Nursing, which must be one of the public's most trustworthy institutions, many of those jobs are specialist nursing roles. These are the nurses who, after spending two or three years in the profession, decide they want to work in specialist heart units, or with children, or cancer patients. They are the front-line when it comes to healthcare workers. Doctors only operate on you or pay you a visit in your bed every couple of days; the nurses are there with you throughout. They've got to help you cope with the despair illness brings and fortify you in your battle to get better. The figures I looked up showed that 22,000 jobs like these have disappeared in the NHS since the start of 2006, when cuts were introduced because the books weren't balancing. But with all that extra money the Chancellor has pumped in over the years the books shouldn't just have been balancing, there should have been a surplus for emergencies. The NHS gets more money than many Third World countries generate in one year.

I've found some examples of where the money is being wasted. In an earlier chapter I mentioned the £20 billion computer that is to be built to serve the whole country with patients' records. The project was started in 2003 with a budget of £6 billion. Even at that price somebody should have thought again about whether or not the country was getting value for money. The cost of the exercise then doubled to £12 billion, and now, because of the delays, the projected cost is £20 billion. I accept that you have to have computers in modern life and that they are expensive, but you could build and equip 30 brand spanking new hospitals for the same amount. That's one for every major city in the country. A report from MPs looking into the whole sorry mess has advised the Health Secretary to scrap the project altogether and write off the £2 billion that has already been spent. Yes, that's right, just whistle farewell to £2 billion of our money. Portsmouth Naval Dockyard is in danger of closing down because of Defence spending cuts of £500 million – a miserly quarter of what has been wasted so far on a project that will never be built. So we might lose one of the greatest symbols of our heritage, the naval base where Henry VIII saw the sinking of the Mary Rose, and we'll have to sell off about a third of the fleet of the Royal Navy, the one that held Hitler at bay, because some idiot politician completely screwed up on a plan to build a computer for the NHS. Oh, and on the actual need for the computer, the report from the MPs said that they weren't sure it was going to be fit for purpose even if it is completed because 'doctors and nurses were left out of the planning and the design'.

The whole thing is an absolute scandal. Imagine building an ocean-going yacht to take part in the America's Cup without actually seeking any input from the sailors who were going to crew her. Or buying a load of expensive footballers for a club without asking the manager if he thought they were any good or not. It is the most blatant example of incompetence and waste, but it is not the only one. There are hundreds of depressing stories just like it.

How about this one: civil servants at the Department of Health are being paid a total of £1.5 million a year for doing nothing. They are described as 'displaced', which means that they have been taken on but there is nothing for them to do. They can join a voluntary exit scheme, but unsurprisingly there is nothing which says they have to. Free money. Why would they want to leave? Of the many other unbelievable stories that come out of the NHS is this one: money is being spent on sending staff on comedy courses to cut stress and raise productivity!

The NHS is a vast, lumbering monolith which is so inefficient that if it was a private enterprise it would have gone bankrupt years ago. Only politicians could get away with running such a laughably incompetent operation. The person who should be running the NHS is the same individual who founded Specsavers, or maybe the guy who runs one of those pharmaceutical companies that make millions.

Yet at the heart of the NHS are doctors and nurses who are among the finest in our society. Is it any wonder that thousands of these doctors are now spending more of their time working in private medicine than in the NHS? It's not just that they make more money by doing so – and they have every right to in my view – they are also working in hospitals that operate efficiently. A private hospital in England is like every hospital in America – except that American hospitals are better. Private hospitals don't appear to have the same problems with MRSA and other superbug diseases which routinely kill people. Where have these superbugs come from? Nobody knows, but their emergence coincided with budget restraints on cleaning facilities. According to a doctor pal of mine, as many as 50,000 English patients a year now go abroad for treatment because of lengthening waiting lists and the fear of being killed by an infection in an NHS hospital.

I believe we have got to look at how we fund the NHS. The problem with Gordon's billions is that there is absolutely no accountability to those who provide the funds – i.e. you and me. Public spending is without responsibility. The deal is that once a government is elected you hand over your dosh and somebody else wastes it. But by the time you have discovered it has been wasted it is too late to do anything about it. I think we should hand the power in health spending back to the provider – once again, you and me. In much the same way that it is compulsory to have motoring insurance, everybody should have to take out their own health insurance policy. Health is such a huge part of the national budget that if the government were no longer responsible for funding it they could introduce big tax cuts. With that money restored to the people who earn it, we could all afford a decent health insurance policy. And those who genuinely couldn't would have their needs looked after by the rest of us. Because there would be a business motive in this equation, i.e. insurance companies trying to tempt you into taking out their policies and hospitals encouraging you to use their services, there would be a high level of efficiency. It would also have the benefit, in theory, of wiping out about one sixth of the jobs in Whitehall. Those people who previously worked at the Department of Health would soon get a job in the private sector if they had the right attitude and commitment.

The NHS is like a very heavy weight around our nation's neck. It was a commendable idea when it was set up after the Second World War, but it no longer works. No other modern country so completely commits such a huge amount of public money to supplying healthcare.

Over the last 25 years dozens of organisations have broken away from being funded with public money and are now financed in an alternative and more efficient way. These include British Airways, all of our gas, electricity and refuse collecting companies, and even those despicable people who go around clamping our cars. We are at a tremendous disadvantage compared to our European neighbours. This is probably why, despite the fact that countries such as France have higher proportions of spending on social welfare than we do, they have roads and railway systems that work. Their streets look cleaner, and because their health services are partly privatised, they have much better healthcare too.

'Think the unthinkable' is an oft-used political mantra. But reforming the National Health Service is not the 'unthinkable', it's the absolutely necessary. Our doctors and nurses are magnificent people and they deserve a better infrastructure in which to work.

***

In addition to my little girl being put right by dedicated medical staff, I have another reason to be grateful to those who dedicate their lives to looking after the rest of us: they almost certainly saved the life of my broadcasting partner and very great friend Mike 'Porky' Parry.

The story of his health decline and how he was rescued is quite remarkable. This is a man who was told that if he hadn't been taken into hospital on the night he was, he would have been dead within hours. Even then he was given only three months to live because his heart had virtually exploded. The fact that he is alive today, let alone working again as a broadcaster, is nothing short of a miracle.

Porky nearly worked himself to death, and I saw his deterioration from day to day. During a break in our breakfast show one summer morning in 2004 I went down the corridor towards the bathrooms and heard what I thought was a dog barking. I went into the first bathroom and found Porky on his hands and knees, coughing so violently that his whole body was shaking. His eyes were watering as though he was crying and he didn't seem able to catch his breath. I thought he was having a heart attack. I grabbed him and pulled him to his feet. He bent over a sink and was violently ill. His body was heaving, but in short gasps of conversation he told me he thought he had a chest infection and he wouldn't be able to finish the show.

I took him that day to a doctor in Harley Street, the spiritual home of great physicians, off Oxford Street in London. The doctor told him that he was suffering from a stress-related illness and gave him some sedatives. As soon as we were out of the consulting rooms Porky threw the tablets away. He didn't suffer from stress. He actually lived on it. He got up, like me, at four a.m. every day, six days a week, to do the breakfast show. But whereas I was free to do whatever I wanted after we finished at ten, Porky wasn't because he was the programme director of the station. He'd usually leave the office at about three o'clock.

It was a week before Euro 2004 began in Portugal that I found Porky on his hands and knees, coughing his guts out. The golden boy of English football at the time was Everton's Wayne Rooney. He had exploded on to the scene eighteen months earlier, scoring a goal against the champions, Arsenal, which ended a year-long unbeaten run. Porky, who comes from a family that has supported Everton Football Club for a century, had been talking about Rooney for a couple of years as whispers emanated from Merseyside about this extraordinary youngster from Croxteth who had blow-torches in his boots. He had become the youngest player ever to turn out in an England shirt, and then the youngest to score for his country.

Although I knew Porky was a fanatical Evertonian, he did have a point about Rooney. I had rarely seen such a young kid dazzle senior professionals with his talent. He was confident, bordering on arrogant. He would stand with his foot on the ball and his hands on his hips, taunting defenders to try to take the ball off him. In my day somebody would have put him in hospital to teach him a lesson. But in the modern game, rightly enough, that sort of behaviour is frowned upon.

On a very cold night in February 2003 Porky and I went to West Ham's ground where it was anticipated that Rooney would make his full international debut in a friendly game against Australia. He started the second half to become the youngest player ever to have put on a shirt for his country, at the age of seventeen years and 111 days. Porky was ecstatic. He talked about nothing else to the end of the season. He became a Rooney bore. As far as he was concerned the Croxteth kid was going to win the following year's European Championship single-handedly.

So, even though there was definitely something wrong with Porky in the run-up to that competition, he was very reluctant to admit it because he feared somebody would tell him he could not go to Portugal. He told me that he had been to see several doctors but they'd all said he had either a chest infection or it was stress. Amazingly, in March that year he had gone for a full private health check and had been given the all-clear. He was worried that he might have damaged his liver after what he described as '25 years of social drinking', but he was given a clean bill of health on all counts. He was in a bad way, though. He had been putting on weight for some time, which I couldn't figure out because he never ate very much and he had become a virtual non-drinker. He said he had lost the taste for wine because everything he tried tasted like vinegar. I also learnt that he had recently bought some groceries but couldn't carry them up the stairs to his flat so he had thrown them in the bin instead.

We went to Portugal via Spain. We flew to Madrid, where we were doing a show, and then we were going to drive a sponsored Ford car to Lisbon. In the Spanish capital we went out for dinner with our old pal Paul Breen-Turner. To get back to our hotel we had to walk up a hill. Paul and I got to the top of the hill, but we lost Porky. He was sitting on a wall at the bottom. We urged him to hurry up but he just waved and said he would be up in a minute. Half an hour later in the hotel bar there was no sign of him. I went out to find him. He was sitting on the same wall. I thought he might have had a cigarette, which he did occasionally. I went down the hill and asked him if he was OK, and he told me he couldn't make it up the hill. I put my arm around his shoulders and we shuffled up together, but it took a good ten minutes. He was completely breathless.

The following day I urged him to go home. Not only did he dismiss that out of hand, he made me vow not to contact anybody. He actually said, 'I'm not going home until Rooney does. England are going to win this competition and I am going to be there to see it.' I didn't really know what to do. It was no good me ringing alarm bells in London if Porky was going to dismiss them as me being melodramatic. And in his position I knew I would probably be doing the same. We come from similar backgrounds and have always regarded illness as weakness.

On the morning we set off for Portugal I had to do some television work at short notice, so Porky was going to go in the Ford with 'Big' Jim Brown, our chief engineer, doing the driving. I was going to fly out that evening. About three hours after they set off, I got a call from Jim. He was in a bit of a panic. Porky had had a bad turn, probably due to the intense heat, which he found difficult at the best of times. They had stopped in a tiny godforsaken town on the Spain/Portugal border. Porky was having trouble breathing. Jim didn't know whether to keep going or to bring him back. I told him to keep going because the whole talkSPORT caravan was setting up in Lisbon for the three-week-long championship and if help was needed that was where it would be.

The terrible irony of that journey was that Porky was desperately ill but he couldn't have been with a fitter man. Jim Brown went to the gym every day of his life, except for Christmas Day. He was tough and muscular and didn't have an ounce of fat on his body. Yet Porky is still with us whereas Jim died at home in his sleep eighteen months later. He was a great professional and a tremendous bloke to have on your side. God rest his soul.

Porky couldn't sit up in the car because he couldn't breathe. The vehicle was a Ford Ranger, a sort of 4x4 pick-up truck. Jim had to find a blanket and let Porky lie down flat in the back with a cover to protect him from the sun. I had this image in my head of a spaghetti western-style scene, Jim arriving at our hotel with Porky prostrate in the back.

Over the next three weeks, all Porky did was get up for the breakfast show and go back to his room. He did the rest of his work on the phone, emerging only for England games. He seemed to be getting better, and then we had to travel out of Lisbon for England's second game against Switzerland. We went up to a dusty little town called Coimbra. It was a boiling hot day, even by Portuguese standards. The stadium was a new one and had not been completed in time, and there was no roof over our seats. I like the sun, but I felt very uncomfortable. Porky was wilting by the minute. His spirits were lifted, however, when Wayne Rooney scored the opening goal and got a second to seal England's 3-0 victory.

We decided to leave as early as possible to try to beat the traffic out of town back to Lisbon. Jim had to stay until the final whistle to gather up all the gear so I volunteered to go and get the truck and bring it down as close as I could to the stadium. I was sitting in the car with the engine running, a couple of hundred yards from the ground, when Jim rang. Porky couldn't physically make it. Jim was having to carry him. A few minutes later he came round the corner, a case of broadcasting equipment in his left hand and Porky slung over his right shoulder. The man was a Colossus.

On the way back we had to stop at a booth on a toll road. The Ford vehicle we were driving was covered in talkSPORT logos. A load of England fans surrounded the car and wanted us to sign their programmes and have their pictures taken with us. Porky is usually very good at the PR side of the business and would normally have got out and mingled with the fans, but he couldn't move. He just smiled weakly and waved his arm as the supporters banged on the semi-tinted window. I got out instead and did all the hand-shaking and pictures, but then the fans started moaning about Porky. One individual opened the door, saw Porky slumped in his seat and announced, 'He's pissed. Porky's completely out of it. He's been on the old rosé.'

Nothing could have been further from the truth. I hadn't seen him have a drink since he'd been in Portugal. But unfortunately, a Chinese whisper started and soon the internet was full of stories of Porky drinking for England. There's no justice, because on our only day off, Sunday, I had gone down to the Algarve to join a few other ex-footballers in one of their villas for a mammoth session which ended up with me waking up in the middle of the night on a golf course. I still don't know how I got there.

The next morning I once again urged Porky to go home. The veins in his neck were bulging terribly. But he wouldn't entertain the idea while England were still in the competition. They had to win their third qualifying game to ensure that they got through to the knockout stages. For me, it had got to the point where I was wanting England to go out so that we could take him home. Not only was he very ill, he was now not sleeping because he said that every time he closed his eyes he got the sensation that he was drowning.

I don't know if he'd had a premonition, but he nearly drowned in reality. One day he decided to sit outside in the shade to help his breathing. After a while he took a dip in the pool to cool off. But as he slipped into the water he just kept going down to the bottom of the pool like a bag of cement. Fortunately one of the lads spotted him and he managed to scramble him out, but Porky was in a hell of a state. He said he felt like he had lead weights in his boots, and when you looked at his ankles that wasn't surprising. They were terribly swollen.

In hindsight, of course, it was ridiculous not to have taken him to a hospital. But remember, he was the boss of the whole operation and nobody could tell him what to do.

England beat Croatia 4-2. Rooney scored two more goals, and Porky was in his element. The team was now due to meet the hosts, Portugal, in the quarter-finals. It was a tough task, but everybody, me included, thought England looked like winners. And we were all converted now to the Rooney cause.

Everything seemed to be going to plan when Michael Owen opened the scoring for England in the third minute. But disaster struck after 27 minutes when Rooney's foot seemed to collide with the heel of a Portuguese player. He went down, then limped to the bench where he sat down again with his legs outstretched. I knew exactly what had happened. He hadn't been able to put any weight at all on his foot as he came off the pitch. He was staring at his boot, because he knew, like I did, that he'd broken a bone.

The crowd had gone quiet around us. I turned to Porky and said, 'He's busted his foot. He's out of the competition.'

Porky looked at me with incomprehension. 'How do you know that?' he said.

'I just do. He won't be playing again until the new season. He might not even make it then. He's had it.'

My forecast was exactly right, and England went on to lose the match on penalties. I don't dislike England and the English, as I sometimes pretend to on the radio, but I was mightily relieved that they were not going any further in this competition for the sake of my pal. He was now definitely going home tomorrow.

That night, probably to drown his sorrows, Porky had his first drink of the competition. Bizarrely, all he would take was Baileys Irish Cream. He said it was the only thing he could keep down. He tried white wine and then red but said that everything except Baileys tasted of vinegar. He drank two bottles of it, and for a few hours the old Porky returned. There were a few talkSPORT bigwigs around and I think for the sake of appearances, and to numb the disappointment of England going out, he was back on the razzle.

But he paid for it the following morning. Jim and I and a porter at the hotel had to carry him downstairs. He was a deadweight. He didn't want to go on the plane because he was frightened he might stop breathing in the pressurised cabin. But by now he was desperate to get home and he knew there was no other way. Actually, I'm amazed he was allowed to get on the plane. He was almost unconscious when we checked him in at the airport.

Porky went ahead of me. When I got back to England a few days later nobody had even seen him. I thought he'd probably gone home, locked the door and switched his phone off. But I was wrong. That evening I got a call from him. He had been rushed into hospital that very afternoon. He had been diagnosed with acute heart failure.

His heart had sort of exploded. Apparently the left-hand chamber is the one that pumps blood around your body. Porky's wasn't pumping at all. It had packed up. As a result the fluids that usually move around your body weren't going anywhere. They were settling on his lungs, which was why he couldn't breathe. Fluid had also collected in all parts of his body, which was why he had put on weight and had swollen ankles and bulging veins. The drowning sensation happened because every time he tried to lie down the fluid in his body poured into his lungs and stopped the breathing function. He was, in fact, in danger of drowning in his own fluids.

He had been to see two different doctors when he got home. One said he had a chest infection, the other, again, said it was stress, listened to his heart and pronounced everything normal. Only when he walked into the surgery of the third did the doctor immediately suspect a major problem. He rang a heart specialist and sent him there straight away. As soon as the cardiologist saw him he phoned for an ambulance. He said he didn't even need to examine him to be able to tell that his heart was failing. He found that he had hardly any blood pressure at all. At any time Porky could have died because when your blood is not moving around your body it clots, and if a clot moves into your heart, you die. If it goes to your brain, you have a stroke. The doctor told Porky, 'I'm not sure you would have got through another night.'

Three days later I went to see him in hospital. He was wired up to some sort of heart machine. He looked much better than he had done for a long time. That was unsurprising because since he had been admitted he had had pumped out of him pint after pint of the water that had been causing him so much distress. But his heart was incapable of coping on its own. A few days after that he rang me very early to tell me that he was being transferred to Harefield Hospital in Middlesex, Britain's leading cardio-thoracic centre, where he would be under the care of some of the world's leading cardiologists. This had been decided after he was told that his heart wouldn't last more than about three months.

Harefield is the hospital where so much pioneering work was done by the world-famous surgeon Sir Magdi Yacoub. I visited Porky there several times. Because he was so ill he had his own room and visitors were allowed at any time. It was nice to be able to go up there and sit in the gardens with him. He had been diagnosed with dilated cardio-myopathy. His left ventricle was stretched out of all proportion and his heart was working at about one-third efficiency. He was terribly weak. I pushed him about in a wheelchair.

At first the doctors believed that his illness had come about as the result of a virus attacking his heart. Research shows that in some extreme cases perfectly healthy people can be reduced to critical illness in just a few days if they're unlucky enough to be infected. But it now seems more likely that my pal might have inherited an illness that killed his father 25 years ago. His dad had all the same symptoms – shortage of breath, water retention and sickness – but in those days the first heart transplant had not even been done in this country and obviously there wasn't the detailed knowledge of heart disease we have today. His father died when a blood clot hit his heart.

The thing that always impressed me at the hospital was the care and dedication of the staff. I felt so humble about having been a footballer when I saw the suffering, and the work doctors and nurses were doing to try to alleviate it. There were young men there who pushed what looked like a little suitcase around on a trolley in front of them. The 'suitcase' was in fact the battery to a pump which was attached to their chests and kept them alive. Everywhere they went the trolley and battery had to go with them. It was literally a life-support unit, and that was their existence until they got a heart transplant. On one occasion, Porky told me, three doctors came into his room and sat and discussed with him a plan to give him a similar pump because his heart was fading. He dreaded the thought of the pump because it meant you were a prisoner in the hospital, whereas now, on a good day, he could be taken out for a ride in the car.

Porky was very positive throughout his illness. He was terribly relieved finally to be given a proper diagnosis. At least now, he figured, the doctors knew what they had to put right. And he was very anxious to get his life back on track. He kept telling the doctors and nurses that he wanted a transplant as soon as possible.

I was very concerned to keep Porky involved with the station, and I wanted him to talk to us on the phone from the hospital. But when we eventually got it all fixed up with the doctors and the hospital it came as a complete shock to hear him. It so happened that he was having a bad day, and we did it from his bed while he was lying down. He explained as simply as he could about what had happened to him. Many listeners contacted us to say how weak he sounded. Porky has always had a robust broadcasting style and we weren't used to hearing him talk in little more than a faltering whisper. I probably hadn't noticed because I had seen him on quite a regular basis. On reflection, he didn't just sound weak. Whenever we asked him a question it took him a few seconds to summon up enough breath to answer. The listeners wouldn't have known it, but he also looked very frail. His movements were like those of a cripple. He shuffled rather than walked, and his head movements were like those of somebody with bad rheumatism, almost robotic.

After a while Porky was allowed home for short periods, but he always seemed to go downhill and ended up back in hospital. He said he felt safe at Harefield because he didn't think there was anywhere else in the world that could look after him so well.

He was taking an awful lot of drugs and tablets. Some of them were clearly life-saving, like the diuretics that drained the water off his lungs, but some of the others, for instance the beta-blockers that help strengthen the heart, had to be tested on a trial basis. Apparently, one patient's life-saver may produce a violent reaction in somebody else. His 'diet' of drugs was being changed all the time.

Towards the end of November that year, about five months after he had first been admitted to hospital, he rang me to say that he was starting to feel better. He added that each day over the last two weeks he had felt a bit stronger, and in one tremendous victory he had been able to walk to the post-box near his house, which was about 100 yards away. Believe it or not, considering how ill he had been, this was a big breakthrough.

Soon after that he had a meeting with his doctors to discuss the transplant position. Porky was frustrated that while he was waiting for a new heart he couldn't restart his life. The problem about waiting for a new organ is that you have no idea how long it will take. It's a strange irony these days that safer motor vehicles mean fewer people dying on the roads, which means fewer hearts and lungs for transplants. Porky had heard of cases of people who had a transplant a week after going on the list, but others waited months, and in some cases years. And all the time you have a little bag packed that is permanently with you in case you get the call to go to the hospital, which has to be done very quickly.

The doctors were pleased with his progress and put it down to the latest combination of drugs. Apparently, some of those he had been taking earlier had not agreed with him and now he was taking a mixture of tablets that seemed to be working together. The doctors agreed to take him off the transplant list and to monitor his progress. And ever since that day he has got stronger. To look at him today you would not believe there was anything wrong with him, even though he has to be very careful with his lifestyle. I call him the 'pill-box' (a play on the word 'pillock') because of the amount of tablets he still takes.

What I found surprising during my brief association with Harefield is that the people who run the National Health Service appear to be hell-bent on getting rid of it. It is a most delightful hospital. None of it is more than three storeys high. It is on a greenfield site on the edge of a small market town, surrounded by countryside. Most of the staff who work there live in the town or the surrounding villages. There is a lake in the grounds where patients, most of whom are very ill, can sit on a bench under a tree and spend time with family and friends. There is also a little shop that serves tea and buns, staffed by volunteers. Porky and I sat there once watching rabbits running in and out of the bushes. He showed me a sett where a family of badgers lived. Songbirds hovered in the sky. It was like something you'd see in a Disney cartoon film. It is the most perfect setting you can imagine for people who are sick and whose lives have been terribly traumatised. Yet the number-crunchers wanted to close it down. Some believe they still will.

Harefield is a stellar medical facility. It is the premier facility for heart disease and transplants. You would have thought with all the budget-deficit chaos that abounds in the NHS that they could leave things as they are. It works marvellously, to the satisfaction and delight of patients and staff. Yet for years it was programmed to be swallowed up in a huge new development in Paddington, inner-city London. The reason given was that the NHS would be more efficient if everything was centralised. Presumably that is the view of the same jerk who is responsible for all the other efficient elements of the service, which have plunged it into a cash crisis.

You cannot put a price on the spiritual aspect of Harefield Hospital. I suspect there are plenty of other places like it around the country which the medical planners would say, despite their life-enhancing qualities, are 'old-fashioned' and 'out of date'. But where do you think a patient would prefer to be treated, in the lovely, leafy surroundings of a smallish, friendly hospital in the country, or in a tower block in the big city where smog and belching fumes replace fresh air and daffodils?

In my view it is all down to politicians again. They love to have control. They love to be able to say 'We've got everything under one roof' because by saying that they can run the show instead of leaving it to the professionals. They don't want to take the risk of allowing a superb facility like Harefield to have a mind of its own. It has escaped their attention that the NHS belongs to, and is paid for by, the patients.

A couple of times a year Harefield has fund-raising days – a summer fair, or a Fun Run day. They are wonderful occasions when the true camaraderie and spirit that exists at specialist institutions come to the fore. So many people labour so hard to make the place work. Not just the medical and ancillary staff but former patients like Porky and the families of those who have been treated there. Unfortunately, that includes the relatives of those who weren't lucky enough to get a transplant in time and who remember their loved ones through the care and devotion that was given to them at Harefield. You simply can't generate that sort of love and inspiration if you are part of a soulless operation, reaching up 30 floors into the sky and lacking any specific identity.

The other issue is this: I am terrified of falling ill in this country in case I catch something in hospital that kills me. I thought that the outcry over the MRSA bug was hype until I had a look at the figures. People are dying every week. I read recently that a thousand people a week are now travelling abroad for medical treatment. They are fed up of waiting lists in this country and the high cost of private treatment if you want to relieve yourself of pain before the NHS can do it for you. But another reason put forward was the fear of catching a killer bug.

Once again, I find it astonishing that with all the tens of billions of pounds that have been thrown at the NHS you have a very real chance now of dying of something you catch inside a hospital. With the greatest respect to the countries concerned, what has happened to the United Kingdom when people are prepared to spend their hard-earned cash to fly to places such as India, Turkey and Hungary for safer medical treatment?

I never saw any evidence of the presence of killer bugs at Harefield. The cleaning ladies were the sort of people who could be anybody's mother. They lived locally and took as much pride in cleaning the hospital as they did in their own home. You felt confident that no killer bug would ever be safe with these ladies around. For some reason so-called 'health executives' never like to face up to the fact that the answer to some of their problems lies right in front of them. They would rather splash out millions on cleaning contractors than employ people who know more about cleaning than any of us – mothers and housewives.

The scandal – for that is what it is – of wasted money in the NHS goes way beyond incompetence. It is actually a very serious moral issue. I've already highlighted huge areas of waste. I didn't think I could find any more surprises in the way money is spent on healthcare, but then I learnt about the latest pay offer to nurses. A ridiculous and insulting 1.9 per cent, at a time when inflation alone is running at over 3 per cent. Some nurses will barely make £20,000 a year. At the same time GPs and consultants – the very top specialist doctors – are said to have been given pay rises that have taken their average salaries to over £100,000. Good. They richly deserve it. But nurses also deserve a much more realistic reflection of their worth in society.

As usual, it's cowardly politicians who shy away from bullies and take advantage of the compliant. If you start threatening trouble, you usually get a deal. But that's not the way nurses work.

CHAPTER EIGHT

THE MEN WHO WOULD BE KING

*'There are many who think that footballers
who hail from working-class homes should
not be allowed to accumulate great wealth.
I could not agree less.'*

FOOTBALLERS ARE AMONG the most powerful people in our society. Much more powerful than politicians. Certainly as powerful as top rock stars. In their own right, a lobby with the strength of a business that generates billions of pounds.

Power has everything to do with popularity. Diana, Princess of Wales, who in 1997 so tragically died in a car crash in Paris, was often described as the most powerful woman in the world. That was because everybody loved her, or thought they did. They felt she had been rejected by the royal family and that she was truly the people's princess. She was the first person in the royal family to show the common touch. Whenever she saw her two little boys again after being away she would sweep them up in her arms with the delight of any young mum. This sort of 'normal' behaviour had never been seen before in the royal family, who appeared to have been trained to be emotionless at all times. Diana was young and vivacious, a complete contrast to Prince Charles, who was old beyond his years and so remote from most of us that sometimes it was hard to believe we were all part of the same race. And that is why charities were so keen to have Diana as their patron. One picture of her holding a little child whose leg had been cruelly blown off by a land-mine was enough to generate hundreds of thousands of pounds to help those poor people in distress.

John Lennon's popularity had a different effect altogether. He left Britain in 1973 to live in the United States and never returned. But he fought a constant battle to stay in the country, let alone get there in the first place. President Richard Nixon hated him for his outspoken criticism of the war in Vietnam, a horrifying conflict in the jungles of south-east Asia during which tens of thousands of young, mostly poor, Americans were killed. The world of pop music was the biggest voice of protest against the war, and at the pinnacle of that movement was Lennon, who had moved on from being the most outspoken member of the world's biggest ever group, The Beatles, to being something akin to a guru to young people around the world.

In my day, footballers were popular with their own fans. If you played for a successful team and you were an international, that popularity was played out on a bigger stage. Footballers were popular because millions of little boys dreamt of playing for the club they supported and emulating the heroes they worshipped. Almost all of them never made it, which is why those who did were held in such high regard by the rest. But despite all that, the players of my generation didn't have the impact on society that today's footballers have, because, in addition to popularity, they have tons of money.

Adults revere footballers today because to a bloke who is earning £30,000 a year, trying to pay the bills for his house, his car and his kids, a footballer, by comparison, has the perfect life. Rich people are powerful because they control wealth. They employ other people. They can ask others in society to do things that benefit them because they can afford it. In short, they call the shots. When you put popularity and wealth together, you have a dynamic force.

The first footballer to really understand how to exploit his popularity in order to make himself very wealthy, thus acquiring great power, was David Beckham. The boy who was brought up in east London and who can truly be described as a world superstar must be one of the brightest footballers ever. OK, I agree he might not have a grasp of nuclear physics, but he made himself one of the most famous people in the world. I read one poll that said he was the second most recognised face on the planet after the President of the United States.

Too many people have never understood how clever Beckham has been. In the latest Rich List published annually by The Sunday Times he was said to have increased his wealth by £25 million in just one year to take it to £112 million. Some of this might be to do with the fact that to wrap up his career he has signed a deal with American club Los Angeles Galaxy which could earn him up to £150 million over five years. Even before he started playing for his new club, the 'Becks Effect' had trebled the revenues Galaxy would normally have expected to raise pre-season as a result of a combination of a big increase in season-ticket sales with shirt sales, endorsements and sponsorships.

A mark of the man's overall worth to a football club is that he was regarded as a huge success at Real Madrid for the three years he was there despite the fact that they won just a single trophy during that time. His value to them was a commercial one. Sponsors scramble aboard the wagon in which Beckham is riding. Real's relative lack of success on the field, due to an ageing squad, seemed almost immaterial.

Despite the constant denials from the football authorities, and from Beckham himself, there was no doubt that he wielded tremendous influence over the England national team. Once he became captain at the start of the Sven-Goran Eriksson era he was, in my view, the most powerful man in English football. Sven treated him almost like a blood brother rather than keeping him at a reasonable distance, which is what most managers do with all players, even if they are the captain. And some believed that Beckham had real influence on the England set-up too, and that sometimes the manager even deferred to him.

I was told of one occasion when Sven was addressing a group of coaches and scouts during the build-up to an England game. The door opened slightly and Beckham pushed his head around the door. He wanted to see Sven, but Sven indicated that he had to get on with his meeting. Beckham wasn't having it. He made it very clear that he wanted to see him there and then. Sven sighed, apologised to his aides around the table and left the room. He was absent for fifteen minutes. One of the people at that meeting told me, 'We were all stunned. It was like David summoned Sven out of the meeting. We've all worked with strong-willed players but we've never seen one with the confidence to interrupt a manager's meeting because he regarded his issue as more important.'

The story illustrates the power Beckham acquired after spending years carefully cultivating his image. He became the 'coolest' man in Britain. In my day, no footballer would have been allowed to captain England, let alone play for them, with a Mohican haircut. The idea that Bobby Robson or Brian Clough would have allowed one of his players in the ground, let alone out on the pitch, looking so 'trendy' is unthinkable. But Becks and other England players have established new rules about the relationship between footballers and the authorities. The pendulum has swung massively in favour of the players. The top footballers are more in charge now than they have ever been. They are so wealthy they don't have to be humble with their masters. And the more money that is injected into the game, the more it chases the very best players.

The worth of a footballer and the judgement of his ability is relative to whoever else is around at the time, and no matter what era you are in there are only ever going to be a limited number of very top players. In 2006/07, Cristiano Ronaldo, the 2007 PFA Footballer of the Year, set the benchmark with a blistering season for Manchester United. United did the sensible thing and tied him down before the end of the season with a new contract said to be worth £125,000 a week. Frankly, I think they got him cheap. Real Madrid started a campaign of drum-beating at Christmas. The message that went out from the Bernabeu was that they were after Ronaldo. They wanted him to become their star Galáctico. You can see why. His skill is breathtaking. He scores as regularly as the main strikers while playing out wide, and he is young and good-looking – all of which fits the Real image and makes him a big money-spinner as he captures the admiration of fans around the world.

Everybody, including me, thought Ronaldo would go to Spain. He had expressed a wish in the past to play for the Madrid giants, often referred to as the biggest club in the world, and he hails from Portugal, a neighbouring country with a similar Mediterranean culture. Madrid had enjoyed unusually fallow years and I thought there was nothing they would not do to try to secure one of the world's best and most charismatic footballers. That's why if I had been involved at United I would have called his agent in and put an offer on the table of £150,000 a week. I know that sounds ridiculous, but that's market forces at work. Just think about what a club will have to pay to secure his services when his contract is renewed, at the latest in three years' time. It could be twice or even three times that amount.

I am certain that the first million-pound-a-week footballer is playing today. It might be Ronaldo, or it might be the astonishing Argentinian youngster Lionel Messi of Barcelona. I can't see why wages won't exceed £50 million plus a year within a decade. Those sorts of salaries are already being paid to American sports stars, some of whom compete in games like baseball and American football which are not even global. It doesn't really matter how many people fill a stadium to watch their sports stars, the true wealth of the game comes from TV rights. And football will always attract bigger around-the-world audiences than baseball. When every third house in China and India has some form of cable or digital television that supplies football, today's salaries will seem relatively small. The Premiership is the world's favourite league. Manchester United and Liverpool have vast overseas armies of fans, particularly in the Far East, and that is where there has been the biggest growth in revenues for televised football.

I believe the players are worth every penny they are paid. For nearly a century the people who most benefited from football were the men who ran them. When regular crowds of 60,000 or 70,000 crammed into places like Goodison Park, Maine Road and The Valley, where did all the money go when footballers were on £4 a week if they were beaten, £5 for a draw, and £6 for a win? In fairness, that was not a bad pre-war wage, but it still meant that the club centre-forward could be the bloke in the terraced house next to yours. Again, in fairness, the game was not seen as a money-spinner in those days and the entrance money to stand on the terraces could be pence rather than shillings. Nevertheless, the club chairman and directors were usually the only people who left the ground in a motor car. But everybody benefits today. Salaries are massive for both players and the top employees of a club. Some chairmen, like Bill Kenwright of Everton, don't even take a salary; others take a handsome one, as they are entitled to do if they are running a successful business.

I don't understand the call for salary-capping. Why would any profession want to introduce disincentives into the pay structure? How can a manager say to a young player, 'OK, you've done very well and you're getting a pay rise. But I have to tell you that even if you do better next season I can't give you a better deal because you're getting as much as I am allowed to pay you.' I would happily listen to an argument to put players' salaries into a trust to make sure the money didn't get squandered during their more impetuous early years, but even that is probably not necessary because such high earners are surrounded by advisers and experts.

Instead of trying to restrict the amount of money these young people earn, we should look at the benefits brought to society by this new class of multi-millionaire.

For a long time now there has been a very distinctive class structure in Britain. It started with the upper class and the working class with a thin middle-class filling. As the decades went by, wealth was created and the economy grew at a faster rate than it ever had before. The middle class became the biggest and most distinguishable group. But almost all footballers came from the working class, unlike cricketers and rugby players who came from the middle class, or even occasionally the upper class, and most footballers earned enough for the good life only while they were still players. The smart ones moved into business or some form of new career – in the media, for instance – but I know dozens of ex-pros who these days drive a taxi or work as security guards.

That should never happen again to any young man who has played even a few seasons in the Premiership on a modest salary, which by today's standards is around £20,000 a week. That means that what has been created by the huge explosion in players' wages is a new stratum of immensely wealthy young people. It's not like they have gone from working class to upper class in one generation as, say, Sir Alan Sugar's family have done. Some of these people have gone from the proletariat, and often the most basic level of it, to lifelong financial independence by their 21st birthday.

There are many who think, purely through meanness of spirit or snobbery, that footballers who hail from working-class homes should not be allowed to accumulate great wealth. I could not agree less. They are paid vast salaries because they are the very best at what they do in a business that is easily the biggest leisure pursuit in the world. Virtually every male wishes he could be or could have been a footballer. It is the dream job. Fame, wealth, girls, cars – when you are a footballer you can have it all. But there is one big proviso: you have to keep producing the goods.

Sometimes, even if the early promise fizzes out a young man will have enough to keep him comfortable for the rest of his life. I know of one young footballer who came through the youth ranks at a middle-ranking Premiership club and was quickly snapped up by one of the big four teams. He then spent two frustrating years trying to establish himself but never really made the breakthrough, and over the next few years was subject to a number of transfers and loans until he seemed to settle down at a Championship club. Yet I know for a fact that he has few financial worries because a good mate of mine has a villa next to his in Portugal.

For those who consistently perform, of course, the rewards are fantastic. But those young men do not get there by accident. They are very tough and very intelligent people. Some might guffaw at the idea that I class players as intelligent, but I do. Porky once produced an equation that he said proved that Wayne Rooney was as bright as Albert Einstein because of the way his footballing brain worked out angles and velocities. Well, I don't know about that, but there is no doubt that when you are catapulted from a council housing estate to mega-stardom and wealth in the space of a year, you have to brighten up or you will not survive.

I heard Wayne Rooney being interviewed when he was nineteen and I'm not sure I would have coped as well at that age. Questioners can't catch him out because he has a cunning and a guile about him that he probably learnt from the tough environment in which he grew up. One interviewer once asked him after news broke of a new, improved pay deal, 'Well, Wayne, what are you going to do with all the extra money? Buy Coleen some more handbags?' A thick young man might have smiled weakly and mumbled something behind an embarrassed laugh in response to such a crass enquiry, which branded the footballer and his girlfriend as a couple of simpletons. But Rooney hit straight back. 'I don't know who you are, but you're very stupid,' he said. The interviewer went red in the face and received the wholesale condemnation of his fellow journalists. And rightly so. This interviewer had clearly not picked up on it, but Rooney had a lot more to talk about than his girlfriend's handbags.

So-called 'new money' has in fact been around for a few decades. People like the entrepreneur Richard Branson would be described as 'new', whereas the Duke of Westminster, who is usually labelled Britain's wealthiest man, is very much 'old' money. The aristocratic landowner inherited his billions from his forefathers, who centuries ago were lucky enough to pick up cheap plots of land in London which is now some of the most expensive real estate on earth. Branson has made his fortune, totalling hundreds of millions if not a billion pounds, in his own lifetime.

There used to be tremendous snobbery towards new wealth in Britain because of our deep-seated class divisions. New wealth was always seen to be vulgar and there was always the fear among the aristocracy that when new-money people had the sort of spending power that allowed them to dine at the Savoy, they might not know which knife and fork to pick up when they got there. But over the last two or three decades that sort of elitism has gradually disappeared. People like Sir Alan Sugar and retail king Sir Philip Green have rightly taken their places alongside old wealth.

I put a lot of this down to the change in society brought

about during the Thatcher years. Margaret Thatcher was Prime Minister of this country for eleven years, from 1979 to 1990, during which time old, inefficient state industries, loaded down with debt and disincentive, were swept away. They were replaced by a new generation of self-starters who saw the opportunity to cash in on a wave of business opportunity brought about by lower taxes and incentives to make profits. Not everybody agreed with the principle, because as a result of these sweeping changes many were left behind. The coal industry was almost closed down altogether, which left whole communities in traditional working-class areas in a desperate struggle to find new life. Nevertheless, it was the start of an era of wealth creation which goes on today. All the time new money is coming into the economy as technology provides more and more opportunities for new business.

Some of the wealthiest among the new industrialists are those who started up mobile phone businesses. Cellular phones went from being a luxury that you carried around in a briefcase, or installed in your car, to a device the size of a packet of cigarettes in ten years. Those who got in early, like my dear friend Simon Jordan, chairman of Crystal Palace, made huge fortunes.

The activities of men such as Mr Jordan became so prolific that within a few years the new money had moved alongside the old money and the two started to sit very comfortably next to each other. That then left a vacancy for a class of person whom both new and old money could look down upon and sneer at as 'very new' money. That void has been filled by footballers.

Footballers at the very top of their profession are mega-rich because of the same thing that made Charles Dunstone, the boss of The Carphone Warehouse, very wealthy. Technology. In the case of the footballer it was the advent of digital television. When Rupert Murdoch set up Sky TV in the early 1990s it was because of the advent of digital broadcasting. And when he needed something to bring in the viewers, he did what had already been done in America and bought up big tranches of sporting rights all over the world. The most valuable were for football. The game was completely reorganised to accommodate television. The FA Premier League was set up to form a separate body to the Football League, largely to allow the top division to skim off a very high percentage of the money coming into the game. It has been spectacularly successful too, each successive three-year deal bringing in two or three times the money of the previous one. More recently the Premiership has cashed in on overseas rights. Sums approaching a billion pounds a year are now rolling in.

For the 2007/08 season each club in the top flight will receive a minimum of £30 million TV money. If they are one of the top four clubs that figure could exceed £50 million. That does not take into account the gate money the club receives and the funds that are put in by sponsors queuing up to get their endorsement on a shirt or a perimeter board in front of audiences of millions.

The biggest part of a club's expenditure by far is the wage bill. Ronaldo, as noted above, is probably the highest-paid player in the country. His £125,000 a week equates to more than £6 million a year. Market forces say that he has to be paid that amount. If he wasn't, he would probably go to Real Madrid who have an even better TV rights deal because more of their money comes to them directly without having to be shared out, through the league, to other clubs. So it's no good talking about a wage-capping policy. That would just result in salary avoidance schemes, as would a plan to restrict a club's wage bill to a certain percentage of turnover. The point is, without some of the world's best players, clubs cannot be successful; and without success they would not draw in huge sums of money. One is a product of the other.

I simply can't understand why anybody would even entertain the idea of trying to restrict free market forces. Would anybody advocate that a record company should only pay its top solo singer a set amount of money, even if he was topping the charts week after week? Of course not. Such a decision would have no purpose. Those people who demand restraint on footballers' wages don't seem to be that bothered about the vast sums paid out to traders in the City of London. Some of those individuals take home annual bonuses of anything between £10 million and £50 million, which I am sure they richly deserve. Very few of us know what they do for their money, whereas footballers bring us unbridled entertainment. So why are people constantly having a dig at the footballers?

The answer is that class snobbery is alive and well in England. Add to that the rather unattractive traits of resentment, envy and malice, and you'll begin to understand. I think there is a general view that a group of very young men who have usually not had the benefit of a great education have no right at all to become multi-millionaires and live the lives we all dream of.

Every time a list of the wealthiest players is published there seems to be an outcry about their spectacular earnings. But it's not as if somebody has created a monopoly and only these young men can enter the club. Anybody who has the talent they possess will be allowed in. The problem is, of course, that not many of us have such a talent. What happens to footballers is that they are viewed in society like Lotto winners: they just happened to fill in the right numbers on the pink slip. But they didn't. They simply used their natural skills to improve their life and maximise their earnings. Nobody castigates rock stars for earning millions of pounds out of one tour. But then musicians are seen to be more artistic – even though I bet you Jamie Carragher's IQ is higher than some so-called Liverpool musicians I could mention.

Society doesn't frown on businessmen building big houses, or even other sports stars such as Nick Faldo and Michael Schumacher who have designed and built their own mansions. So why do people sneer when a footballer decides to make the best provision for his family by spending some of his wealth on a custom-built house? I was appalled when I saw the treatment England full-back Gary Neville, the Manchester United captain, received after somebody took a picture of his £6 million house under construction. An aerial shot of the building on the Lancashire moors showed what I thought was a rather tasteful building being constructed in the sort of stone that is typical of that area. It seemed to have pretty traditional woodwork, and the grounds looked as though they were being landscaped.

One criticism was that it was replacing traditional buildings going back a few centuries. But at the same time it was admitted that some of those older buildings were dilapidated. Wouldn't the critics be better off finding out why politicians have ordered the demolition of thousands of perfectly sound terraced houses across the north of England, including some just a few miles from Neville's new home?

One headline said that the 31-year-old footballer had built his twelve-bedroom house because he was 'a super-rich soccer star with mates and WAGs to impress'. Talk about total baloney. Neville's mates include Rio Ferdinand, Wayne Rooney and Cristiano Ronaldo, all of whom make more out of football than he does, and who, by the time their careers come to an end, will be ten times as wealthy as he is. When you have mates who drive around in Bentley Continentals at the age of 21 and who wear watches that cost £65,000, who exactly would you be trying to impress?

Another criticism was why did the house have twelve bedrooms. Well, why not? What about family get-togethers at Xmas? Sneeringly, it was reported that he had that many bedrooms so that his Manchester United team-mates could all go round for a sleep-over, as if they were a bunch of children.

Footballers can't live on ordinary streets. They would have people hanging around outside their gates all day long. They have to live in exclusive estates with security, or in gated mansions. They are not exactly a drain on the local authority's housing budget if they decide to build their own home.

Local historians were also said to have objected to the house as it was an 'eye-sore'. Well, as I said, it seemed to me to fit perfectly into its surroundings. If it breaches any by-laws in terms of its size or specification then it is the local council's planning officers who should be criticised.

And I object to the loathing that is directed at footballers' wives and girlfriends, or WAGs as they are called. It's just another aspect of footballers' lives which comes under criticism and which I think is far too personal and vicious. OK, so the expression 'WAGs' has become a stock-in-trade for the ladies you find on the arm of a footballer. That is journalistic licence, like 'yuppies' for the young up-and-comers of the eighties and nineties. It's the personal abuse that accompanies the expression that I don't like. Their husbands and boyfriends earn huge amounts of money, so why shouldn't they dress in expensive clothes? You never see the wife of a Hollywood movie star being derided for the cost of her outfit. I think it is particularly nasty to pick on a young girl whose life has probably been transformed from normal to extraordinary in a matter of months. She has been thrust into the public eye without any preparation in terms of defending herself against a wholesale onslaught simply because her boyfriend is a famous footballer.

A couple of years ago I was at Aintree with Porky for the Grand National meeting. The Friday was Ladies' Day, and as some of the top players are with the Liverpool teams, or, like Wayne Rooney, have Liverpool connections, it was not surprising that football's first ladies were in attendance. I thought they all looked lovely, especially Coleen McLoughlin and Alex Curran, the respective girlfriends of Rooney and Steven Gerrard. Porky couldn't take his eyes off them. Not just the WAGs but all the ladies of the north-west of England who, admittedly, do have a tendency to totter about on high heels looking like they've been enjoying a glass or three of champagne. The following day there were sneering pieces in the newspapers about the way the girls were dressed or the way they behaved. No distinction was made between what I clocked as the very demure behaviour of the football girls and the rest, who, without the sort of financial clout to hire a box and dress in designer clothes, were just out to have a great day. I don't think it's very brave to do that from behind the shield of a pen.

I would argue that footballers and their wives are portrayed to the world very unfairly when you consider the way other sportsmen and their spouses are treated. Wives accompany their husbands on cricket tours but do not get pilloried publicly in the same way. Nasser Hussain once took his wife on tour to Australia when she was expecting, and in an effort to be present at the birth had to zig-zag across the country, sometimes leaving the team camp. The cricketers themselves get treated more leniently too. In the middle of the 2007 cricket World Cup in the West Indies, England's outstanding cricketer, Freddie Flintoff, was reported to have nearly drowned at four a.m. one morning when he was out on a pedalo after a huge night on the beer. Now, I'm not being judgemental about that. But if he had been a footballer there would have been a national outcry and calls to bring him home. Footballers in the past have been expelled for drinking in the middle of competitions. Flintoff was merely stripped of the vice-captaincy, despite having been fined before as a result of his 'socialising activities' while on tour. In 2005 he established himself as a folk-hero for leading England to Ashes glory, and for being intoxicated and red-eyed for about three days afterwards, which included a visit to see the Prime Minister in Downing Street. 'Getting Freddied' is now a well-established expression in cricket for having a few too many. And after England crashed out of the World Cup in the Caribbean, Flintoff was again pictured in the early hours in a bar in Barbados looking very much the worse for wear.

The woman who comes in for the worst treatment in this country is Victoria Beckham. 'Posh Spice' is a constant target of the poison-pen. The usual portrayal is that she spends her life with a pout on her face and does nothing except hang off David Beckham's arm. But nobody ever mentions that she was a member of The Spice Girls, the most successful girl group that ever hit the charts, with nine number one hits. Whether the rest of society likes it or not, people like the Beckhams are forming a new social stratum that will last for many generations.

Footballers are generally regarded as being of average education, even though there are plenty of examples of graduates, such as Steve Coppell and Ian Dowie, getting to the top in the game. Frank Lampard is probably the only footballer in Britain who has a top O-level pass in Latin. His father, of course, Big Frank, was himself an England international footballer with West Ham. But there are going to be plenty of children of footballers who distinguish themselves academically in the future. I know a lot of young pros who have put their sons' names down for Eton, our top public school, which has produced more than twenty Prime Ministers.

I am all for giving your kids a great education if you can. When I was a footballer my girls went to private schools. It is the best gift you can give to them. In one generation, the very new money will have merged with the old money as the kids of soccer stars rub shoulders with the youngsters whose fathers are captains of industry or lords and knights of the realm. Maybe then society will start to accept that footballers have a real place in the structure of our society.

Their presence in society has been called the FB Index, i.e. FootBaller Index, a play on the FT or Financial Times Index. They are massive wealth creators. By definition they then become big consumers. That stimulates demand, which is the vital component that keeps the economy going. Part of the reason why properties at the top end of the housing market go up by as much as 30 per cent a year is because so many rich people are chasing them. Among them are footballers. Some car showrooms in Surrey and Cheshire exist largely to supply the pros with cars, often tailor-made to their needs with specially woven cloth on the seats and hosts of extras. One small town in the home counties is home to dozens of fashion shops and very little else to cope with the insatiable demands of the WAGs.

Football has created its own trickle-down economy. For instance, a big house needs a housekeeper, and somebody to care for the gardens. Somebody has to maintain the estate too. Drivers are needed, as well as nannies and childminders. A collection of other people surrounds every footballer: an agent, accountants, financial advisers, people to run fan clubs and handle merchandise.

David Beckham, for instance, is a one-man industry. With all the endorsements he has, people have to be employed to facilitate the business. He earns about £30 million a year, and his total wealth currently is £112 million. Any company producing that sort of turnover could easily be employing twenty people, and Beckham is no exception.

Many other footballers have used their earning power to create even more wealth. Robbie Fowler of Liverpool, for instance, recognised very early on the value of property and how it would continue to soar in value. One estimate of his wealth as a result has been put at £80 million. Michael Owen is recognised as one of the richest footballers of the current era. He was named as the wealthiest player under the age of 30 in Britain with a fortune of £37 million. And just like Robbie Fowler, his one-time Liverpool team-mate, he has made his money work for him in property. He has also set up a yard for racehorses and apparently intends to move into bloodstock full-time when his playing career is over.

There are no guarantees when you invest in racehorses. Believe me, I know that to my cost. But you only have to look at the examples of the legendary Robert Sangster, Irish investor John Magnier and the Maktoum family of Dubai to realise that if you get it right there are vast fortunes to be made. In order to launch his business, Michael, 27, has bought himself a big spread with up to 50 boxes for a reported £9 million.

I don't think the world has yet fully appreciated the economic power of the football industry. It generates billions of pounds a year all around the globe. In terms of individual British footballers alone, the spending power is phenomenal. The Sunday Times Rich List assessed the top twenty players under the age of 30 to be worth a collective £300 million. That figure does not of course include the richest footballer of them all, David Beckham, nor players who cashed in at the start of the big-money era but are now retired, such as Alan Shearer. Economists say that collectively the 'grey brigade' could represent another billion pounds of football money.

The high-profile role footballers now have in society has been used both for good and for bad. There are far too many cases of young players misbehaving and abusing their wealth, and I would rather not have to read about those things. But there are countless acts of generosity too which do not receive anything like the same amount of coverage. David and Victoria Beckham have given millions to charity, particularly to help disadvantaged children. Niall Quinn, now the chairman of Sunderland FC, gave away his entire million-pound purse when he was given a testimonial. Many other players have done the same.

Rio Ferdinand came in for a lot of stick when he was hassling over his latest pay deal. What is less well known is that he gives away hundreds of thousands of pounds to causes which include helping youngsters who are growing up in the tough neighbourhood where he was born. Steven Gerrard is another man who has not forgotten his roots. Footballers from both of the Merseyside giants, Everton and Liverpool, spend hours visiting local children's hospitals, a policy pursued by many other clubs across the country. Everton player Lee Carsley supports a Down's syndrome trust in the Midlands, where he comes from, as one of his own children has the condition.

One young footballer who never fails to impress me with his generous spirit is Chelsea's Joe Cole. It did not surprise me when I learnt that 25-year-old Joe stuck his hand in his pocket to fork out £20,000 to help a former Chelsea footballer who had fallen on hard times. Peter Brabrook played in Chelsea's 1955 league championship-winning squad. Joe's father George, a lovely, down-to-earth man, heard that 69-year-old Brabrook was struggling to find the money for two knee operations, the legacy of his footballing career. George knows the value of a pound, having brought young Joe up by rising at three o'clock every morning in all weathers to run his fruit and veg business, and he realised that the cost of reconstruction work on the knees was probably beyond the old Chelsea player. Brabrook had had the job done on his left leg but couldn't afford to go ahead with similar work on his other knee. When Joe heard of the problem he bunged a cheque in the post for the full amount. Unsurprisingly, Brabrook said later, 'It is hard to comprehend someone showing such kindness.'

I know a lot of people will say that £20,000 is not a lot to a footballer who probably earns three or four times that a week. But for anybody to hand over a sum of money like that – still a year's wages for some workers – shows a generosity of spirit that is not associated often enough with footballers.

I'd had previous experience of Joe Cole's kindness. I've already told you about the traumatic times of Porky's illness and his struggle back to reasonable health. As a consequence of the fact that he has made such a spectacular recovery, Porky now does a lot of work for heart charities, in particular for Harefield Hospital where he is still an out-patient. When the hospital organised a Summer Fair to celebrate 25 years of heart transplants and 22 years of transplants for children, to help make the day go with a bang Porky tried to find a current footballer who would be prepared to go along to Harefield for a few hours on a Sunday afternoon. He got a phone call from George Cole who said that Joe would be very happy to do it providing that Jose Mourinho didn't keep the players back in the afternoon as they were in intensive pre-season training.

I remember it was a boiling hot day, and down at the hospital there were dozens of little kids running around the edge of the lake. There was a marquee so that those who were still ill, either recovering from or waiting for a transplant, could get some shade with their families. Porky's phone rang to say that Joe was on the way. But you never really believe these things until they happen. Harefield is just off the M25, one of the most notorious roads in Europe for traffic snarl-ups. I've already ranted about the motorways in this country. I have lost count of the number of hours I have sat motionless on the 'London orbital'. It is so notorious that the pop star Chris Rea wrote his hit song about it – 'The Road to Hell'. Anything could have happened, especially as Joe had to get from the Chelsea training ground in Cobham, Surrey, down the A3 to the M25 and then around the M25 to the M40 where he would have to head a couple of miles 'inland' to Harefield. On a bad day that could take up to two hours.

But we were lucky. Within an hour, Joe and his father arrived. Perhaps because I was a footballer myself, I sometimes forget the excitement a real-life star can generate. After all, most people only ever see their heroes on TV, or as a distant figure on the field. Joe is a diminutive figure and the children were running around him in circles, calling him 'Coley Joe'. Within minutes of arriving a large crowd had gathered around him. Autographs, pictures, a kickabout with the kids – nothing was too much trouble for him. He even did an interview on the stage with Porky, extolling the virtues of healthy living and making the point about how lucky he and his team-mates were to enjoy good health when so many people are unlucky enough to be struck down. I got the overwhelming impression that inside that young man was the genuine feeling that life is a lottery, and he wanted to use his good fortune to help those who had been unlucky.

Part of trying to deal with any illness is how you cope with it mentally. When people feel good, they are better equipped to fight back. When Joe left the hospital that afternoon he left behind him a sea of smiling faces. He stayed for more than three hours and he worked non-stop. He had trouble getting out of the car park because scores of people surrounded his car. I've seen players getting away from Wembley easier when they have won the FA Cup.

Another footballer who is immensely kind is Wayne Rooney. That statement may stop a few people in their tracks, because the public image of the England striker is one of a snarling pitbull terrier who never stops mouthing off at referees. But there is a different person off the pitch. His girlfriend Coleen has an adopted sister, Rosie, who is severely disabled. The little girl needs constant care and often has to visit the world-famous Alder Hey Children's Hospital in Liverpool. Wayne was little more than a child himself when he burst on to the footballing scene at the age of sixteen by scoring a spectacular goal against Arsenal. He must have been so proud of that introduction to adult football. It was his first goal in the Premiership. But instead of taking his match boots home for posterity, he gave them to the Alder Hey Hospital so that they could auction them and use the money to help sick children. He gave one of his first England shirts to another children's charity which auctioned it for thousands of pounds.

I have, in the past, described my pal Porky as Rooney's love-child. It's fair to say that he was obsessed with the emergence of such a raw young talent in an Everton shirt. As I have already described, Porky and I were in Portugal together for Euro 2004 when Rooney was storming the football world and Porky became very ill. One of the reasons why, even after he was transferred to Manchester United, Porky continued to revere Rooney as a footballer was the kindness he showed him. Not many people have a 'Get Well Soon' card from one of the world's top footballers pinned up on their wall. Porky also got a shirt. Just as those patients at Harefield felt better when Joe Cole was around, so Porky felt elated when his shirt from Rooney arrived on the ward. Nobody has been able to explain how my pal pulled himself back from the position where he needed a heart transplant or he was going to die. He swears his recovery started the minute he saw that sloping Rooney signature on that shirt. He's often told me, 'Wayne Rooney saved my life.' And that is why to this day he is reluctant to rise up against him whenever the world is baying for his blood.

Prior to the emergence of Wayne Rooney, Porky had been just as obsessive about another Everton footballer, and that was Alan Ball. As you know, I was very, very saddened when I heard the news that Bally had died. I've just talked about modern young superstars. I think it's fair to say that along with George Best, Alan was one of the first of that breed. People forget that he was only 21 when he was clutching a World Cup winner's medal, something Ronaldo, Rooney, Messi and Kaka will never do.

He was a big mate of mine, and I had been going racing with him for years. He was infectious in his enthusiasm for everything. I'll never forget that time at Newmarket when Porky made a complete fool of himself. I think it was probably the first time I had introduced him to Alan and it was clear that he was completely star-struck. He wanted to know all about the World Cup victory and even more about his conquests with Everton. After a few glasses of wine Porky suddenly fell to his knees in front of him and started bowing and chanting, 'We are not worthy of you.' It was very embarrassing. Here was a grown man and a national broadcaster acting like a teenager. But Alan just laughed his head off. He could see Everton Football Club burning a hole in his heart.

While I feel that footballers are generally maligned, I have never heard anybody say one bad word against Bally. How could you?

When I say that footballers are given a bad time, I know a lot of you will think, 'Well he would say that, wouldn't he?' Of course there are modern footballers who misbehave. They are young men, full of energy and adrenalin, with a huge competitive spirit. But for the most part, because they have by definition had to be disciplined to get where they are, they are a force for good in our society.

In 2007, Manchester United's Ronaldo picked up both the Footballer of the Year and Young Footballer of the Year awards. When I saw him picking up his trophies I felt pride as a former footballer, even if the 'bling' is something we weren't into in my day. The Portuguese winger with wizardry in his feet looked strong and confident. At 22 years of age he gave a gracious acceptance speech in perfect English, and you can only say he is a credit to our game.

In addition to my wife Jill, of course, the three people most precious to me are my beautiful daughters. If somebody asked me, 'After what you know about footballers, would you let your daughter marry one?' my answer would be, 'Of course. But can he cut down on the earrings, please?'

CHAPTER NINE

FLOWER OF SCOTLAND

'If you had told me when I was a twelve-year-old kid that one day I would eat at the same table as Tommy Gemmell inside the hallowed portals of Celtic Park, I would never have believed it.'

MY OLD international team-mate Alex McLeish had just been made the Rangers manager. I was making my way with Porky to the champagne bar at Stansted airport, and a friend from Glasgow had just rung to tell me the news. I am a Celtic man, but I was nevertheless delighted that my '82 World Cup campaign pal had risen to the top. The chair at Ibrox was one of the choice domestic jobs in British football.

Amazingly, as I chatted to Porky about playing for my country with McLeish, we turned a corner and literally bumped into the boy himself.

'Bloody hell, Alex,' I said in astonishment, 'I've just heard the news.'

We greeted each other warmly. He had just flown down from the north. Until that day in December 2001 he had been the successful manager of Hibernian; now he was in the hottest seat in the game. Rangers had been having a reasonably successful time under the Dutch coach Dick Advocaat, but now the young and dynamic Martin O'Neill was busy reinvigorating my own club, Celtic. Alex had been handed the poisoned chalice.

But knowing him as I did there was no doubt in my mind

that he was the right man for the job. Alex had always been the quiet man in the squad, he was very understated, but he had an almost menacing presence about him when he was in charge of things. He had spent a lot of his career as a player working under Sir Alex Ferguson, his manager at Aberdeen, and later in charge of the national team. He had never shirked a challenge in his life. In fact, as a 'Hoop' I was rather disappointed that the Rangers board had been astute enough to appoint him.

I congratulated him on his success and said, 'Crikey, you're going to feel the pressure there, aren't you?'

With a mischievous smile on his lips he replied, 'Oh, I wouldn't say that. All I've got to do is win every game.'

'Yeah, well, if you could just lose the odd four plus a couple of cup games each season, we won't fall out,' I said.

We laughed heartily.

The news of the appointment could not have come at a better time, as Porky and I were on our way to Glasgow. We were going to do our breakfast show from a pub in the city the following morning before going off to the Celtic v. Rangers game at Parkhead. For me, it was going to be one of the great weekends of the year. I never need an excuse to visit my homeland, and if there happens to be an Old Firm game on at the same time, that is an added bonus.

I have often been accused of being a belligerent Scotsman. I'm not belligerent, I'm just unashamedly proud to be Scottish. There is no greater honour than to play for your country. I did that thirteen times at the top level and donned the shirt many more times at under-21 and junior levels. I represented my country in a World Cup. I played at Hampden Park, the national stadium I could see from my bedroom window throughout my childhood. I walked out for Scotland at Wembley. Contrary to popular belief, I do not dislike the English. But on a weekend like this you tend to become very 'Jockish', and if there happens to be an Englishman nearby whom you can wind up in a merciless fashion, the Sassenach is going to get it. It was therefore tough luck on Porky. He had never been to a Glasgow derby game before so he was about to find out all about fervour and passion.

Porky had just settled into a corner of the bar and started sipping champagne when he gave me my first golden opportunity to catch him out. He piped up that he had forgotten to bring a tie, which he would need for the lunch we had been invited to at Celtic Park the following day. I offered to go with him to Tie-Rack. I knew his suit would be dark blue because it was the only colour he ever bought. He was looking at all sorts of dopey yellow patterns when I pointed out just the tie he needed. It was broad blue with red stripes and a thinner white one. I convinced my pal that it would be perfect, and he agreed.

But it was cruel of me. To him it was a boldly coloured tie. To me and my rather fiendish sense of humour it might as well have been a Rangers club tie. And as we were going to be guests at the holy Celtic shrine the following day he was certain to come in for bucket-loads of stick. I couldn't contain my laughter when Porky asked the shop assistant if he thought it was right for a dark blue suit. When he asked me what I was laughing at I just shook my head and said, 'Wee Alex McLeish. I'm so pleased for the boy. He's done so well.'

The flight north was full of Glaswegians going home for

the big game. It was an incredible atmosphere, and the juices for my homeland bubbled through my veins. I was among my own, and apart from being with the family on a skiing holiday or around the pool at home, there isn't a better feeling in the world.

That night I took Porky on a tour of the city. The longer I spent in the company of my old mates the more guttural my Scottish accent became. By the end of a great night in an Irish piano bar just off Glasgow's George Square, Porky couldn't understand a word I was saying, nor could he make out the string of insults being delivered to him one after the other by my old friends. This was no night to be an Englishman in the city, though Porky was oblivious to the fact. Everywhere we went it was like a rowdy eve-of-battle party. And each time one of the lads patted the lone Sassenach on the shoulder and told him in the local dialect that he was a complete dickhead, or something far worse, he just smiled broadly and gave it the thumbs up. This prompted the rest of the lads to collapse in mirth. Porky, who thought he had just been told a very funny joke, would then laugh even more.

Word had got around that we were in town. Until I arrived in Glasgow I hadn't realised what a large and loyal audience we had north of the border. Every taxi we got into that night was tuned in to our station, talkSPORT, and the minute we opened our mouths they knew who we were. We had great trouble even paying the fares as people seemed to be genuinely pleased to see us – well, me anyway.

The next morning we broadcast our Saturday morning breakfast show from the Lismore pub on the Dumbarton Road, one of the best drinking establishments in the city. In charge was an old pal called Steve. Incredible care had been taken to keep the place in shape. The craftsmanship on parts of the pub was quite beautiful. The windows had been fashioned in stained glass and told historical tales of the Scottish people. The floors were polished wood and the bar and the fittings were like burnished gold. Steve doesn't allow anybody in the pub to wear a football shirt, which gives it a great atmosphere no matter which part of the city you hail from. Dozens of people came down to see us and it was all very good-natured. I intermittently chuckled because Porky had left his tie on the seat behind our transmission desk. I wondered how much trouble that was going to cause that afternoon.

I soon found out. A car came to take us to the ground, and though we could have got out right by the main entrance I insisted we go down to the far end where we would encounter the main bulk of Celtic fans. As I got out of the car I got a big cheer from the fans. I'm a very well-known Celtic fan in my own city. My tally of 62 goals in one season for Celtic Boys Club is still a record. In a lot of places Porky and I visit I am usually the better known, but he is automatically recognised by association. So as soon as he stepped out of the car, Rangers tie and all, the cheers turned to boos.

Ever since we had begun working together I had regularly baited him that he was a secret Rangers fan. That way, if, on a rare occasion, Celtic got beaten by 'the auld enemy', Porky would get a load of abusive e-mails and callers, and that would make for great radio. In truth, he had no feelings at all for a Scottish team. If anything, he should have been accepted as a 'Hoop' because he and his family from Chester are lifelong Everton fans. He once told me that the origins of Everton were

Catholic as the club had derived from St Domingo's Church, though the religious attachment had long since disappeared. Certainly there is a well-established connection between Celtic and Liverpool. The clubs share the same anthem, 'You'll Never Walk Alone', and the transfer in the 1970s of Kenny Dalglish to Anfield created strong bonds.

Porky was puzzled by the booing. It was quite mild as he eased himself out of the car, but then, when the army of Celts saw that he was wearing a 'Rangers' tie, they went mad. The booing turned to baying, as if they were after blood. Porky was completely mystified as to why he was so instantly unpopular on his first ever visit to this classic fixture.

Unfortunately, I had also misjudged the mood. It was so long since I'd been a kid on the terraces at Parkhead that I'd forgotten the extent of the burning animosity that can sometimes exist between the two sets of fans. I quickly sensed that the best thing to do was to get out of the way. I grabbed Porky's sleeve, bolted for the door and dragged him with me. But as we went I saw some form of missile coming over the top of the crowd. Porky yelped as a heavy roundish object caught him. Then another, and another. It was a volley of oranges, and by now my pal was trying to shield his head from the attack. I can only assume that his tormentors were using oranges because of the connection between Rangers and the Protestant king William of Orange. The Celtic fans at the front of the crowd had started to laugh when the barrage began, but when they saw it was turning into less than a bit of fun they turned on the orange throwers.

I cursed myself for buying the tie. It certainly wasn't supposed to have turned out like this. Still, we'd managed to get inside. No damage to Porky that a couple of glasses of Chardonnay wouldn't put right.

I ate lunch sitting next to 'Lisbon Lion' Tommy Gemmell, the full-back who scored in the glorious European Cup victory of 1967. It didn't matter at that moment that I had played for my country, as Tommy had. It was irrelevant to me that I too had achieved European glory, with Ipswich and Spurs. Anyway, it wasn't at anything like the level Tommy had reached. The fact was, I was sitting down for lunch with a Lisbon Lion. If you had told me when I was a twelve-year-old kid that one day I would eat at the same table as Tommy Gemmell inside the hallowed portals of Celtic Park, I would never have believed it. Forget the footballing achievements, this was one of the great moments of my life, as great for me as it would be for a young boxing fan to sit down to lunch with Muhammad Ali.

Celtic won the game, and we were invited to a celebration party in honour of the New Jersey, USA, branch of the Celtic Supporters Club. Sixty American fans had come over for the game and there was a huge party in the basement of one of the Glasgow hotels.

Porky was still wearing his 'Rangers' tie. He would not take it off on a point of principle. He argued that as he wasn't a Rangers fan and wasn't wearing their colours, he had no intention of bowing to the orange throwers he'd met on the way in. Nevertheless, he accepted that it did look as though he was a Rangers supporter, and as we were guests of a group of Celtic fans and we were at a huge 'Hoops' party it looked a bit provocative.

In the crazy world of Porky's logic, he bought a Celtic hat and a lapel badge in the belief that it would even things up.

All it did was confuse people.

We were invited up on the stage to say a few words about the game. I was full of joy at the result whereas my pal, who had been working on anaesthetising his orange wounds with wine, started out on a long, rambling speech about uniting the communities in Glasgow. It was such a disjointed load of old rubbish that people actually thought it was supposed to be funny. He talked about 'hands across the Forth', which of course is the river that runs through Edinburgh. The Clyde is what he meant. He tripped over his microphone lead and crashed into a musician's guitar, which emitted the most terrible high-pitched whining that nobody seemed to be able to stop. When he finished, Porky waved to the crowd and wandered off as though he had solved the problem of sectarianism in Glasgow which had, after all, only been around for about 500 years.

But then somebody else played a cruel trick on my mate. Porky's Celtic cap was whipped off and replaced with a sort of 'Noddy' hat in the colours of the Irish tricolour. There was a blue flash. Somebody had taken a picture of him, and within a few days that image had started to appear on Rangers websites. Websites were still in their infancy in those days, but when the picture was later published in some sort of Rangers fanzine, Porky managed to completely alienate himself from both sides of Glasgow. Each set of fans accused him of being a secret supporter of the other side. The truth was that he wasn't a supporter of either, he just didn't understand the culture of the city.

This became overwhelmingly clear when on another occasion I foolishly took him to the most fiercely pro-Celtic bar in the whole of Scotland, Heraghty's in the east end of Glasgow. It is an Irish bar, so not unnaturally there were a few individuals in there I suppose you could describe as having Republican sympathies. We were going in there to meet a few old mates, and to watch on the telly a rugby international between England and Ireland from Lansdowne Road.

This was probably my worst mistake ever when it came to winding up Porky. It is no exaggeration to say that he was the only Englishman in an absolutely packed bar full of rabid Scotsmen of Irish descent. Most of them had a look on their face like the warriors in *Braveheart*, just before going into battle. There was no semblance of reason in the place. The noise was like being in a railway tunnel with a steam locomotive coming towards you. Even I remember shuddering at the intensity of the support for Ireland, and I was among my own people. Men were actually hanging off the ceiling, from a light-fitting or a water pipe, to make sure they got the best possible view of the big screen.

Now, if there is one thing that Porky most definitely is, it is a proud Englishman. At first his lone voice could not be heard amid the raucous din that erupted every time Ireland picked up the ball. But then England scored. I put my finger to my lips to indicate to Porky not to make too much of it. But he wasn't having it. He started singing 'Land of Hope and Glory'.

Beer started flying in his direction, and soon he was soaked. But as England had the upper hand he didn't seem to care. Then more madness afflicted him. He climbed up on a chair and started berating the fans around him, accusing them of being traitors to their country. I remember him shouting things like 'That's why Scotland will always be a joke country. You lot don't know whether you want to be Irish or Scottish. Why are you all supporting Ireland, eh? It's not Dublin that pays out your social security, it's London. If you like Ireland so much, why don't you all push off back there and save the English taxpayer a few quid?' The amazing thing is, we had only been in the bar for about ten minutes and he'd hardly had anything to drink.

Needless to say, his rantings caused a furore. People started poking him and threatening to shut him up. I kept telling Porky to shut up, but he was only spurred on by their reaction.

'Why do you lot want to take on the identity of another country?' he continued. 'Are you ashamed of your own? I don't call myself French just because William the Conqueror got lucky on the beach at Hastings when Harold wasn't looking.'

Now a group of people surged over to Porky, and somebody grabbed him round the throat. I tried to grapple with his attacker. But again, instead of quietening down, Porky was emboldened by the maelstrom of aggression he had whipped up. As I desperately tried to intervene, he was wrestled to the floor. As he went down, he shouted, 'You lot should be supporting England, not Ireland! What has Ireland ever done for you? We gave you rugby, not them!' And, just as he disappeared completely under a pile of bodies, I heard a muffled 'God save the Queen!'

Now I had to get stuck in. Fortunately I had a couple of pals with me. We rolled into the fray and somehow hauled Porky out. At that moment the pub manager came bursting through the crowd. Amazingly, it was Danny, a classmate from my school, Holyrood. We'd seen each other on and off over the years.

Danny was boiling with anger. 'For Christ's sake Al, get him out of here before he wrecks the place,' he said. Then, pointing his arm very resolutely towards the door like a referee sending off a player, he barked out, even louder, 'Take him out or I'll knock him out!'

Still Porky wasn't having it. 'I'm not going anywhere!' he stated, even as other angry Scotsmen were trying to get at him. We hauled him towards the exit, using our forearms to ward off swinging fists and bottles. 'What happened to free speech?' he wailed. 'This place is a banana republic!'

At that point I punched him in the ribs. It had the desired effect: he let out a gasp and his knees buckled. We dragged him out and frogmarched him down the street.

Porky has always had an unfortunate relationship with Scotsmen. In turn, they have always had a strained relationship with him. I put it down to the England v. Scotland game in June 1977 when we descended from north of the border to beat England at their hallowed home, Wembley. I think it badly affected him, and warped his mind. It wasn't so much the result, more the conditions that surrounded it. One night when we were in the Carlton George Hotel in Glasgow he told me the full story.

He lived in the north of England at the time and was a cub reporter on a weekly newspaper in his home town of Chester. He went down to London with his mate from Birkenhead, and it was the first proper visit, apart from school trips, they had ever made to the capital. From the time he got off the train at Euston, Porky was appalled to be surrounded by Scotsmen. He was even more horrified that when they got to Wembley there were virtually no other Englishmen in sight.

He was learning one of the truisms of life: when the oldest international fixture gets played in England, Wembley gets taken over by Jocks. It had happened for years, and it was still happening when I played for my country in front of the twin towers in 1983.

Worse still, he had suffered a dreadful experience with some Scottish fans on a tube train to the ground. He was crushed in next to a man with a shock of wild ginger hair wearing a kilt and a Scotland shirt who was clutching a bottle from which he was swigging neat vodka. Thinking he was being amusing, Porky said to the Scots fan, 'You've already had too much, mate. You're a Scotsman. You're supposed to be drinking Scotch. What's with the vodka? You're pissed.'

The Scotsman gave him a steely-eyed look, then said very lucidly, 'I prefer vodka. I think it's a very civilised drink. Don't you?'

Porky realised that his stab at a bit of humorous camaraderie with the Scottish fans had completely failed. And as he and his mate were outnumbered by about 300 to one he nodded his head heartily, raised his thumb and said, 'Absolutely.'

The Scotsman lowered his head right into Porky's face and said with barely disguised menace, 'In that case I insist that you join me for a wee dram.' He thrust the bottle into Porky's hand.

Porky had never drunk neat vodka before, but, under the circumstances, he thought it would be a good idea not to refuse. He lifted the bottle to his lips and, deciding not to look at the rim in case it was too horrible, took a very quick swig. The firewater hit him in the back of his throat, almost catapulting his eyes out of his sockets and creating a burning sensation down his gullet and into his stomach which almost made him retch.

'Did you enjoy that?' said his Scots friend.

Porky's voice had gone. Gasping for breath and swallowing intently to keep everything down, he nodded vigorously.

'In that case you must join me for another. And this time, don't just cover it with your tongue. Have a real drink.'

The Scotsman was with a whole gang of pals. Porky had no choice. He raised the bottle gingerly to his mouth again, trying to constrict his throat against another intense attack. But just as the rim rested on his bottom lip an arm appeared from somewhere and pushed the bottle up. The vodka didn't just run down my pal's throat. It went up his nose, into his eyes, down his shirt and even around the back of his neck. As Porky coughed and spluttered and tried to regain his composure, a gaggle of Scotsmen, and even Porky's mate, gripped their sides with mirth.

But it wasn't even that unfortunate experience that warped Porky's view of his cousins north of the border. The game was the one after which the victorious Scottish fans tore Wembley apart. The goalposts and bars disappeared, as did seats and other artefacts from the most famous football stadium in the world.

To cap it all, what I think really disturbed Porky's mind happened later that evening, when he and his mate were trying to find a bar in Piccadilly Circus that was not full of Scotsmen. As he staggered from one kerb to another he came across a Jock sleeping on the pavement. He was comfortably settled on what looked like a dark-coloured duvet. Porky tripped on the edge of the duvet and it squashed under his foot. He looked closer and discovered to his total angst that the boy on the floor was actually lying on a huge sod of turf.

The horror of the situation hit Porky immediately. He had already had to endure the humiliation, as an Englishman, of watching Scotsmen tear Wembley to pieces. What he had not realised until now was that in addition to the goalposts and bars, they had taken huge chunks of the hallowed turf with them as well. Mentally, it knocked Porky out. He wondered whether his hero the late, great Alan Ball had covered every blade of the grass that was now deposited like an old rug on a dirty pavement. I think he's held a grudge against the Scots ever since.

Despite my rantings on my radio show on talkSPORT, I don't hold any grievance at all against the English. Well, except maybe for one.

Those of us from north of the border don't believe that Scots footballers have ever been given the credit they deserve for the success of British football. Remember, when Celtic became the first team from these isles to capture the European Cup, they were made up of eleven Scots lads all born within a 30-mile radius of Celtic Park; and when Manchester United, Liverpool and Nottingham Forest were storming through the Continent, their teams were bolstered by Scotsmen. The Celts didn't need any Englishmen to help them, but the English clubs needed the Jocks. And we are talking about world-class players such as Denis Law – who, though he didn't play in the 1968 final, did so much to get United there – Kenny Dalglish and Alan Hansen at Liverpool, and Kenny Burns and little Johnny Robertson at Forest.

Even that wouldn't be a problem – we're happy to help out in our missionary work – if it wasn't for the spectre of 1966. Every single day of my life I hear about England winning the World Cup. Ramsey's wingless wonders; that glorious day under the twin towers; blah, blah, blah. It's enough to drive you mad. Move on. Germany keep winning World Cups. Italy have just done so, and Brazil and Argentina always will. England can't get themselves into perspective. Yes, they did brilliantly to carry off the top trophy in football. But it was on home territory, there were only sixteen teams in the finals compared to 32 today, and, most importantly, it happened 41 years ago now and they have never been able to repeat the feat.

People like Porky drive me mad. He makes wild predictions that England are going to win every competition they enter. It is an arrogance that generally infects the English. Maybe it's because England was at the heart of the British Empire. Perhaps English people still have a thing about gunboat diplomacy. Are the natives being rebellious? Well, send a couple of frigates and as soon as the locals see the White Ensign fluttering on the horizon they will flee back to the hills. This is the sort of attitude I pick up all the time while working with my friends in London.

I took absolutely no comfort in England's poor performance in the World Cup in Germany in 2006. Their predicament echoed the public debate that has been taking place in Scotland for decades. Under German coach Berti Vogts Scotland were absolutely awful as a national team, though, in fairness, he had very few talented players to work with. But previous coaches have had tremendous talent to work with. Dalglish and Hansen I've just mentioned; then there's Peter Lorimer, Gordon McQueen, Joe Jordan, Charlie Cooke, Jim

Baxter, the Lisbon Lions, Danny McGrain, Gary McAllister – the list of truly world-class players is endless. I'm not sure I was ever good enough to join that exalted company, but I have to mention my Ipswich team-mate Johnny Wark, who could have stood his ground with any player in history. But for some reason no coach was ever able to pull the talent together to make a concerted impression in international competitions. And that is precisely what England have been accused of in recent years.

Most recently, England were said to have had a 'golden age'. When the squad set off for Germany there was tremendous optimism about their chances. All the factors were in their favour. The competition was in Europe. The hosts, Germany, were not as strong as they normally were. There was no great threat from South America either, Brazil having laboured their way to the finals. Football, in fact, was looking for a great international team. Against all expectations Greece had won the European Championship two years earlier in Portugal, and they didn't even qualify for the World Cup finals. The 1998 World Cup winners, France, were having to rely on a number of players returning from international retirement just to be able to assemble a credible squad.

Against this backdrop, I agree that England had a great chance of glory. Player by player they had a formidable team: great defenders in John Terry and Rio Ferdinand, and outstanding midfielders such as Steven Gerrard, Frank Lampard and Joe Cole. They also had a potential world-beater in Wayne Rooney, and the 'oomph' factor in their captain, David Beckham. On paper it looked very good, and as usual the English went barmy about their chances. Months before the tournament even came into sight it seemed as if every second car on the road was flying the flag of St George, and every kid was walking around in an England shirt. But that's not necessarily a problem. What irritates the non-English is when you read that plans have already been drawn up for a victory party at Downing Street.

Porky is the very worst sort of English fan, totally arrogant about the English and horribly dismissive of the other home countries and the Republic of Ireland. He questions whether it is worth Northern Ireland having a team at all, and dismissed the Welsh as makeweights in their World Cup qualifying group. He said from the start that England would win it. There was no rationale behind his approach. As far as he is concerned, when England are playing abroad, they are doing the world a favour just by turning up. Every other country England were due to play were either 'second rate', 'fallen giants' or 'banana republics'. He regularly deluded himself by telling everybody that the mere sight of Wayne Rooney in the tunnel would reduce opposition defenders to quivering wrecks.

Porky was way over the top in the lead-up to the 2006 World Cup, and most English fans I meet are exactly like that. According to Porky's mob, it is a conspiracy that England have only ever won one World Cup. The world's footballing authorities are plotting against them all the time, and 'foreigners' are treated more leniently on the pitch than Englishmen. What Porky doesn't realise is that by adopting a superior attitude he is actually fuelling the superiority complex of the Englishman. And it's not just the Scots that resent this way of thinking. It irks all football people around the world. I genuinely believe that the reason why England fans get singled out sometimes when they are abroad is because of the superior attitude they exude.

Compare them to Scottish fans. I played in a World Cup for my country and not one single fan got arrested during our campaign that summer in Spain. The tartan army felt privileged to be there. We are a small nation, and it takes a supreme effort to get on to the world stage and take our place with the likes of Brazil. It is something most Scotsmen pray for, and when it comes about they feel they have been blessed. When the fans travel out there, they realise they are guests in somebody else's country and they respect that. It's all very well to say it's only a minority of England fans who have caused trouble over the years, but the majority have an obligation to deal with the minority. With the tartan army, anybody who stepped out of line would be whipped straight back in.

I became aware of an example of that during the 1982 World Cup. When you are away with an international squad you always have a few fans hanging around the camp whom you've seen before. They are devotees; they just like to be in the same arena as the players. If they saw Graeme Souness or Kenny Dalglish coming back from training it just gave them a good feeling. They weren't anoraks. In fact it was OK to have them nearby because through them you got direct feedback from the fans.

One of them told me about an incident that had taken place in Marbella. They were in a Chinese restaurant having a big nosh-up with a few beers. They were boisterous but well behaved. Another group of supporters were sitting at the table nearest the door. They were quiet and sullen. They seemed to be whispering to one another, plotting something. This group eventually called for their bill. Too soon after it arrived, they complained as one about being overcharged and demanded to see the manager. The waiter disappeared behind a curtain. The fan who was telling the story said he knew exactly what was going to happen next. Sure enough, the quiet bunch kicked their chairs back and all of them sprinted through the door.

Before the Chinese waiters had even realised what was going on, the boisterous mob also kicked their chairs back and sprinted out. But this second bunch weren't trying to avoid paying their bill, they were after the first lot to try to stop them. There were more of the second group than the first and they caught the runners and overpowered them. They dragged them back to the restaurant where they then had to protect them from knife-wielding waiters. They made the boys pay up. And when the 'runners' couldn't produce enough money, those who had apprehended them made up the difference. The police never got called, but the good guys told the bad guys that if they ever saw their faces around the Scottish contingent again, they would give them a kicking. It is assumed that they went home.

I was very proud of my countrymen when I heard that story. I don't know who those boys were, but the way they dealt with that situation leads me to believe that they could sort out the nightmare of Iraq a lot more quickly than the thousands of diplomats and politicians who created the quagmire in the first place.

I think the problem with the English is that they don't actually have a national identity. Indeed, they have had to invent one. The flag of St George, as far as I can remember, has only been the symbol of English football for the last few decades. The flag of St Andrew and the golden Scottish lion on a blue flag has been the symbol of my country since time immemorial. For some reason the English gave up on the Union Jack some time between winning the World Cup in 1966 and Italia '90. If you look at all the old pictures of 1966 you will see that the multi-coloured flag is the national symbol. But the English ditched it.

It has been said that the reason for that was because it became over the years a symbol of the National Front. The extremist party started using it and it therefore became unfashionable to fly it or wave it in a football ground. To me, that is a terrible indictment of the English. When you go to an international football match you see the national flags of the two competing countries in abundance. It shows national fervour and pride. Everybody knows what the French and German flags look like. The idea that they would suddenly ditch them because some minor, rather unsavoury political party had taken the flag as their symbol is ridiculous. By caving in and choosing to resurrect the flag of St George, the English actually gave their national flag to the National Front. How crazy is that? I hardly ever read about the NF. In fact, it is so long since I read anything about them that I had to check that they had not broken up. What happened to simple national pride? If some weird political group in Scotland suddenly sprouted up and started using the flag of St Andrew as their symbol there would be a public outcry. Then the boys would get round to the group's first rally and make it clear that we, as a nation, were unamused by the desecration of our national symbol.

As I said, England does not have an identity like Scotland, Ireland and Wales. The one thing they did have, the Union Jack, the most colourful flag in the world that was once a symbol of world domination, they let go in the most feeble fashion. This was the flag, as I alluded to above, that used to send fear throughout the world. When a Royal Navy gunboat was despatched to a far-flung part of the Empire to quell a rebellion, the Union Jack flew from the top of the main mast. It was the first thing the rebels saw on the horizon. The history books show that on many occasions the very sight of this distinctive flag was enough to put down the uprising. You would have thought that as the English have always taken the attitude that they are the total sum of Great Britain and the Celtic nations are just the water-carriers, they would have fought to keep this flag.

You can spot a crowd of Scots supporters from a mile away. It's the same with the Welsh and the Irish. But the English just look like a group of fairly neutral people. They don't have distinctive accents. There is no tartan or green, no thistles or shamrocks, no distinctive songs that identify the country and its culture, and no national dress, unless you include the preposterous image of a man in pinstripe trousers and a bowler hat. English rugby fans have more of an identity than football fans. They do have distinctive songs and patterns of behaviour, such as a picnic in the car park at Twickenham, which don't inhabit football.

To all intents and purposes, my daughters are English. They have grown up in Suffolk and they speak as if they are English. But when we all went to an England v. Scotland rugby match they turned up wearing the tartan. I didn't put any pressure on them. Sure their dad played football for Scotland and my two older daughters have skied for Scotland, but every day they are thoroughly immersed in English culture. I just wonder if they have trouble identifying with it.

Please don't get me wrong. Most of my friends are English. I love living in England, particularly in Constable country, and I played all my football there. Like millions of others of my fellow countrymen over the centuries I believe that I have put as much into England as I have taken out. I certainly have in terms of the amount of taxes I've paid. And from the appreciation that has been voiced for my work as both a footballer and a broadcaster, I think England has been as happy to have me as I have been to be here.

This leads into another strange thing for me about the English: the way they have let the Scots run their country. I have some sympathy for the fact that while Scotland and Wales have their own regional assemblies, at massive cost to the taxpayers, including me, the English don't have any such representation. Scotsmen can sit in the British Parliament and make decisions about the way of life of Englishmen, but Englishmen do not sit in the Scottish regional assembly and influence the lives of the Scots. Frankly, I am amazed that the English put up with this. Not just the regional assemblies, but the fact that the British Parliament, the only political representation they have, is run by Scotsmen. Prime Minister Gordon Brown is so Scottish he is almost a political liability; his Chancellor, Alistair Darling, also hails from north of the border. The Speaker of the House of Commons is Michael Martin, MP for Glasgow North East. The leader of the opposition, David Cameron, carries an unmistakably Scottish name. Even Tony Blair's roots were Scottish: he was educated at Fettes College in Edinburgh, a sort of Scottish version of Eton. I think the issue of representation by Scotsmen in England will come into far sharper focus over the coming years following the recent surge of support for the Scottish Nationalists, which has resulted in them gaining a slender majority in the assembly.

I firmly believe that England and Scotland should co-exist. The union has lasted for 300 years now, during which time this country has established itself as one of the permanent leading nations of the world. Once, that was in the form of colonial power and vast military strength. Today it is about economic organisation. The home nations are good for one another. Breaking up into separate countries won't benefit anybody. Home Rule, independence or whatever you want to call it is a pipe-dream. Next you'll have Cornwall and Devon asking for total autonomy. The Braveheart factor is very romantic but it belongs back in the days when Scotsmen were virtual slaves to the English.

Strange as it sounds, I think the film *Braveheart*, a creation of the Australian-raised actor Mel Gibson, had quite a lot to do with the resurgence of the independence movement north of the border. For those who have not seen it, *Braveheart* is the story of a brutal English army of occupation that forced the Scots into serfdom. Gibson plays the part of the Scottish rebel William Wallace who vows vengeance on the English after they attack and kill his girlfriend. He then raises an army, boots the English out and invades England to the extent that he is seen laying siege to York.

The accuracy of a lot of the historical content has been

challenged. It has also been claimed that the English were portrayed as too barbaric and the Scots as too civilised. Porky, who among other academic boasts says he is an expert on British history, claims that Wallace was a drunken vagabond and a sheep-rustler who deserved all he got when he was hanged, drawn and quartered at Smithfield in London. And in typical English fashion, he couldn't just dismiss it as a film. He wrote to Mel Gibson at his Californian film studios to complain and advise him about historical facts and to this day berates the Hollywood superstar for his anti-Englishness, and for not writing back to him.

I am no economist, but I have a lot of Scottish friends in the City, the financial sector of London, and after talking to them at length, usually late into the night over quite a few glasses of bubbly, I've concluded that if Scotland was ever going to seek independence it should have been done a few decades ago.

The major claim for the last 40 years or so has been the ownership of the oil and gas to be found in the North Sea. When it was first discovered the energy industry was a nationalised corporation. It belonged to the whole of Britain; it would have been difficult to construct an argument in those days to allow only Scotland to benefit from the massive revenues. Through decades of decline in heavy industry and manufacturing, oil money was Britain's lifeline. The problem these days is that most of the revenues from the North Sea have now disappeared.

What a lot of Scottish Nationalists apparently believe in is the power of the 'Celtic Tiger'. They have seen Ireland enjoying a boom by developing radical economic policies that have created tremendous growth. One of these seems to be incentives to attract investment from overseas by reducing taxes on profits – something that has been tried out successfully in many other countries in Europe. But I'm not sure it would work for an independent Scotland. Ireland, as a separate sovereign state, has benefited greatly from membership of the EEC/EU. When they entered they were one of the poorer countries. They enjoyed big financial support, and they built on it. Scotland has not been eligible for that, though it has received high amounts of taxpayers' money. Whether we Jocks like it or not, public spending is higher in Scotland than most other areas of the UK.

Far from separating the two countries, I would actually like to see them brought closer together.

I simply do not understand why all the English want to live in the same corner of England, i.e. the south-east. I have to go there to work because my studios at talkSPORT are in central London, but my main house is in East Anglia – a glorious location with lots of space, and saturated in the culture and history of the ages. I live in the heart of Constable country. Ten minutes from my house is Flatford Mill, the setting for one of his most famous paintings. In my opinion, more people should move out of the south-east. Similarly, the population of Scotland is concentrated in two major centres, Glasgow and Edinburgh, and then spread out pretty thinly over a very big area.

But in this day and age of highly sophisticated communications you can virtually work from anywhere in the world. That is why big businesses set up their call centres in India. I have been frustrated by trying to communicate with people in India when trying to change my mortgage or something, but

I wouldn't be if I was talking to somebody in Scotland. The government should introduce big incentives for businesses to go there and create jobs in areas that need them. Better than that, they should also set up tax-free development zones, a bit like the New Towns that were built in England in the second half of the twentieth century.

Scotland is a beautiful country. The problem is that people don't think there are enough opportunities there. That problem has to be addressed. If Scotland became more prosperous through importing people, businesses and skills, there would be less call for independence. We could also solve the problem of chronic overcrowding in the south-east of England. Already towns such as Stirling are not so much suffering from the explosion in immigration, discussed elsewhere in this book, as benefiting from it. Controlled growth is good for communities when it is properly handled.

***

Who knows, under the Brazil plan we might be able to resurrect the England v. Scotland fixture at Wembley without our boys having to take the goalposts home. And Porky might be able to go to Glasgow again without giving people the urge to punch him in the face wherever he goes. Though that's probably pushing it.

INDEX

Abramovich, Roman 15, 16, 111

Adams, Terry 133

Adrian (Hare Krishna member) 187-190, 191

Advocaat, Dick 269

America 24-25, 26-27, 37-38, 120, 156-157, 209, 212

Arsenal FC 94, 193, 222, 264

Asians in Britain 151, 152, 154

Atkinson, Ron 55, 56

Australia 40, 43-51

Bailey, Gary 55-56, 57

Ball, Alan 9-15, 265-266, 282

Ball, Jimmy 10, 11, 15

Ball, Lesley 11

Barrow FC 58

Baxter, Jim 283-284

BBC programmes 59, 89-90, 92

Beckenbauer, Franz 25

Beckham, David 243-245, 258, 259, 260, 261, 284

Beckham, Victoria 258, 261

benefits, people living on 158-159

Berezovsky, Boris 109-112, 113, 114

Bernie (rock musician) 127, 128-129, 130-131

Best, George 13, 23-24, 25-35, 36, 265

Birmingham 155, 158

Blackburn 96-98, 152-153

Blair, Tony 103, 104, 291

Bob (pub customer) 133-134, 135, 136, 137-140

Bobby Robson Classic golf tournament 14, 194

Bognor Regis 155

Bollinger 183-184, 185-187, 189

Brabrook, Peter 261-262

Branson, Richard 250

Braveheart 291-292

Brazil, Alan, parents 67, 145, 176

Brazil, Jill (wife) 32-33, 39, 40, 41, 49, 52, 77-78, 101, 127, 200, 266

Brazil, Lucy (daughter) 170, 171, 175, 266, 289-290

Brazil, Michelle

(daughter) 98, 101, 170, 171, 175, 266, 289, 290

Brazil, Mike (brother) 68

Brazil, Steffie (daughter) 89, 170, 175, 215, 266, 289-290

Breen-Turner, Paul 162-169, 170, 224

Bristol Rovers FC 58

Brown, 'Big' Jim 225, 226, 229

Brown, Fred 120-121

Brown, Gordon 209, 211, 216, 217, 290

Brown, Judge Robert 58-59

'Bullet, The' 75-77, 78

Burns, Kenny 282

Bush, George W. 209

Butcher, Terry 74-75

Byrne, Liam 149

Callaway 193, 195

Cambridgeshire, policing in 120-122

Cameron, David 290-291

Campbell, Sir Menzies 290

Canavan, Peter 19, 20-21, 22-23, 74

Canterbury Cathedral 115-116

Capel St Mary 19-20

carbon tax 209-210,
211
Cardiff 30, 95
Millennium
Stadium 90, 94
Carling Cup final
(2007) 94
Carnoustie 181
Carragher, Jamie 254
Carsley, Lee 261
Carter, Andrew
16, 17
Carter, Jimmy 212
Carter, Judith 16, 17
Carter, Phil 15-18
Celtic FC 67, 75, 76,
269, 270, 271, 273,
274, 275, 282
Celtic Supporters
Club, New Jersey
branch 275
Charles, Prince 241
Chelsea FC 15, 16,
94, 261
Cheshire schoolboy
126-127
children, risk-taking
by 176-177, 178-179
Coimbra 226
Cole, George 261-262,
263
Cole, Joe 261, 262,
263, 264, 265, 284
Cooke, Charlie
283-284
Copford, Windmill
night-club 19, 20
Coppell, Steve 258
Cornell, George 136
Cotterill, James

58-59, 65, 66
Cotton, Henry 181
Coutts bank 138-139,
140
Crewe 155
criminality in
Britain 119, 131-133,
136, 160
Croatia national
team 228
Curran, Alex 256

Dalglish, Kenny 274,
282, 283, 286
Daniel (dining car
maitre d') 105-106
Danny (Holyrood
classmate) 278-279
Darling, Alistair 290
Dave (assistant
producer) 9, 10
Detroit Express
football team 24-25,
26, 27
Diana, Princess of
Wales 241-242
Dickin, Mike 18
Doherty, Brian 199,
200, 201, 202
Dowie, Ian 258
driving 84-85, 87,
88-89, 90, 95-97,
98-102
Dubcek, Alexander
145
Dunstone, Charles
252

England national
rugby team 65

England national
team 14, 91, 223,
226, 228, 229, 244,
277, 279, 283, 284,
285
English national
identity 283,
284-285, 287-289
Eriksson, Sven-
Goran 244
Eton public school
258
European
Championship
(2004) 223, 224, 225,
226-227, 228, 264
Everton FC 13, 222,
247, 261, 265, 266,
273-274

Faldo, Nick 181, 254
Ferdinand, Rio 255,
261, 284
Flatford Mill 293
Flintoff, Freddie 257
flying 37-38
football, the law and
58-63, 65
Football Association
59
FA Cup (1978) 21, 24
FA Premier
League 252
footballers' earnings
243, 245, 246-247,
248-249, 251-254,
259-260, 262
footballers'
generosity 261-262,
263-265

footballers'
  popularity 242, 243,
  244, 245-247
footballers' wives
  and girlfriends
  ('WAGs') 255-257,
  258, 259
Fort Lauderdale
  Strikers football
  team 25, 26
Fort William 100-101
Fowler, Robbie
  259-260
France national team
  284

Gangs of New York
  72-73
Gardner, Steve 196,
  198
Gates, Eric 19, 22
Gatting, Mike 64
Geddis, David 19,
  20-21, 22, 74, 75
Gemmell, Tommy
  275
Generous 30
Gerrard, Steven 256,
  261, 284
Gibson, Mel 291, 2
  92
Glasgow 67-73,
  75-77, 145, 270-271,
  272-279
  Carlton George
    Hotel 279
  Heraghtys bar
    276-279
  Holyrood School
    67, 278

Lismore pub
  272-273
Mr Singh's
  restaurant 154-155
global warming
  209-210
golf 179-189, 190-202
government advisers
  and ministers
  212-214
government
  spending 214,
  219-221
Graham, Arthur 70
Grand National
  meeting 256-257
Gray, Eddie and
  Frank 70
Greaves, Jimmy
  35-36
Greece national team
  284
Green, Sir Philip 250

Hall, Sir John 169-170
Hammond, Richard
  103, 104
Hansen, Alan 282,
  283
Hare Krishna
  movement 187-190
Harefield Hospital
  230-232, 233,
  234-237, 262-263,
  265
Harrison, George
  189
Hawthorne, Rob 98
Hill, Richard 65-66
Hobson, Jason 65, 66

Houghton, Ray 70
Hungary 145
Huntley, Ian 116-117
Hussein, Nasser 257

immigration 147-157,
  159-160, 161
Indian Haven 170,
  171-172
Ipswich 29, 129
  Black Adder pub
    127-131, 133, 199-200
Ipswich Town FC 14,
  18-19, 21, 22-23, 24,
  27-28, 47, 73, 144,
  146-147, 195-198
Ireland 293
Irish 2,000 Guineas
  170, 171-172

Jamieson, Alex 47,
  49-51
Jeff (Krays'
  godfather) 134, 135,
  136-138, 139
Joe (Glasgow pal)
  69
Johnson, Martin 65
Jordan, Joe 283-284
Jordan, Simon 251

Kate (pub cleaning
  lady) 127, 128-129,
  130
Keegan, Kevin 91
Kenwright, Bill 247
Keys, 'Bruiser' 41-44,
  45, 46, 47, 48
Khodorkovsky,
  Mikhail 111

Kissinger, Henry 157
Kray, Ronnie and Reggie 136
Kuala Lumpur, Hilton Hotel 39-40, 43, 45
Lampard, Frank 258, 284
Lavenham 134-138, 139
Law, Denis 23, 282
Lennon, John 242
Lewis, Denise 93
Lisbon 224, 225, 226
Lithuanians 155-156
Littleport, Cambs. 120-121
Litvinenko, Alexander 111-112, 113, 114
Liverpool, Alder Hey Children's Hospital 264
Liverpool FC 246, 261, 274, 282
Livingstone, Ken 206, 207
Llanelli 155
Lodz, Poland 143-144, 145-147
London 109-110, 112-113, 120, 138-139, 206-208, 281-282
Blackfriars Bridge 207
Blind Beggar pub 136
Caxton Wine Vaults

163-167
'Congestion Charge' 208
East End 151-152
Four Seasons Hotel, Canary Wharf 14-15
Guy's Hospital 215
Harley Street 222
House of Commons 88
Lanesborough Hotel 16-17
Langan's 12
The Oval 64
Longchamp 30, 104
Lorimer, Peter 283-284
Los Angeles Galaxy football team 243
Lugovoy, Andrei 113

Madrid 224
Magnier, John 266
Maktoum family 134, 260
Manchester 158
Manchester City FC 96, 97
Manchester United FC 23, 55-57, 245, 246, 255, 282
Marbella 24, 77-78, 132, 162, 286-287
Markov, Georgi 114
Marsh, Rodney 169
Martin, Bill 12
Martin, Michael 290
Mayer, Louis B. 157

McAllister, Gary 284
McGrain, Danny 284
McLeish, Alex 269-270, 271
McLoughlin, Coleen 249, 256, 264
McLoughlin, Rosie 264
McMenemy, Lawrie 211
McQueen, Gordon 56-57, 283-284
McVitie, Jack 'The Hat' 136
Mendes, Pedro 59
Messi, Lionel 246, 265
Michaels, Harry 39, 40-41, 43-45, 46, 47, 48
Monaco 17
money, 'new' and 'old' 250-251, 258
Murdoch, Rupert 177-178, 252
Murray, Andy 182

National Front 288
National Health Service 89, 148, 150, 214-219, 220, 221, 234, 235, 236, 237
Neville, Gary 254-255
New York 38, 120
Newmarket 15, 133, 171, 196, 265-266
Bedford Lodge Hotel 132

Nixon, Richard 242

North American Soccer League 25, 26

Nottingham Forest FC 55, 282

O'Leary, Michael 210-211

O'Neill, Martin 269

Open, The 182-189, 190-192, 193

Orwell, George 146

Osborne, Roger 21

Owen, Michael 228, 260

Oz Aerobics 39, 48

Pakistan cricket team 155

Parry, Mike 'Porky' 17, 34, 38, 52, 88, 169-170, 171, 172, 256, 269, 292

and Alan Ball 14, 265-266

charity work 262, 263

at Chinese restaurant 124-126

and England team 283, 285

father 231

and Glasgow visit 270, 271, 272, 274-278, 294

and golf 181, 184-187, 189, 190-195

health decline and recovery 221-222, 223-230, 231, 232-234, 236, 262, 264

and Paul Breen-Turner 162, 163, 164-168, 169

and Scotsmen 277-282, 294

train incidents 82-83, 84, 85, 86

and Wayne Rooney 222, 223, 224, 226, 249, 264-265, 285

at Wembley 91-93

Pele 25

Phillips, Ian 74

Poland/Poles 143-144, 145, 146-147, 155-156, 157, 159

policing in Britain 114-123, 124-127, 131, 160

politicians 87-88, 90, 104, 149-151, 158, 159, 205-206, 208, 211-213, 235

Popovich (Yugoslav footballer) 39

Portsmouth Naval Dockyard 218

Portugal national team 228

Prague 145

Puerto Banus 161-162

Sinatra's bar 171

Vinnie Samways' bar 170-172

Purdis Heath golf club 196-197, 198

Pursey, Alex 34

Putin, Vladimir 111, 112, 113

Quinn, Niall 261

Rangers FC 75, 76, 269-270, 273

Rea, Chris 263

Reagan, Ronald 212

Real Madrid football team 243, 245-246, 252-253

Redgrave, Sir Steve 91-93

Reid, John 149-150

Rigg, Sean 58-59

road-pricing 87, 88-89, 102, 103, 208-209

Robertson, Johnny 282

Robson, Sir Bobby 14, 19, 21, 26, 27, 146, 194, 195-196, 197-198, 244

Robson, Bryan 56

Romania 160

Ronaldo, Cristiano 245-246, 252, 255, 265, 266

Rooney, Wayne 222-223, 224, 226, 228, 249-250, 255, 256, 264-265, 284, 285

Rose, Justin 180

Ross, Hamish 121
Royal College of
  Nursing 217
Royal Lytham St
  Annes golf club
  182-187, 190-192
Royal Navy 218,
  289
Royal Society for
  the Prevention of
  Accidents 178-179
rugby, the law and
  65-66
Russia 111-112, 113,
  114
Ryanair 210-211

Samways, Vinnie
  170-171
Sandwich 193
Sangster, Robert
  134, 260
Scholes, Paul 11
Schumacher,
  Michael 254
Schwarzenegger,
  Arnold 154
Scotland national
  team 75, 93, 270,
  271, 279-281,
  283-284
  fans 279-282,
  286-287, 288, 289
Scots in government
  290-291
Scott, Richard 170
Scottish footballers
  282-284
Scottish Highlands
  98-100

Scottish
  independence 291,
  292-293, 294
Shatila, Mary 30,
  31, 32
Sky TV 29, 177-178,
  252
Southampton FC 13
Spain 161-162,
  169-172
Spice Girls, The 258
sports facilities,
  outdoor,
  withdrawal of
  176-177, 179
Steel, Jim 9, 10
Stein, Jock 94
Steve (Lismore
  publican) 272-273
Stirling 294
Stobart, Eddie 213
Suffolk 36, 102-103,
  124-126
  landlady in 20
Sugar, Sir Alan 248,
  250
Sunday Times Rich
  List 17, 243, 260
Sydney 40, 43-45,
  46-48
Sydney Cricket
  Ground 46-47
Sydney Olympic
  football team 40,
  41, 46-47, 48
Sydney Opera
  House 48

talkSPORT 9-10,
  51-52, 64, 90,

162-164, 166, 168,
  182-183, 185, 186,
  221-222, 225, 229,
  232, 272, 282, 293
teachers 61-62, 63
Tenors Unlimited
  17
Terry, John 284
Thatcher, Ben 59
Thatcher, Margaret
  251
Tignes 101
Townsend, Andy
  194
train journeys 30,
  31-32, 81-84, 85-87,
  94-95, 104-106

UEFA Cup 18, 28,
  144, 146-147

Vale of Glamorgan
  golf course 192-193
Vickery, Phil 65, 66
violence in sport
  56-66, 75
Vogts, Berti 283

Wade, Virginia 182
Wallace, William
  291, 292
Waller, Jonathan
  17-18
Wark, John 75, 77,
  284
Wembley Stadium
  90, 91-94, 271, 279,
  280, 281, 294
Westminster, Duke
  of 250